The Bible Speaks Today

Series Editors: J. A. Motyer (OT)
John R. W. Stott (NT)

The Message of Nehemiah
God's servant in a time of change

Kevin Ray

Titles in this series

OLD TESTAMENT

The Message of **Genesis 1—11**
David Atkinson

The Message of **Genesis 12—50**
Joyce G. Baldwin

The Message of **Deuteronomy**
Raymond Brown

The Message of **Judges**
Michael Wilcock

The Message of **Ruth**
David Atkinson

The Message of **Chronicles**
Michael Wilcock

The Message of **Nehemiah**
Raymond Brown

The Message of **Job**
David Atkinson

The Message of **Proverbs**
David Atkinson

The Message of **Ecclesiastes**
Derek Kidner

The Message of the **Song of Songs**
Tom Gledhill

The Message of **Isaiah**
Barry Webb

The Message of **Jeremiah**
Derek Kidner

The Message of **Daniel**
Ronald S. Wallace

The Message of **Hosea**
Derek Kidner

The Message of **Amos**
J. A. Motyer

NEW TESTAMENT

The Message of the
**Sermon on the Mount
(Matthew 5—7)**
John R. W. Stott

The Message of **Mark**
Donald English

The Message of **Luke**
Michael Wilcock

The Message of **John**
Bruce Milne

The Message of **Acts**
John R. W. Stott

The Message of **1 Corinthians**
David Prior

The Message of **2 Corinthians**
Paul Barnett

The Message of **Galatians**
John R. W. Stott

The Message of **Ephesians**
John R. W. Stott

The Message of **Philippians**
J. A. Motyer

The Message of **Colossians & Philemon**
R. C. Lucas

The Message of **1 & 2 Thessalonians**
John R. W. Stott

The Message of **2 Timothy**
John R. W. Stott

The Message of **Hebrews**
Raymond Brown

The Message of **James**
J. A. Motyer

The Message of **1 Peter**
Edmund P. Clowney

The Message of **2 Peter & Jude**
Dick Lucas & Christopher Green

The Message of **John's Letters**
David Jackman

The Message of **Revelation**
Michael Wilcock

The Message of Nehemiah

God's servant in a time of change

Raymond Brown

Inter-Varsity Press
Leicester, England
Downers Grove, Illinois, U.S.A.

InterVarsity Press
P.O. Box 1400, Downers Grove, IL 60515
World Wide Web: www.ivpress.com
E-mail: mail@ivpress.com

Inter-Varsity Press
38 De Montfort Street, Leicester LE1 7GP, England

InterVarsity Press® *is the book-publishing division of InterVarsity Christian Fellowship/USA*®*, a student movement active on campus at hundreds of universities, colleges and schools of nursing in the United States of America, and a member movement of the International Fellowship of Evangelical Students. For information about local and regional activities, write Public Relations Dept., InterVarsity Christian Fellowship/USA, 6400 Schroeder Rd., P.O. Box 7895, Madison, WI 53707-7895.*

Inter-Varsity Press is the book-publishing division of the Universities and Colleges Christian Fellowship (formerly the Inter-Varsity Fellowship), a student movement linking Christian Unions in universities and colleges throughout the United Kingdom and the Republic of Ireland, and a member movement of the International Fellowship of Evangelical Students. For information about local and national activities write to UCCF, 38 De Montfort Street, Leicester LE1 7GP, England.

All Scripture quotations, unless otherwise indicated, are taken from the Holy Bible, New International Version®. NIV®. *Copyright* ©*1973, 1978, 1984 by International Bible Society. Used by permission of Hodder and Stoughton Ltd. All rights reserved. "NIV" is a registered trademark of International Bible Society. UK trademark number 1448790. Distributed in North America by permission of Zondervan Publishing House.*

USA ISBN 0-8308-1242-3

UK ISBN 0-85111-580-2

Typeset in Great Britain by The Midlands Book Typesetting Company.

Printed in the United States of America ⊖

Library of Congress Cataloging-in-Publication Data

Brown, Raymond, 1928-
   The message of Nehemiah: God's servant in a time of change/
Raymond Brown.
     p.   cm.—(The Bible speaks today)
   Includes bibliographical references.
   ISBN 0-8308-1242-3 (USA: pbk.: alk. paper).—ISBN
0-85111-580-2 (UK: alk. paper)
   1. Bible. O.T. Nehemiah—Commentaries.   I. Title.   II. Series.
   BS1365.3.B76   1998
222'.807—dc21   *98-26065*
                                                     CIP

British Library Cataloguing in Publication Data

A catalogue record for this book is available from the British Library.

21	20	19	18	17	16	15	14	13	12	11	10	9	8	7	6	5	4	3
15	14	13	12	11	10	09	08	07	06	05	04	03	02					

Contents

General preface

The Bible Speaks Today describes a series of both Old Testament and New Testament expositions, which are characterized by a threefold ideal: to expound the biblical text with accuracy, to relate it to contemporary life, and to be readable.

These books are, therefore, not 'commentaries', for the commentary seeks rather to elucidate the text than to apply it, and tends to be a work rather of reference than of literature. Nor, on the other hand, do they contain the kind of 'sermons' which attempt to be contemporary and readable without taking Scripture seriously enough.

The contributors to this series are all united in their convictions that God still speaks through what he has spoken, and that nothing is more necessary for the life, health and growth of Christians than that they should hear what the Spirit is saying to them through his ancient – yet ever modern – Word.

J. A. MOTYER
J. R. W. STOTT
Series Editors

Author's preface

Among the treasures of the Louvre is one of the great masterpieces of French art, Théodore Géricault's 'The Raft of the Medusa'. The huge painting depicts the true story of fifteen people shipwrecked after the sinking of a frigate in 1816. It is sunrise, and the survivors on the raft divide roughly in two. One group, in the forefront of the picture, burdened by dark memories and the possibility of increasing anguish, have their backs to the horizon. Those on the other half of the raft are waving frantically to a tiny ship in the distance. They too have suffered but, at that moment, the adversities of a grim past are dwarfed by the hope of a better future.

The survivors illustrate the contrasting despair and hope of the opening verses of the book of Nehemiah. Hanani reflects despondently on Jerusalem's desolation; Nehemiah treasures the possibility of change. More than once in the narrative, Jerusalem's governor turns the faces of his compatriots towards a brighter horizon. The striking characteristics of Nehemiah's story have been repeated throughout history as trusting and resourceful individuals have urged their contemporaries to believe in God's transforming purposes.

Throughout my Christian life, like millions of others, I have been challenged and inspired by Nehemiah's story, and I have endeavoured to interpret his book in the three Baptist churches at which I have been privileged to serve as Minister – Zion in Cambridge, Upton Vale in Torquay, and Victoria in Eastbourne. Nehemiah's leadership ideals were also a rich incentive during my years as Principal of Spurgeon's College, London. More recently, I have expounded some chapters of Nehemiah during Bible weeks and conferences at various places in England and Northern Ireland, and at both the Hong Kong and Japan 'Keswick' Conventions. The message of Nehemiah 8 formed the substance of the first Mandy Lee Memorial Sermon, when a large congregation gave renewed thanks for the life and witness of a vibrant young Christian, whose spiritual journal reflected her profound conviction that 'the Bible speaks today'. I offer this afresh to her parents and sister as a token of continuing love.

I am grateful to the Old Testament editor of this Bible Speaks Today series, Alec Motyer, for his invitation to write on Nehemiah, and especially for the inspiration I have often received from his spoken and written exposition of Scripture. I greatly appreciate the editorial help of Colin Duriez and his colleagues at IVP, and wish to thank my wife, Christine, for her love, encouragement and practical support across the years.

I should like to dedicate this book to the memory of a friend, Stuart H. Cook, a minister in his early fifties who 'went ahead' on the first day of this year. He frequently encouraged me in my writing and, even during prolonged illness, often enquired about the progress of this book. He confidently faced the better horizon, and 'glorious it was to see how the open region was filled with horses and chariots ... to welcome pilgrims as they went up and followed one another in at the beautiful gate of the city'. The Lord 'did not ... abandon them', for he is 'a gracious and merciful God' (Nehemiah 9:31).

St Neots   *Raymond Brown*
March 1998

Bibliography

Commentaries

Ackroyd, P. R., *I and II Chronicles, Ezra, Nehemiah*, Torch Bible Commentaries (London: SCM, 1973).

Batten, L. W., *Ezra and Nehemiah*, International Critical Commentary (Edinburgh: T. & T. Clark, 1913).

Blenkinsopp, J., *Ezra, Nehemiah*, Old Testament Library (London: SCM, 1988).

Bowman, R. A. and C. W. Gilkey, 'Nehemiah', in *The Interpreter's Bible*, vol. 3 (New York: Abingdon, 1953), pp. 551–567, 662–819.

Brockington, L. H., *Ezra, Nehemiah and Esther*, New Century Bible (London: Nelson, 1969).

Browne, L. E., 'Ezra and Nehemiah', in *Peake's Commentary of the Bible*, ed. M. Black and H. H. Rowley (London: Nelson, 1962), pp. 370–380.

Cave, D., *Ezra & Nehemiah*, Crossway Bible Guides (Leicester: Crossway, 1993).

Clines, D. J. A., *Ezra, Nehemiah, Esther*, New Century Bible (Grand Rapids: Eerdmans, 1984).

Coggins, R. J., *The Books of Ezra and Nehemiah*, Cambridge Bible Commentary (Cambridge: Cambridge University Press, 1976).

Cundall, A. E., 'Nehemiah', in *New Bible Commentary Revised*, ed. D. Guthrie and J. A. Motyer (Leicester: IVP, 1970), pp. 404–411.

Evers, S. K., *Doing a Great Work: Nehemiah*, Welwyn Commentary Series (Darlington: Evangelical Press, 1996).

Fensham, F. C., *The Books of Ezra and Nehemiah*, New International Commentary on the Old Testament (Grand Rapids: Eerdmans, 1982).

Hamrick, E. W., 'Nehemiah', in *Broadman Bible Commentary*, vol. 3, ed. C. J. Allen (London: Marshall, Morgan & Scott, 1971), pp. 470–506.

Holmgren, F. C., *Ezra and Nehemiah: Israel Alive Again*, International Theological Commentary (Grand Rapids: Eerdmans, 1987).

Kidner, D., *Ezra and Nehemiah*, Tyndale Old Testament Commentary (Leicester: IVP, 1979).

Klein, R. W., 'Nehemiah', in *Harper's Bible Commentary*, ed. J. L. Mays (San Francisco: Harper, 1988).

McConville, J. G., *Ezra, Nehemiah and Esther*, Daily Study Bible (Edinburgh: St Andrew Press, 1985).

Myers, J. M., *Ezra–Nehemiah*, Anchor Bible (Garden City: Doubleday, 1965).

North, R., 'The Chronicler: 1–2 Chronicles, Ezra, Nehemiah', in *The New Jerome Biblical Commentary*, ed. R. E. Brown, J. A. Fitzmyer and R. E. Murphy (London: Chapman, 2nd ed. 1989), pp. 391–398.

Ryle, H. E., *The Books of Ezra & Nehemiah*, Cambridge Bible for Schools and Colleges (Cambridge: Cambridge University Press, 1907).

Short, S. S., 'Nehemiah', in *The International Bible Commentary*, ed. F. F. Bruce (Basingstoke: Marshall Pickering, 1986), pp. 497–507.

Throntveit, M. A., *Ezra–Nehemiah*, Interpretation: A Bible Commentary for Teaching and Preaching (Louisville: John Knox, 1992).

Williamson, H. G. M., *Ezra, Nehemiah*, Word Biblical Commentary (Waco, Texas: Word, 1985).

———, 'Nehemiah', in *New Bible Commentary*, 21st Century Edition, ed. D. A. Carson *et al.* (Leicester: IVP, 1994), pp. 432–441.

Yamauchi, E. M., 'Nehemiah', in *The Expositor's Bible Commentary*, vol. 4, ed. F. E. Gaebelein (Grand Rapids: Zondervan, 1988), pp. 678–771.

Other works

Ackroyd, P. R., *Israel under Babylon and Persia*, Clarendon Bible (Oxford: Oxford University Press, 1970).

———, *The Chronicler in his Age*, Journal for the Study of the Old Testament: Supplement Series 101 (Sheffield: JSOT Press, 1991).

Coggins, R. J., *Samaritans and Jews* (Oxford: Oxford University Press, 1987).

Cook, J., *The Persian Empire* (London: Dent, 1983).

Cowley, A. E., *Aramaic Papyri of the 5th century BC* (Oxford: Oxford University Press, 1923).

Davies, W. D. and L. Finkelstein, *The Cambridge History of Judaism*, vol. 1 (Cambridge: Cambridge University Press, 1984).

Ellison, H. L., *From Babylon to Bethlehem* (Exeter: Paternoster, 1976).

Frye, R. N., *The Heritage of Persia* (London: Weidenfeld & Nicolson, 1962).

Hoglund, K. G., *Achaemenid Imperial Administration in Syria–Palestine and the Missions of Ezra and Nehemiah* (Atlanta: Scholars Press, 1992).

Motyer, J. A., 'A Single, Steady Aim', in *Keswick Seventy-Six*, ed. J. Hywel-Davies (Eastbourne: Coverdale House Publishers, 1976), pp. 69–112.

Olmstead, A. T., *History of the Persian Empire* (Chicago: Chicago University Press, 1948).

Packer, J. I., *A Passion for Faithfulness: Wisdom from the Book of Nehemiah* (London: Hodder & Stoughton, 1995).

Porten, B., *Archives from Elephantine: The Life of an Ancient Jewish Military Colony* (Berkeley, California: University of California Press, 1968).

Redpath, A., *Victorious Christian Living* (Glasgow: Pickering and Inglis, n.d.).

Simons, J., *Jerusalem in Old Testament Times* (Leiden: Brill, 1952).

Southwell, P., *Ezra–Job*, Bible Study Commentary (London: Scripture Union, 1982).

Stern, E., *Material Culture of the Land of the Bible in the Persian Period 538–332 BC* (Warminster: Aris & Phillips, 1982).

White, J., *Excellence in Leadership: The Pattern of Nehemiah* (Leicester: IVP, 1986).

Wiersbe, W. W., *Be Determined* (Amersham on the Hill: Scripture Press, 1992).

Widengren, G., 'The Persian Period', in *Israelite and Judean History*, ed. J. H. Hayes and J. M. Miller (London: SCM, 1977), pp. 489–538.

Williamson, H. G. M., *Ezra and Nehemiah*, Old Testament Guides (Sheffield: JSOT Press, 1987).

Wiseman, D. J., *Peoples of Old Testament Times* (Oxford: Clarendon, 1973).

Wright, J. S., *The Date of Ezra's Coming to Jerusalem* (London: Tyndale Press, 1947).

———, 'Nehemiah', in *Ezra–Job*, Bible Study Books (London: Scripture Union, 1968).

Yamauchi, E. M., *Persia and the Bible* (Grand Rapids: Baker, 1990).

Chief abbreviations

NEB   *The New English Bible* (NT 1961, 2nd ed. 1970; OT 1970).

NIV   *The New International Version* (1973, 1978, 1984).

RSV   *The Revised Standard Version* of the Bible (NT 1946, 2nd ed. 1971; OT 1952).

Introduction

God finds his servants in surprising places: an innocent sufferer in an Egyptian dungeon, a terrified farm-worker hiding behind a closed door in Ophrah, a young shepherd on the hills of Bethlehem. Though raised to prominence and plenty, such men did not begin so. But with Nehemiah it was different. His story opens in the luxurious surroundings of a Persian court. It is a dramatic narrative which exemplifies obedience, demonstrates heroism, encourages prayer, emphasizes partnership and inspires confidence. Before embarking on an exposition of the book, we will consider its background, date, sources, author, themes and relevance.

1. Background

When Babylon's soldiers marched out of Jerusalem in 586 BC, they left a desolate city behind them. Its magnificent temple, built by Solomon four hundred years earlier, was reduced to heaps of fallen masonry and charred timber. The city's gates and all its important buildings were enveloped in flames, and its strong walls demolished to ensure that the impoverished citizens could not organize another revolt such as the one recently attempted by the hapless Zedekiah. Only the poorest of Jerusalem's people were left behind, the rest led off as captives to distant Babylon.

As the despondent exiles tramped the thousand miles of desert highway their steps were heavy; a burning city was behind them and an unknown future lay ahead. Worst of all were the tormenting thoughts that their present desolation, frequently threatened by the sensitive and courageous Jeremiah, was nothing other than the chastising hand of God.[1] The punishment inflicted by Nebuchadnezzar was dwarfed by the intensity of their guilt and despair. If God was against them, who could be for them?

[1] Je. 1:14–16; 2:16–30.

Yet, all was not lost. The time would come when Isaiah's prophetic word would come gloriously true; their iniquity pardoned, they would emerge from exile as people refined by suffering.[2] Across the centuries, Israel had been led by great people. Although costly, Abraham obeyed God and a new race was born, a people destined to make their unique mark on world history. Overcoming adversity, Joseph saved not only his own people but other nations as well. Moses, another imperilled by hardship, led the Israelites to freedom. Other great leaders had followed in their steps. Joshua conquered a hostile country. Gideon raised an unlikely army. David established a city. Solomon built a temple.

But to the despondent exiles such echoes of the past seemed but taunting memories of a remote story. Their blinded king, shackled and humiliated, was alongside them as they trudged the long road to an alien land. Yet, though they could scarcely have believed it, better days were ahead. God prepares new leaders for fresh challenges. In distant Babylon they were not alone; men and women were equipped for crucial service. Ezekiel's ministry confronted the exiles with higher standards and unfailing resources. In a pagan environment, the stories of Daniel and his companions recalled enduring values. The God who was chastising them would raise up an unknown Persian prince to be their deliverer. The Israelite people would return to their war-torn land and begin again – and with resourceful leaders to inspire them. Challenged by new prophets, God's people would think again about noble things. Haggai, Zechariah and Malachi brought persuasive truths to the returned people. In God's strength, Zerubbabel organized the rebuilding of a temple. Ezra proclaimed the centrality of God's Word, and Nehemiah made possible the rebuilding of those broken walls. In every generation God equips trusted servants for effective leadership.

2. Date

Nehemiah provides his narrative with a firm mid-fifth-century BC date. There is little reason to doubt his historical and contextual data, that he worked in the Persian king's winter palace at Susa (south-western Iran), already famous from the exploits of Daniel and Esther. He served in the court of Artaxerxes, who reigned over the vast Persian empire from 464 to 423, and the dramatic events related in Nehemiah's story began around 445 BC. Although there has been some difference of opinion among Old Testament scholars regarding the date of Ezra's coming to Jerusalem (some asserting the priority of Nehemiah), the precise date of Nehemiah's work has not been

[2] Is. 40:1–2.

seriously questioned. In this exposition we shall follow the dating provided in the biblical material that Ezra came to Jerusalem around 458 BC, to be followed by Nehemiah about thirteen years later. A fuller discussion of these chronological issues can be found in the major commentaries: see especially Kidner (pp. 146–158), Clines (pp. 14–24) and Williamson (1985, pp. xxxix-xliv); but see also Williamson (1987) and J. S. Wright's fine monograph (1947).

3. Sources

The narrative is impressive for numerous reasons, not least because of its historical value and literary character. From a historical perspective, Nehemiah's memoirs provide us with 'one of the most trustworthy sources of Jewish history in the Persian period',[3] whilst, as literature, both Ezra and Nehemiah preserve an unusual mixture of personal reminiscences and historical archives. Autobiographical memoirs are hardly common in the Old Testament. It contains huge sections of national history, and monumental stories of particular distinct events were used to direct, control, secure and correct God's people, but it is comparatively rare to read personal recollections such as those contained in sections of the books of Ezra and Nehemiah. They make the reading all the more compelling because of the high sense of drama, involvement and immediacy they bring to their treatment of history. Nehemiah's reference to 'this wall' conveys the strong impression that the narrative was written in Jerusalem, though with time to reflect on the events he is describing (6:1b; 7:1).

In addition to these vivid autobiographical passages, Nehemiah's book preserves considerable archival material, occasionally paralleled in Ezra or Chronicles, and probably indebted to temple sources. This material takes the form of lists and genealogical data concerning the returned exiles, priests and people, their role in the rebuilding of Jerusalem's walls, settlement in the city and surrounding countryside, and participation in an impressive dedication ceremony. Williamson (1987) notes that each of the lists reveals 'a particular interest in the temple and its personnel'.[4]

It has been suggested that originally the first-person narrative may have formed the substance of Nehemiah's report to the Persian king, later presented afresh for a wider audience and with a different purpose, either by the writer, a colleague or successor. The supplementary lists may have been added to provide a rich sense of continuity, an important theme in the book. At one time, it was

[3] B. W. Anderson, *The Living World of the Old Testament* (Harlow: Longman, 4th ed., 1988), p. 513. [4] Williamson, *Ezra and Nehemiah* (1987), pp. 28–29.

widely held that editorial work on the narratives of both Ezra and Nehemiah was in the hands of 'the Chronicler', a view supported by the repetition of 2 Chronicles 36:22–23 in Ezra 1:1–3, but more recently this view has been challenged. Japhet and others have suggested that, for a variety of reasons, Chronicles and Ezra–Nehemiah ought to be viewed as separate works with common interests but different emphases.[5]

4. Author

Nehemiah must surely be regarded as one of the most inventive and resilient personalities in the rich tapestry of Old Testament biography. He was called to serve God at a time when the Israelite people were emerging from their traumatic years in exile, a stunned and uncertain people. Under Babylonian then Persian domination they lived as a subject people, without their Davidic king and his embodiment of national security and spiritual ideals. The exiles had been without land and temple and the great days of vigorous prophetism mainly belonged to earlier centuries. Now that many were back in Judah, it was important for them to have a sense of continuity with the people of God in earlier days. Nehemiah is not a king, but his work reminds the people of great regal enterprises. He is not a prophet, but speaks and acts in a manner reminiscent of the best of them. He does not belong to the priesthood, but supports the priests with enthusiasm and manifests priestly characteristics in everyday life. He is a visible reminder that the great days of Israel's life and witness are not locked away in a distant past.

This dedicated layman was involved in national projects normally associated with kings, such as major building enterprises, repopulation projects and spiritual reformation.[6] He appears as Hezekiah and Josiah redivivus, summoning the people to renewed dedication focused on great festivals, urging them to hear and obey the message of God's Word.

He is not a prophet in the usual sense of the term, but his recollection of how he was called to service in Jerusalem begins with a literary formula ('The words of Nehemiah'), also found in prophetic literature,[7] and there are times when he functions as a prophet, boldly declaring what God had said to him and how the people are to bring

---

[5] S. Japhet, 'The supposed common authorship of Chronicles and Ezra–Nehemiah investigated anew', *Vetus Testamentum* (1968), pp. 330–371; H. G. M. Williamson, *Israel in the Books of Chronicles* (Cambridge: Cambridge University Press, 1977), pp. 60–69; and M. J. Selman, *1 Chronicles*, Tyndale Old Testament Commentaries (Leicester: IVP, 1994), pp. 65–69.   [6] Ackroyd, *The Chronicler in his Age*, pp. 38–46.
[7] Je. 1:1; Amos 1:1.

a like obedience to a divine call (2:12, 17–18). In outspoken confrontation with oppressively materialistic Judeans, he addresses social questions with the same directness and determination as the great eighth-century prophets, and confirms the seriousness of his intentions by a symbolic act (5:13), also typical of earlier prophetic ministry. Like some great Old Testament prophetic figures, he too was harassed by the deceitful message of false prophets (6:10–14).

Neither is Nehemiah a priest, but he encouraged the ministry of the priests, participated with them and their Levitical colleagues in public occasions of spiritual renewal (5:12; 8:2, 9; 12:27–47) and promoted the ideals of a holy, exemplary priesthood (7:65; 12:1–26; 13:4–9, 28, 30–31). Moreover, in penitential prayer and the recollection of God's former mercies and promises, he performed priestly functions as he interceded for his people (1:4–11) and took a leading part in occasions for national witness and worship (8:9–12; 9:38 – 10:1; 12:38).

Nehemiah is a visible reminder to the Israelite people of the unchanging mercy of God. Life has changed for them, and some of their treasured institutions were no more, but the Lord was with them, raising up new people to refine and invigorate the vulnerable community. A trusted wine steward in a pagan palace becomes God's instrument for Israel's renewal.

5. Themes

Although a gifted raconteur, Nehemiah has a greater purpose in writing than merely to recount an impressive story. He is recording educative history and uses the narrative to convey great doctrinal, moral and spiritual ideas. The book is both an artless personal testimony and a dynamic theological confession. It skilfully unites the subjective experience of a man deeply conscious of God's leading in his life (2:4, 8, 18; 6:10–14; 13:3–31) with the great objective truths which God has revealed not simply to one gifted leader but to all his believing people (1:5–11; 4:14; 8:1–12; 9:1–37). The book adds to the story of Israel's distinctive message and witness as it interprets four great themes: Nehemiah's doctrine of God, his passion for Scripture, his experience of prayer and his example in leadership.

a. Nehemiah's doctrine of God

Throughout his memoirs Nehemiah emphasizes both objective truth and subjective experience, a balance not always maintained throughout Christian history. We live in a period when the subjective awareness of God's immanence is more prominent than the objective reality of his transcendence. David F. Wells maintains that

17

'the church's identity vanishes when transcendence melts into immanence' and 'where theocentric faith [*i.e.* faith centred on God as an objective reality] becomes anthropocentric faith [*i.e.* faith centred on therapeutic interest in the self]'.[8] Nehemiah's teaching about God as holy and true is a healthy antidote to highly subjective aspects of Christian experience which, under the subtle and unrecognized influences of modernity, emphasize more about how the believer feels than upon what God has declared, more about novel and mercurial experience than the unshakeable foundation of revealed truth.

Nehemiah's contemporaries needed to be reminded of *the reality of God's uniqueness*. In the post-exilic period there was an understandable sense of wistfulness. Judah had lost her political freedom (an issue not ignored in this book, 9:36–37) and could no longer pledge her allegiance to her own king. Although recently rebuilt, the temple lacked the impressiveness of Solomon's magnificent construction.[9] Things were certainly not the same, but Nehemiah emphasizes the continuity of the great realities still at the heart of Israel's faith. Most of all, God was on their side. He had not changed, and throughout the narrative the author warms to his primary theme of the greatness of God (9:32), a message for dispirited people in every generation.

God is *universally sovereign*. The 'God of heaven' (1:5; 2:4, 20) was a divine title in Persian religion but Nehemiah uses it as dramatic apologetic: the Lord Yahweh, he alone (9:6) is God of heaven, not Ahura-Mazda, the non-existent 'god' of his Persian contemporaries. Nehemiah hears of Jerusalem's distress whilst living in distant Susa but God is in control of the entire world and is shaping the destiny of his people wherever they are, guiding an unknown cupbearer into his sovereign purposes. Moreover, in his sovereignty he can not only clear the way for those who honour him, but also frustrate the designs of those who oppose him (4:15). He alone can turn a cruel curse into an immeasurable blessing (13:2).

He is *totally reliable*, the God 'who keeps his covenant of love with those who love him and obey his commands' (1:5; 9:32). He is true to his promises (9:8). The events leading up to the threatened exile were a stark illustration of Israel's disloyalty. They had not honoured their covenant obligations but, as Isaiah's message assured them, they were disciplined though not abandoned. His 'unfailing love' would not be shaken nor would his 'covenant of peace be removed'.[10]

God is *utterly holy*. The first word of those who are burdened

---

[8] David F. Wells, *God in the Wasteland* (Leicester: IVP, 1994), pp. 121–122, 133–151.   [9] Hg. 2:1–3.   [10] Is. 54:4–17.

with grief (1:3–4) is to acknowledge that their greatest need is not immediate relief from present trouble but eternal forgiveness. Nehemiah confesses that he is a sinner whose personal life is set in the wider context of human rebellion, past and present (1:6–7; 9:2). Once forgiven, God's people do not shape their moral standards by contemporary, variable ethical norms. They live not to win human approval but according to the pattern of God's holiness. They must be holy because he is holy.[11] Nehemiah was determined to do everything in life 'out of reverence for God' (5:15) and others treasured the same ambition (7:2).

God is *compassionately merciful*. When he entered into a covenant with them, God knew that his people would fail him and warned them of the serious consequences of their inevitable transgressions. They would be 'exiled ... at the farthest horizon' but, if they returned to him in penitence, he would bring them back to the land he had given them as a token of his mercy (1:8–9). Time without number they grieved him, but he pardoned their offences and restored them (9:16–19, 26–31). He is, literally, 'a God of forgivenesses' (9:17).

God is *uniquely powerful*. He encounters no difficulties in accomplishing his purposes for them. The God who created the universe (9:6), who enabled childless Abraham to become the 'father of a multitude' (9:7) and 'redeemed' (1:10) his oppressed people from Egyptian slavery by his 'great strength' and 'mighty hand' (Exodus language) could certainly bring the exiles home. Moreover, his deliverances are not restricted to the outstanding events of their history but are markedly evident in everyday life when his people are threatened by powers too strong for them. On days when they felt totally overwhelmed by their enemies, their God would 'fight' for them (4:20). Finding their true joy in their spiritual resources (8:12, 17), their physical strength would be perpetually renewed (8:10).

God is *infinitely gracious*. Nehemiah's project was given royal approval, not because he was in the right place at the right time, but because 'the gracious hand' of his God (2:8, 18) was upon him. He does not deal with individuals or communities as they deserve but desires and designs things for their highest good.

He is *intimately near*. The transcendent 'God of heaven' is not detached and distant; he draws close to his dependent people and keeps on putting (2:12, present tense) the right and best things into their hearts. When they are in danger, he makes them sensitive to his promptings (6:12), and when they are uncertain of the way ahead, he reveals his will to them (7:5).

---

[11] Lv. 19:1; 1 Pet. 1:14–17.

God is *completely just*. Like many of God's servants across the centuries, Nehemiah was plagued by bitter opposition. He and his contemporaries had to know that a day would come when life's wrongs would be put right, when evil people will be brought before the bar of God's judgment. His enemies had not merely insulted Nehemiah; they had despised God (4:4–5; 6:12). But their righteous God was aware of Israel's sins as well as those of their enemies. If they ignored his command to love their neighbours[12] and robbed the poor (5:1–13), they too would experience his severe judgment (9:33). Ezekiel told his contemporaries that the people of Sodom came under divine condemnation not only on account of their sexual obscenities but because they had ignored the cry of the distressed poor.[13] What Sodom suffered would be Jerusalem's fate if they persisted in such unloving conduct to their destitute neighbours. God did not have rules for one people which he overlooked in the case of others.

Nehemiah's life was totally devoted to such a God. He found 'delight' (1:11) in seeking God's face (1:4), revering God's name (1:11), pursuing God's will (1:11; 2:4–5), acknowledging God's goodness (2:8, 18), serving God's people (2:12, 17), trusting God's power (2:20), confessing God's holiness (4:14; 5:9, 15), sharing God's Word (8:9), showing God's love (8:10), remembering God's generosity (8:13–18), recalling God's faithfulness (9:5–37), obeying God's commands (10:29) and encouraging God's servants (10:37–39; 13:10–13).

b. Nehemiah's passion for Scripture

One of the most fascinating aspects of the post-exilic literature is the manner in which these later biblical writers reflect on what God has said and done in earlier days. They treasure his unique revelation in Scripture and the story it unfolds of his saving work in the life of the nation, and seek to interpret its message afresh to their contemporaries. At the heart of Nehemiah's narrative is the story of a unique Bible Reading in the centre of Jerusalem. It was not a temple gathering, thereby restricting attendance either to religious officials or to those privileged few who might gain entry to a restricted area. It was held in the city's main square and everybody, young and old, men and women alike, were eager to attend. Although Ezra leads this occasion,[14] it is Nehemiah who joins with Ezra in encouraging the people's response to Scripture (8:9–11). Nehemiah was inspired, taught and fashioned by God's Word.

[12] Lv. 19:18.   [13] Ezk. 16:49.

[14] Some scholars believe that the narrative in Nehemiah 8 is misplaced and that the event 'actually occurred in the year of *Ezra's* arrival in Jerusalem (458 BC), the seventh year of Artaxerxes I, and not in the year of *Nehemiah's* arrival (445 BC, the twentieth year of Artaxerxes' (Clines, p. 181).

Nehemiah was *inspired* by Scripture. The story of how God had called, equipped and used men and women over the centuries never ceased to encourage him. The personalities of the Old Testament story ennobled and challenged him. Abraham believed God's promise (9:7–8, 23), Moses shared God's Word (1:7–8; 8:1, 14; 9:14; 10:29; 13:1), Aaron entered God's service (10:38; 12:47), David (12:24, 36–37, 45–46) and Asaph (12:46) encouraged God's praise and, more recently, Zerubbabel (7:7; 12:1, 47) built God's temple. But Nehemiah has also taken to heart the warning stories of Scripture – Solomon forgot God's holiness (13:26) and ignored God's warning, with disastrous consequences.[15]

Nehemiah was *taught* by Scripture. It was not only the characters of Scripture which attracted him. From his youth onwards, the uplifting language of God's Word, its enriching truths, clear warnings and dependable promises took possession of his receptive mind. Some of the great books of the Old Testament became special to him. In the Pentateuch, the stories and sayings of Genesis (9:7–8), Exodus (1:10; 9:9–18), Leviticus (8:13–15), Numbers (9:20; 13:3) and Deuteronomy (1:8–9; 9:21–23, 29) are never far from his mind, nor the narratives of Joshua (9:23–25), Judges (9:26–28), 1 Kings (13:26) and 2 Kings (9:6). There are echoes of prophetic teaching by Isaiah (6:9), Jeremiah (13:18), Ezekiel (13:17–18) and Daniel (1:4–7), as well as reminiscences of some great psalms (9:13).

Nehemiah was *fashioned* by Scripture. Obedience to Scripture was life's highest priority. From his youngest days, Nehemiah will have become increasingly aware of its authority, persuasiveness, power and relevance. McConville points out that every group needs 'emblems of its identity'.[16] Prior to the exile, the Israelite people had gloried in the emblems of land, temple, throne, book and day. Removed from the land, bereft of temple and robbed of king, they turned with greater commitment to the book God had given them, to his revealed Word embodied particularly in the Mosaic law. Obedience to that law in terms of observing the Sabbath became a confirming 'sign' of their uniqueness, but Sabbath-allegiance was derivative; the Word was paramount. Nehemiah came to love that law, and his commitment to Scripture is evident from his prayers, service, testimony and conduct. He was encouraged by its promises (1:5, 9; 4:20; 9:7–8, 17), challenged by its warnings (1:7–8; 5:9; 9:30, 37; 13:17–18, 26–27) and enriched by its ideals.

c. *Nehemiah's experience of prayer*

Nehemiah uses the narrative to convey to his readers the importance of prayer. Great prayer-passages are found throughout the entire

[15] 1 Ki. 11:1–13. [16] McConville, p. 34.

book. It begins with prayer in Persia (1:4) and closes with prayer in Jerusalem (13:31). The story reminds us of the great dimensions of prayer: adoration (8:6; 9:3, 5), thanksgiving (12:24, 27, 31, 40, 46), confession (1:4–7; 9:33–34), petition (1:11; 2:4) and intercession (1:6). There are prayers of anguish (4:4–5; 6:14; 13:29) and prayers of joy (12:43), prayers for protection (4:9), and prayers of dependence (6:9) and commitment (13:14, 22, 31). It is a story of compassionate (1:4), persistent (1:4), personal (1:6) and corporate (1:7) prayer. Prayer provides Nehemiah with perspective (1:11, 'this man'); it widens his horizons (2:4, 'God of heaven'), sharpens his vision (2:12) and dwarfs his anxieties (4:8–9). Here is a believer who hurries to the place of prayer to share his present griefs (1:4), confess his past failures (1:6–7) and discover his future work (1:11).

d. Nehemiah's example in leadership

Nehemiah's memoirs preserve his indelible character. The fact that such a wide variety of gifts, expertise and achievement are crowded into the narrow compass of one life is ample evidence of Nehemiah's qualities as one of Israel's most outstanding leaders. His leadership qualities are as necessary and relevant today as in the fifth century BC.

Nehemiah was a leader with *infinite compassion*. On hearing of his people's needs he 'sat down and wept . . . mourned and fasted and prayed' (1:4). Love matters most in leadership. The loveless leader achieves little of significance. Jerusalem's plight was a thousand miles from Susa's palace but, because he loved them, the anguish of his people reduced everything else in his life to items of lesser importance.

Nehemiah was a leader *under greater authority*. Bewildered as to the right and best course of action in crisis, he sought God for direction (1:5–11). Leaders must be led. In his daily work he was used to receiving the orders of a Persian king, but his greatest priority was to stand as a submissive servant in the audience chamber of God. He recognized that it was more important patiently to discern God's will than to rush to the help of God's people.

Nehemiah was a leader of *transparent integrity*. Coming before God's throne, he speedily recognized his iniquities and longed to confess them. He did not merely acknowledge the nation's sins; he lingered in God's presence to identify his own (1:6). He was not someone who acknowledged himself worse than others in the place of prayer but acted as better than others when he left it. He was not only honest before God but also toward others. When Judah's deprived people complained of injustice, he did not act as a man totally detached and free from blame. However innocently, he had participated in money-lending (5:10) along with others and did nothing to conceal his personal involvement in an issue which must be put right.

Nehemiah was a leader with *a vision for something great*. Believers with vision have 'a deep dissatisfaction with what *is* and a clear grasp of what *could be*'.[17] God planted within this leader's heart (2:12) a strategy which could transform Jerusalem's destiny, relieving its people of ignominy (1:3), insecurity and poverty. Nehemiah became indignant about the city's appalling degradation and could not be at peace until an alternative prospect began to form in his mind.

Nehemiah was a leader *aware of his own vulnerability*. Leaders are not perfect; they all have some point of weakness at which they are on the threshold of possible danger. Sensitive, dependent, honest and venturesome, Nehemiah discovered his potential for crippling fear (2:2). Good leaders do not allow themselves to become so enamoured with their assignments that they forget their temptations. Many a good work has been damaged if not ruined because the leaders have been so busy instructing others that they have ignored a primary leadership obligation, 'Keep watch over yourselves'.[18]

Nehemiah was a leader with *the ability to inspire others*. The rebuilding of demolished walls could not be attempted without galvanizing a unified team, so the task must begin with effective recruitment. Jerusalem's citizens were aware of incipient opposition, and identifying with a new leader could prove dangerous. As a good leader, Nehemiah spoke realistically of the problems, convincingly of the answer and confidently of the resources (2:17, 20).

Nehemiah was a leader who recognized *the necessity and advantages of delegation*. He could oversee the project but was totally incapable of executing it himself. He made sure that responsibility for each section of the wall was entrusted to responsible co-workers (3:1–22), and they in turn recruited their partners who, under agreed leadership, 'worked with all their heart' (4:6).

Nehemiah was a leader who *did not baulk at adversities*. He knew the necessity of perseverance. Difficulties were bound to arise and, within a very short time, external hostility was matched by internal pessimism (4:1–12).

Nehemiah was a leader with *sensitive adaptability*. Things do not always go as well as we hope. When problems arise, the effective leader regards them not as intimidating deterrents but as creative opportunities. After hearing the complaints of despondent and

[17] J. R. W. Stott, *Issues Facing Christians Today* (Basingstoke: Marshall, Morgan and Scott, 1984), p. 328. [18] Acts 20:28.

23

endangered workers, undaunted Nehemiah emerged with a five-point plan. He mustered local protection squads (4:13), reminded them of their spiritual defences (4:14), divided the team into builders and protectors (4:15–18), organized a plan whereby a mobile brigade of troops could be rapidly despatched to any vulnerable part of the wall (4:19–20) and ensured that everyone in the city was guaranteed twenty-four hour protection (4:21–22).

Nehemiah was a leader *prepared to make personal sacrifices*. He had surrendered his luxurious lifestyle and personal safety on leaving Persia; once in Jerusalem he had to forfeit the comfort of necessary relaxation and undisturbed sleep (4:23). He continued to be harassed by known enemies with insidious schemes to destroy him (6:1–9), treacherous friends who valued money more than loyalty (6:10–13), corrupt religious leaders intent on misusing spiritual gifts (6:14), and community leaders whose allegiance to their governor was neither wholehearted nor sincere (6:17–19). Like the apostle Paul centuries later he was 'hard pressed on every side, but not crushed ... persecuted, but not abandoned'.[19]

Nehemiah was a leader with *the ability to enlist dependable colleagues*. Once the wall was rebuilt, practical arrangements must be made for the oversight of its spiritual, social and military needs (7:1–2). The governor chose partners with moral 'integrity' and spiritual commitment. In the work of community administration he wanted people alongside him who 'feared God' (7:1–2) rather than those who pleased others, colleagues who were utterly 'trustworthy' (13:12) and not corrupted by materialistic ambitions.

Nehemiah was a leader who *anticipated the next challenge*. Any achievement for the Lord will be promptly tested in one way or another. The governor knew that the newly secured city must be adequately defended and quickly populated (7:3–5; 11:1–24). His reliable colleagues were required to implement arrangements for the protection of the residents: guards must be appointed at the main points of access and detailed instructions given about appropriate times for opening and closing the gates. A sparsely occupied city could easily be attacked. The enemies who wanted to destroy it during the building operation were unlikely to lose interest in it. He quickly made imaginative plans for recruiting new citizens to take up residence in Jerusalem. Good leaders have the ability to think ahead to identify possible areas of difficulty and be alert enough to develop fresh opportunities for expansion and progress.

Nehemiah was a leader blessed with *enviable tenacity*. He overcame many daunting discouragements which might have ruined another man, but God enabled him to endure even when things

---

[19] 2 Cor. 4:8–9.

seemed at their worst. He coped with a precarious employer (2:1–3), hostile neighbours (2:10, 19), insulting opponents (4:1–3), determined adversaries (4:7–8), disheartened colleagues (4:10), terrified partners (4:11–12), loveless officials (5:1–13), persistent enemies (6:1–11), false prophets (6:12–14), disloyal priests (13:4–9, 28), avaricious traders (13:15–22), and disobedient believers (13:23–27). During a period when he went back to Persia, standards rapidly declined and spiritual and ethical principles were gradually abandoned. On his return to Jerusalem, Nehemiah had to take up the task again with firm resolution to bring a wayward people back into the will of God. Buffeted by trials, committed leaders may be temporarily disillusioned but, following the teaching and example of the perfect leader, they put their 'hand to the plough' and refuse to 'look back'.[20] William Carey suffered innumerable hardships during an outstanding missionary career. In later years he shared his secret with his nephew. Disclaiming every other gift, he said, 'I can plod. That is my only genius. I can persevere in any definite pursuit. To this I owe everything.'[21] Dedicated leaders never give up.

6. Relevance

Although we are separated from Nehemiah by two and a half thousand years, the problems he faced are not peculiar to the world of antiquity. In contemporary society, human problems may appear in a different guise but they were found in ancient communities no less than in ours.

Ours is a constantly changing society. The past few decades have witnessed unprecedented changes: collapsing political structures (the disintegration of the USSR, the termination of apartheid, the repeated incidence of civil wars in Africa), astonishing technological developments, economic pressures (serious unemployment in many countries), and religious tensions (with the greater degree of pluralism in Western society, the rise of Islamic militancy, the increasing attractiveness of eastern religions, and the proliferation of new religions such as 'New Age').

Moreover, these changes are not simply dramatic items for media attention; they have inevitable personal repercussions. Individuals and families are seriously affected by them. Social patterns have changed. Work no longer offers the stability and security it often did; compulsory redundancy is a cruel spectre on the employment horizon. In order to maintain their families, many people have to be prepared for dramatic changes at work, sometimes thrusting them

---

[20] Lk. 9:61–62.
[21] S. P. Carey, *William Carey* (London: Hodder and Stoughton, 1923), p. 23.

into unfamiliar geographical and social contexts. Although some may not have to move from one part of the country to another, they are not likely to escape the challenge of change. Modern technology makes fresh demands, familiar work patterns disappear, different techniques have to be acquired and new opportunities grasped, often at the expense of home and family life.

Nehemiah had to face the problem of change. Obedience to God involved him in vocational, geographical, cultural and social change. When the Lord put it into his heart what he must do for Jerusalem (2:12), it meant moving from one part of the ancient world to another. He had to leave his secure home surroundings for an existence more tentative and uncertain. It involved a change of job from dignified palace steward to building-site manager, leaving a safe and affluent milieu in Persia for a less secure one in Judah. Friends had to be left in Susa, probably forsaking wider family ties as well. It meant exchanging the totally familiar for the largely unknown.

Nehemiah coped with the challenge of dramatic change in work, location and lifestyle. First, he depended upon God, so vividly expressed in his earnest prayers (1:5–7). Secondly, he was conscious that others before him had proved the Lord's generosity in times of geographical, cultural and social change, notably Abraham (9:7–8) and Moses at the exodus (1:10). Thirdly, he faced the future with the deepening assurance that the Lord's 'gracious hand' was also upon him (2:8, 18) and would crown his venture with success (2:20). Nehemiah's name does not appear in what Richard Sibbes called 'the little book of martyrs' in Hebrews 11, but his was certainly a venture of faith. He too 'was commended as one who pleased God'. He 'obeyed and went' and 'made his home in the promised land like a stranger in a foreign country'. In working for God's people he not only reconstructed Jerusalem's damaged wall but 'administered justice, and gained what was promised'.[22]

Modern society is crippled by selfish individualism. The sense of community concern has disappeared from many contexts in contemporary life. The ruthless pursuit of personal satisfaction has left many of our contemporaries with little time for projects which may benefit others. 'Our computers are starting to talk to us while our neighbours are becoming more distant and anonymous.'[23] Voluntary agencies find it impossible to recruit enough people to staff local ventures to help others. Sick, disadvantaged, elderly, immobile, disabled, deprived people in modern communities are denied the practical support they deserve. Nehemiah's memoirs preserve the story of a prosperous individual who put community needs before his own. He left the opulence of palatial surroundings

[22] Heb. 11:5, 8–9, 33. [23] Wells, *God in the Wasteland*, p. 48.

for a dispirited community in a dilapidated city he had never seen, a thousand miles from his home. When he reached Jerusalem, he had to inspire its citizens and people from the surrounding area to forsake their self-interest for a period in order to do something for the broken city, and once the wall was rebuilt he had to persuade others to do a further unselfish thing, come to live in Jerusalem for good. The narrative has compelling things to say about putting God first, about living unselfishly in the contemporary world, and about the joy and satisfaction of serving others. Modern society is becoming increasingly violent. Tragically, aggression and hostility, both personal and corporate, are familiar television scenes all over the world. The elderly are no longer safe and children are especially vulnerable. Minorities are in grave danger in many parts of the world and thousands of twentieth-century Christians have suffered for their faith. Nehemiah's story is also set within a context of social antagonism, verbal onslaughts, persistent ridicule and continuing attempts at physical brutality, not only directed at Nehemiah personally (6:1–14) but also toward all who identified with his work for God (2:19; 4:1–3, 7–12). His memoirs are particularly relevant to those who have to endure persecution in any form because of their love for Christ.

Human rights have a deservedly high profile in contemporary international politics. Millions are aware of appalling inequality, deprivation, homelessness and injustice. The success of Nehemiah's building enterprise was seriously imperilled by heartless Judean nobles and officials who were making money by exploiting the poor, causing widespread poverty, hunger, family disruption and slavery (5:1–5). Nehemiah was a man ready to champion the cause of the needy, and the manner in which he handled this crisis is strikingly relevant in the modern world. He opposed evil practice (5:6–13) and demonstrated by his own lifestyle (5:14–19) that the needs of others will never be far from the believer's mind.

Contemporary Western society is grossly materialistic. Those Judean nobles were not the last individuals to prize money more than people. Materialistic ambitions and economic interests probably figured more prominently than other factors in the opposition of Nehemiah's enemies. With its newly built walls and stable population, Jerusalem would no longer be a downtrodden community but would develop its own opportunities for trade and commerce. Those who had benefited by its earlier poverty were outraged that the new city might enjoy better days.

But, as we have seen, there were materialists in Judah as well as Samaria and Ammon. Israelites who had plenty were also greedy for more. Materialistic gain was a recurrent temptation to Nehemiah's contemporaries. It caused them not only to abuse the poor (5:1–5) but also encouraged unhelpful (possibly business and domestic) alliances (6:17–19). Their lust for money made them indifferent to God's teaching about love for debtors (10:31) and the regular support of God's servants (13:10–13). It caused them to marginalize the importance of the law's requirements for an essential rest day for humankind and animals (13:15–22). When monetarism gains pride of place on the human agenda, selfishness is likely to follow and sadness will never be far away.

Materialistic lifestyles are the congenial soil of secularism and relativism. People who deny God's existence and thereby dismiss his laws have little regard for objective moral standards. Ethical principles become subservient to situational needs. Contemporary Western society is becoming increasingly secularist. One cannot imagine secularism as a serious threat to a religious community in mid-fifth-century Judah. But it did make serious inroads into the life of the Israelite people; they maintained religious ceremonial but without spiritual commitment. Nehemiah had to deal with such insidious dangers. When he returned to Jerusalem after his stay in Persia, he discovered that his Judean contemporaries had adopted an overtly secularist lifestyle, both by what a temple official did and by what the people refused to do.

First, what was done: a responsible religious leader disregarded God's law and allowed an Ammonite (13:1–3) opponent of Nehemiah to take up residence in the temple (13:4–5). When spiritual leaders become indifferent to God's revealed Word, it is hardly surprising if secularist attitudes are adopted more widely by the people. If a temple official could marginalize God's laws about holiness, then the average Judean felt free to ignore his teaching about giving (13:10–11). Nehemiah confronts his contemporaries with the seriousness of both offences. He introduces immediate, public and practical means for diverting the offenders from a God-ignoring to a God-honouring pattern of life expressed in holiness (13:6–9) and generosity (13:12–13). His courageous witness challenges contemporary secularist attitudes and is a rebuke to moral and ethical compromise within the church and beyond it.

Western society is becoming more and more pluralistic. Christian ideals are constantly disputed and the distinctive dimensions of biblical faith seriously questioned. It is reliably estimated that within five years there will be more committed Muslims than committed Anglicans in Britain. Contemporary religious education encourages the notion that all the major world religions are of equal value and that there is nothing unique about Christian faith. Jesus is widely regarded as one religious leader among many, and the New Testament's uncompromising assertion of his deity is dismissed as intolerant religious prejudice. A contributor to *The Myth of*

Christian Uniqueness asserts that the 'idea that Christianity, or even the biblical faiths, have a monopoly on religious truth is an outrageous and absurd religious chauvinism',[24] betraying a dogmatism considered abhorrent in others. Alister McGrath asks how such writers can imagine that their pluralistic theologies are alone 'privileged, detached, objective and correct': 'Is this not also an "outrageous and absurd" imperialism?'[25] With his concern that Israel might hand on to others her distinctive message, pluralism was an urgent problem for Nehemiah. It was a matter of urgency to deal with those who had adopted syncretistic patterns of spiritual life as they provided their children with teaching about the religions of Ashdod, Ammon and Moab (13:23–27). Israelite parents no longer talked about God's Word with their children.[26] Nehemiah's passion for biblical truth ensured that Israel's faith was handed on to the next generation. He knew the role of the family as an effective teaching unit and the importance of communicating the message to the next generation.

In contemporary Britain, like many Western countries, vast numbers of our children have little knowledge of the Christian gospel. Eighty-five per cent of them have no links whatever with a church or Christian organization. Nehemiah's determination to reach the homes and families of his people is an example of one man's attempt to rectify spiritual ignorance and encourage the regular communication of God's truth to his contemporaries.

Like ourselves, Nehemiah lived heroically on the frontier between two worlds: human life as God intended it to be and as people have chosen to make it. In everyday conduct he was confronted, as we are, with the constant tension between life's crucial alternatives: God or self, holiness or sin, love or indifference, courage or weakness, generosity or greed. The temptations he faced and the transgressions he exposed are still rife in our more sophisticated but no less sinful society. His compassionate concern, disciplined prayerfulness, spiritual confidence, resourceful service, moral integrity, resilient faith, biblical principles and exemplary lifestyle continue to be relevant in our different but perilously needy world.

[24] R. R. Ruether, in J. Hick and P. F. Knitter, *The Myth of Christian Uniqueness: Towards a Pluralistic Theology of Religions* (London: SCM, 1987), p. 141.
[25] Alister E. McGrath, 'The Church's Response to Pluralism', *Journal of the Evangelical Theological Society* 35 (1992), p. 494.   [26] Dt. 6:4–9, 20–25.

A. Rebuilding the walls (1:1 – 7:73)

Nehemiah 1:1–11
1. The servant's preparation

Nehemiah treasured no greater ambition than to be a loyal 'servant' of God; the noun is deliberately repeated throughout the book's opening narrative (6, 7, 8, 10, 11). This introductory section of his memoirs sets the scene and explains how God's servant was prepared for new work in far-off Jerusalem. Its story unfolds in five scenes, portraying the attitude of God's servant.

1. Looking out in compassion (1:1–3)

Biblical accounts of a call to God's work frequently begin with an arresting assertion of the divine initiative, though there are occasions when the 'call' is discerned through a known crisis. Prompted by an overwhelming awareness of need, such people do not decide to serve; they believe the decision has been made for them. Nehemiah's call was discerned in that way. Born in Persia a century after the ravages of Babylon's king, he learned of distant Jerusalem only from stories related by fellow-Israelites. He knew of Nebuchadnezzar's ruthless devastation but, as caravans from other countries visited Susa, Nehemiah heard of Jerusalem's more recent troubles. A servant of King Artaxerxes, he was aware from court news that one innocent attempt to rebuild Jerusalem's walls had been dramatically frustrated. At that time, local opponents had written to the Persian king asserting that Jerusalem's citizens were intent on rebellion and, on the king's orders, work on the walls was brought to an abrupt end.[1]

Nehemiah knew that his contemporary, Ezra, had led a second group of returning exiles and was endeavouring to establish the community with God's Word at the heart of its spiritual and moral life, but it had not been easy. So, when travellers came from Judah we can understand why, concerned about his people, Nehemiah

[1] Ezr. 4:6–23.

questioned them about the Jewish remnant that survived the exile, and also about Jerusalem (2). As the story begins, Nehemiah is identified as a man of deep concern, with clear priorities.

First, the narrative illustrates Nehemiah's concern. Although he had a highly responsible job, in a secure environment in a fine Persian city, noted for its opulence and prosperity, magnificent buildings and spacious gardens, he is not remotely preoccupied with himself. Anxious for the welfare of the returned exiles, he enquires about the condition of the city where they lived. The initiative was with Nehemiah, not the visitors. Throughout Christian history, men and women with a deep love for others have been used to transform the face of society. Evident need constituted their call; they could not believe that God was indifferent to the cry of their deprived contemporaries. Profoundly disturbed about prison conditions in England, John Howard and Elizabeth Fry campaigned zealously for reform. The degrading traffic in slaves disturbed the consciences of Thomas Clarkson and William Wilberforce, and they could not rest until the evil practice was abolished. During the Industrial Revolution, Lord Shaftesbury worked tirelessly for improvements in factories where women and children worked under appalling conditions. Tom Barnardo, T. B. Stephenson, George Müller and C. H. Spurgeon carried the needs of orphaned children on their hearts and took practical steps to provide them with food, shelter and security. These eighteenth- and nineteenth-century Christians were people who looked out compassionately on their world and their disturbed consciences led to vigorous action. It was not enough to identify a need; they had to meet it, and with all speed.

Secondly, the narrative identifies Nehemiah's priorities. People mattered more than things. He was naturally troubled about the physical condition of the city. Broken walls meant frightening insecurity, negligible commercial development and serious economic deprivation, but the depressed people within the city were infinitely more important than its shattered walls. Equally, his friends from Jerusalem were more concerned about the city's residents than its fortifications. In Nehemiah's thoughts the *Jewish remnant* took precedence over *Jerusalem*, and his visitors had the same sense of priority: *They said to me, 'Those who survived the exile . . . are in great trouble and disgrace.* Additionally, the *wall of Jerusalem is broken down, and its gates have been burned with fire'* (2–3).

The history of Christian work and witness across the centuries is an inspiring record of sacrificial people who did not think primarily about their own well-being but gave top priority to God's will and the needs of others. Paul expressed it perfectly. Christ gave himself on the cross that those who trust him for forgiveness and new life 'should no longer live for themselves but for him who died for them and was raised again'.[2] Living for Christ means loving and serving others.

2. Looking up in dependence (1:4–6a)

Nehemiah's immediate reaction to the news of his people's troubles was to go into the presence of God. Throughout the book this gifted leader is vividly portrayed as a man of earnest prayer, and this, the first of his nine recorded prayers, offers several perspectives on the quality of Nehemiah's prayer-life.

He was *committed* to prayer. For Nehemiah, prayer was natural, immediate and spontaneous (4). He turned instinctively to God. P. T. Forsyth used to say that in some form or another everybody prays. If we are not praying to God we are towards something else.

> You pray as your face is set – towards Jerusalem or Babylon. The very egotism of craving life is prayer. The great difference is the object of it. The man whose passion is habitually set upon pleasure, knowledge, wealth, honour or power is in a state of prayer to these things or for them. He prays without ceasing. These are his real gods, on whom he waits day and night ... He prays to an unknown God for a selfish boon ... Beware lest the whole trend of the soul fix on a deity that turns a doom.[3]

In Nehemiah's life, far from being a conventional religious exercise, prayer was a vital daily experience. Nothing mattered more than entering the Lord's presence to express his anguish about his people's needs, confess his inadequacy, reflect on his personal response to the news from Jerusalem, and seek for guidance about what might and must be done.

Nehemiah was *genuine* in prayer. Deeply grieved to learn such distressing news, he identifies with the dejection of Jerusalem's citizens: he *sat down and wept* (4). Though separated from them by a vast desert, their needs were close to his heart. He was not the last person to weep over Jerusalem's troubles. During the last week of his earthly ministry, Jesus looked out over the rebellious city and found it impossible to hold back the tears.[4] Like Nehemiah, he too was infinitely more concerned about the people's welfare than his own.

Nehemiah was *sacrificial* in prayer. He believed there was nothing better he could do for his people than pray for them so, in order to give undisturbed time to his intercessions, he denied himself food for several days. When he *mourned and fasted* (4) he was engaging

---

[2] 2 Cor. 5:15.   [3] P. T. Forsyth, *The Soul of Prayer* (1916), pp. 89–90.
[4] Lk. 19:41.

in a practice with notable biblical precedents.[5] In ancient near-eastern countries, meals were not the hurried affairs of busy contemporary life. Normally, they were relaxed and extended opportunities for social contact and leisurely conversation. Missing a meal released an hour or two for undisturbed prayer.

Nehemiah was *persistent* in prayer. For *some days* (4) he continued to seek God; *day and night* (6) he poured out his soul to the Lord. Like the importunate friend in Luke's parable,[6] Nehemiah knocked repeatedly at God's door because there was no-one else to whom he could turn for help. Prayer is the most eloquent expression of our priorities. It confesses our total reliance upon God, exercises our personal faith and demonstrates our love for others. As he approaches God, Nehemiah divests himself of every distracting thought so that he can concentrate his mind entirely on the one who has promised to listen to everyone who calls upon him.

Nehemiah was *encouraged* in prayer. Dependent believers of earlier generations have entered the holy place before him, and phrases and themes from their prayers inspire, inform and shape his own. His prayer deliberately echoes the petitions of Moses, Solomon, David, Jehoshaphat, Daniel, and his contemporary, Ezra.[7] If by prayer these intercessors had received cleansing, found peace, obtained strength and gained confidence, so could Nehemiah. He is not simply inspired by their example; his prayer is enriched by their language. The words they used, preserved in Scripture, became the inspiration of his heart and mind as he entered the divine presence. The great prayers of Scripture ought to be incentives and models for our own.

He was *confident* in prayer. As Nehemiah exalts God, he focuses on eight highly relevant aspects of God's nature. The prayer becomes an adoring octave of divine omnipotence. Although Jerusalem's need has driven him into the presence of God, the city's problem is soon dwarfed by an awesome sense of God's majestic glory. Within moments he is exalting a God who is sovereign, mighty, holy, loving, faithful, vocal, attentive and merciful.

With a sense of submissive awe, Nehemiah approaches his sovereign God. He prayed *before the God of heaven* (4) and said, *O LORD, God of heaven* (5). He was in Susa and his problem was in far-off Jerusalem, but both cities – one rich the other poor, one strong the other weak, one proud the other broken – were like tiny specks of dust under the vast canopy of God's heaven. 'God of heaven' was a brilliantly graphic expression of the universal supremacy of the only true God. The phrase was popular in contemporary Persian

[5] Jdg. 20:26; 1 Sa. 7:6; 1 Ch. 10:12; Ezr. 8:23; Est. 4:3; 9:31; Ps. 35:13; Is. 58:6–8; Je. 36:9; Dn. 9:3; Joel 1:14; 2:15; Jon. 3:5.   [6] Lk. 11:5–10.
[7] Dt. 9:26–29; 1 Ch. 17:20–21; 2 Ch. 6:14–42; 20:6–12; Dn. 9:4–19; Ezr. 9:6–15.

prayers and Nehemiah will have heard it on the lips of pagan courtiers, but he had also known it from the prayers of devout Israelites recorded in Scripture. In an earlier Jerusalem crisis, King Jehoshaphat had sought 'the God who is in heaven'. In a different kind of danger, the runaway prophet Jonah confessed his allegiance to 'the God of heaven, who made the sea and the land'. Surrounded by pagan idolatry, Daniel rejoiced that there was 'a God in heaven'. More recently, Persia's king had described Ezra's God in identical language.[8] Although Nehemiah is deeply troubled, he affirms his commitment to 'the God of heaven', knowing that life's bewildering adversities are all under his sovereign control.

Moreover, although sovereign, God is not remote and distant, untouched by humanity's everyday events, ruling in heaven but detached from life on earth. Nehemiah knows his God is almighty, *the great* (5) God whose power has been evident throughout Israel's precarious history. His power transformed Jehoshaphat's crisis into a triumphant victory, Jonah's plight into a psalm of thanksgiving, Daniel's adversities into persuasive testimony, Ezra's formidable mission into impressive service. Nehemiah also faced an immense challenge; such problems could be effectively overcome but only by a *great* and omnipotent God.

Nehemiah also enters the presence of an *awesome* (5) God, believing that he is not only powerful but holy. Nehemiah is specially conscious of the divine holiness and comes before God with adoring reverence. Like Moses in the desert, he hides his face, metaphorically removing the shoes from his soiled feet. Like Isaiah in the temple, he confesses his need before an *awesome* God. Like Job, his encounter with an *awesome* God ushers him into the place of repentance.[9] It is the holiness of God which identifies and exposes sin as sin. All too easily we give less ugly names to it, rationalize our unacceptable conduct and find excuses for the things undone. But, confronted by a holy Father, we see sin for the offensive thing it is, recognize its malevolent and destructive power, and beg an awesome God's forgiveness.

Nehemiah rejoices that his holy God is also compassionate. He identifies his needs in the presence of a God of infinite grace who has made *a covenant of love* (5) with his people. As he prays, Nehemiah draws especially on the rich teaching of both Deuteronomy and Daniel. Scripture enriches his adoration, supplication, petition and intercession. Its assurance about God's love and power is deliberately reminiscent of Moses' words to the Israelite people on the threshold of the promised land and those of Daniel as

[8] 2 Ch. 20:6; Jon. 1:9; Dn. 2:19, 28; Ezr. 7:12, 21, 23.
[9] Ex. 3:5–6; Is. 6:1–5; Job 42:5–6.

he pleaded with God for his people.[10] Earlier prayers inspire present hope. Whatever the contemporary adversities of Jerusalem's citizens, a God of infinite compassion is eager to meet their needs and deepens Nehemiah's love for others in order to initiate his purposes.

Further, God's love is not fickle and changeable but constant and reliable. He is a faithful God who *keeps his covenant of love with those who love him* (5). His people have not been what they ought to have been, but God has never acted unlovingly towards them. His chastisement has always been purposive, corrective and remedial. He has stood by them during long periods when they were far too preoccupied with marginal things to *love him and obey his commands* (5). During the demanding and dangerous assignment which lay ahead, Nehemiah found himself constantly fortified by the faithfulness of a loving God who would never let him down.

God's servant also worships a vocal God. He is not a silent deity like the gods of the surrounding nations. He has spoken eloquently, patiently and persistently through his servants, as men like Moses faithfully transmitted God's *commands* to his people. A God who has spoken so relevantly and persuasively across the centuries is not going to leave Nehemiah without direct and relevant *commands* concerning his future work.

This compassionate self-revealing God did not only speak; he listened. Israel's God was not like the deaf idols of other nations. Throughout their history his people heard his voice, and he loved to hear theirs. Nehemiah asks that his Lord's *ear* will *be attentive* and his *eyes open to hear the prayer* his servant was *praying ... day and night* (6a). Nehemiah knew that, whatever the problems which lay ahead, the way of prayer was always open and, as he prayed, help certainly came.

Nehemiah offered this prayer knowing that he was addressing a merciful God. His own sins and those of both his rebellious forefathers and disobedient contemporaries must be acknowledged and forgiven before he could embark on any enterprise for God. His servants must be cleansed before they are used. Quiet reflection on God's character intensified his servant's awareness of unforgiven sin.

3. Looking inward with penitence (1:6b–7)

God's servant's exaltation of God's nature prompts a sorrowing acknowledgment of sin. The words of his prayer reveal the intensity, honesty, realism and urgency of Nehemiah's confession.

There was an *intensity* about his confession. Overwhelmed by the

---

[10] Dt. 7:9, 21; 10:17; Dn. 9:4–6.

rebelliousness of human sin, Nehemiah gives himself to prolonged petition and intercession; *day and night* he poured out his soul to God. Since he heard of Jerusalem's distress, he had been haunted by the recollection of the people's failure to honour God and, scarcely able to think of anything else, spent every moment of available time in God's presence.

There was an *honesty* about his confession. He made no attempt to excuse the Israelite people, nor did he pray for them as a man detached from the enormity of their past transgressions and repeated failure: *I confess the sins we Israelites, including myself and my father's house, have committed against you* (6b). As he surveyed the grim record of Israel's past and present failure, he knew he was not exempt from blame. Nehemiah recognized that he was as great a sinner as anyone else in Judah.

There was a *realism* about his confession. Nehemiah knew that the people's frequently overlooked sins of omission (*We have not obeyed the commands, decrees and laws you gave your servant Moses*, 7) were just as serious as the obvious sins of commission. The glaring iniquities, the things done that offended God had to be confessed, but the many things they had failed to do were equally offensive to a holy God. In the teaching of Jesus the servant who 'does not do what his master wants' is deservedly condemned. The early Christians were reminded that 'anyone . . . who knows the good he ought to do and doesn't do it, sins'.[11] Nehemiah knew that to do nothing when he had heard of such a crying need would be a serious transgression. The *laws* God gave his *servant Moses* (7) included the command to love God with all their 'heart . . . soul and . . . strength' and to love their neighbours as much as they loved themselves. Nehemiah's prayerfulness indicated the intensity of his love for God; a response to Jerusalem's need demonstrated the reality of love for his neighbour. That love must not merely be 'with words or tongue but with actions'[12] as well. Nehemiah soon realized that earnest confession must be followed by willing obedience.

There was an *urgency* about Nehemiah's confession. It was vital to seek God's face, for in Scripture's *commands, decrees and laws* he had been taught that sin is not merely a stubborn refusal to obey certain rules which harm the life of an individual or community. It is a defiant act of aggressive personal rebellion towards God. Nehemiah acknowledges the *sins we Israelites, including myself . . . have committed against you. We have acted very wickedly towards you* (6b–7).

When David committed adultery he came to realize that he had not only transgressed against Bathsheba and her husband Uriah; he had also sinned against God. The remorseful offender cried out for

---

[11] Lk. 12:47; Jas. 4:17.   [12] 1 Jn. 3:18.

help: 'Against you, you only, have I sinned and done what is evil in your sight.' In Jesus' famous story the prodigal begins to frame his penitent confession whilst he is far away from home. He too realized that he had not merely hurt his human father but, more seriously, had sinned 'against heaven'. When he returned home he gave expression to the seriousness of his sin. He had grieved God.[13] As Clines observes, in Nehemiah's eyes sin is not regarded 'primarily as a failure to meet standards, but as a breaking off of personal relations with God'.[14]

Nehemiah was sensitive to the fact that all sin, things blatantly or carelessly done, or things selfishly or heedlessly left undone, need to be identified, acknowledged and pardoned. He knew that all such sin can be fully, immediately and eternally forgiven.[15] When John Bunyan was burdened with unrelieved guilt, the promises of Scripture caused him to stop 'and, as it were, look over my shoulder behind me, to see if I could discern that the God of grace did follow me with a pardon in his hand'.[16] He proved that the Lord is always more eager to forgive our sins than we are to confess them.

4. Looking back with gratitude (1:8–10)

Though sin must be confessed, Nehemiah does not wallow in a prolonged introspective examination of his failures and those of his fellow-Israelites. His mind continues to be informed by great passages from Deuteronomy[17] as he reflects on God's greatness and unmerited mercy. His prayer focuses not on his undoubted guilt, bruised conscience or vascillating feelings, but on two unchanging historical realities: what God has said, and what he has done. Within the narrow compass of these brief verses are the two great scriptural dimensions of revelation (8–9) and redemption (10). As Nehemiah prays, he is not only inspired by the experience, example and language of Israel's prayerful personalities. Something greater takes hold of his mind than the enriching thought that others have prayed – the colossal truth that God has spoken and acted decisively in history, both addressing his people and saving them.

a. What God has said (1:8–9)

Nehemiah recalls the realistic words of Moses about the danger of Israel's apostasy and the promise of divine mercy: *If you are unfaithful, I will scatter you among the nations, but if you return to*

[13] Ps. 51:4; Lk. 15:18, 21.   [14] Clines, p. 139.
[15] Ps. 32:1–5; 51:1–2, 7, 9; 103:12; Is. 1:18; 44:22.
[16] John Bunyan, *Grace Abounding to the Chief of Sinners* (1666), para. 173
[17] Dt. 4:27–31; 9:29; 12:5; 28:58–64; 30:1–5; Ex. 32:11.

me and obey my commands, then even if your exiled people are at
the farthest horizon, I will gather them from there and bring them
to the place I have chosen as a dwelling for my Name.

The words are a skilfully arranged mosaic of great Old Testament
warnings and promises originally given to Moses and repeated by
Solomon at the dedication of the temple.[18] Encouraged by the past,
Nehemiah faces the future. God has spoken clearly and unmistak-
ably to his people and will not change his mind: '*I will scatter ... I*
will gather'. He had said that if they broke the covenant they would
be exiled. They disregarded the warning and his word was fulfilled;
their presence in Persia proved the reliability of his word. He also
knew they would regret their disobedience, and he made generous
provision for their penitent return. Nehemiah felt he was at *the*
farthest horizon in Susa, but God was with him and his promise
would never be broken. He had 'returned' to God in a prayer of
confession and dependence, and now sought reassurance through
the promises of God's unchanging Word.

The penitent exiles had returned first under Zerubbabel and then,
eighty years later, under Ezra. Nehemiah realized that now he too
must follow their steps, but there were insuperable obstacles. Those
earlier returnees had left not only with the permission but encouragement of the Persian king. They were at liberty to make the long
journey, but Nehemiah was not a free agent. He was employed by
the king and court at Susa. Yet, if God had spoken so clearly in
Scripture about gathering his people from the farthest horizon,
promising to bring them to the place he had chosen as a dwelling for
his Name, then he was capable of fulfilling that promise in the
personal experience of Nehemiah, whatever the human obstacles,
political problems and natural difficulties. Those who venture on a
work for God recall the unchanging promise of unfailing resources.
What God has said he always does.

b. What God has done (1:10)

But, however inspiring and reassuring, words alone are rarely
enough. God demonstrates the reliability of his Word by the excellence of his deeds. In Old Testament thought, 'God is known for
what he is by what he does'.[19] To the great theme of revelation is
added the complementary truth of redemption. Nehemiah recalls
that his contemporaries are God's servants: *your people, whom you*
redeemed by your great strength and your mighty hand.

For all their undoubted failings, the Israelites are a redeemed community. God acted decisively in their history, doing exactly what he

---

[18] Lv. 26:33–45; 2 Ch. 6:36–39.
[19] C. R. North, *The Thought of the Old Testament* (London: Epworth, 1948), p. 16.

promised. At the burning bush he told Moses that he was going to deliver them, and did everything he said. Uncertain of the future, Nehemiah remembers the past. Like thousands of his fellow-Israelites, he looks back to the great exodus-event as an undeniable demonstration of God's pledge to keep his promise and demonstrate his power. The descriptive language about God's enslaved *people* brought out of Egypt by his *great strength and mighty hand* deliberately recalls the prayer of Moses in a time of immense distress. Now Nehemiah was pleading with the God of Moses, the God of transforming wonders. He was asking that the Lord who acted so dynamically then for a vast community would now do the same for a solitary individual. If he was to make his journey to that same land he too would need a miracle of mercy. God's words and deeds in the past fortified his spirit as he faced the future.

5. Looking forward with confidence (1:11)

Nehemiah's prayer moved from the recollection of what God had said and done to the contemplation of what he will say and do in a new situation. Encouraged by the Lord's former mercies he is assured of present grace. Yesterday had its innumerable blessings but Nehemiah is concerned about *today* with its different needs. We can reflect with gratitude on the mercies of the past but, as Augustine once said, 'it is the present that bites most sharply'. Though it was essential to give his best mind to what Scripture taught, now was the time for something to be done but every action must be preceded by prayer. It would be foolish to rush into the king's presence with the wrong request at any inopportune moment. Guidance was essential so, though it was tempting to push ahead with ideas and plans, Nehemiah must continue to wait upon God.

Believers have not always found it easy to maintain that essential balance between waiting and working. Moses was prepared for his life's work as he cared for sheep in Midian; forty long years of waiting preceded the final forty in service. The greatest ministry on earth was initiated with long years in a carpenter's workshop and those crucial weeks in the wilderness when Christ spent time with God and reaffirmed his priorities for the future. Before the apostle Paul was thrust into his outstanding missionary enterprise he spent time in Arabia. Waiting upon God prepares us for work in the world. On the threshold of his special mission Nehemiah prepared himself by earnest, sacrificial and sustained prayer: *O LORD, let your ear be attentive to the prayer of this your servant and to the prayer of your servants who delight in revering your name. Give your servant success today by granting him favour in the presence of this man. I was cupbearer to the king.* Nehemiah entered the unknown future with a deeper experience of God, a greater indebtedness to his partners, and a wider perspective on his problem.

He enjoyed *a deeper experience of God*. News of Jerusalem's trouble had driven him into the Lord's presence and given him a more alert sense of life's priorities. He would find his greatest delight in revering God's name. In his working life he was surrounded by palace officials whose chief end was to revere their king, but with Nehemiah it was different. Life's greatest pleasure was pleasing God. His spiritual experience echoed the repeated testimony of Israel's psalmists whose 'delight' was in God's unique Word,[20] his great salvation,[21] his perfect justice[22] and, more than all else, in the Lord himself.[23]

Nehemiah had *a greater indebtedness to his partners*. God has heard not just Nehemiah's plea but *the prayer* of his *servants*; they too delight in revering God's name and are equally ready for God's will and work. Others have joined him in the ministry of prayer. In coming days he will be indebted to the loyal partnership of many people who, until he reached Jerusalem, were total strangers to him. God's servants are his brothers (4:14, 23; 5:1, 8, 10; 10:29; 13:13). As he prayed, the realization of partnership with God's people became more inspiring and supportive than ever.

Nehemiah has *a wider perspective on his problem*. With literary artistry, Nehemiah has withheld until this moment in the narrative the nature of his work in Susa. Until now we had no idea that he held the important position of *cupbearer* in the royal palace. Writing in the same century as Nehemiah, the Greek historian Herodotus tells us that the cupbearer's office was highly esteemed among the Persian people.[24] The wine steward was a man of recognized dignity in court circles, entirely trustworthy, the king's confidant and next in rank to princes.[25] Nehemiah knew the protocol which surrounded an eastern court and realized that a huge responsibility now lay on his shoulders. He was to ask King Artaxerxes to change his mind about Jerusalem's wall-building programme. Nehemiah wanted to recommence the work the king had earlier forbidden. It

[20] Ps. 1:2; 119:16, 24, 35, 47, 77, 92, 143.   [21] Ps. 35:9.   [22] Ps. 35:27.
[23] Ps. 37:4; 43:4.
[24] *History* 3.34; see also Xenophon, *Cyropaedia* 1.3.8–9, 11. Describing a palace cupbearer depicted in Persian art at Persepolis, A. T. Olmstead says that in this period such men came to 'exercise even more influence than the commander-in-chief' (*History of the Persian Empire*, pp. 217–218).
[25] For further evidence of the honour in which cupbearers were held in the ancient near east, including the Persian court in this period, see the sources and illustrations in E. Yamauchi, *Zeitschrift für die alttestamentliche Wissenschaft* 92 (1980), pp. 132–142.

was an immense undertaking, and his first obstacle was reversing the king's previous orders.

The more he reflected on it, the more audacious it appeared until God fed a new thought into his fearful mind – the Persian king was only a *man*, nothing more. In a context where near-eastern monarchs were widely regarded as semi-divine beings, it was a salutary reminder of human frailty. The cupbearer must not think of Artaxerxes' status in the eyes of his courtiers but in God's eyes: a mere man. Nehemiah doubtless knew from Israel's wise men that the 'king's heart is in the hand of the LORD'.[26] God could and would direct the heart of Artaxerxes in order to accomplish his sovereign purposes, so Nehemiah confidently prayed, *Give your servant success today by granting him favour in the presence of this man.*

Before leaving this opening section of the narrative, there are important perspectives here on the constantly relevant issue of divine guidance. At this crucial moment in his life, Nehemiah was in urgent need of God's specific direction. Whatever could he do about Jerusalem's need? The initial prerequisite was an open-minded receptiveness to God's leading which, in his case, came through other people's representation of an urgent need (2–3). His immediate response was to pray (4). He reminded himself of the sovereign purposes of a loving God (5) which exposed his own inadequacy and unworthiness (6–7). He then found inspiration in Scripture as he remembered and claimed its specific promises (8–9). He further recalled that the Lord is all powerful (10), the God of the exodus who can accomplish anything for his servants. In seeking guidance, he found support in the prayers of others (11). He cast himself utterly upon God, believing that, however great the obstacles, he would be clearly led and given all the resources necessary for total obedience to God's will. Perplexed about the way ahead, millions of believers have pursued the same steps as Nehemiah and have not been disappointed.

[26] Pr. 21:1.

Nehemiah 2:1–10
2. The servant's guidance

As Nehemiah's story unfolds, it moves from the private aspects of his life to his public duties. We turn from personal times of prayer and fasting to his daily work in a pagan environment, from what he prayed to God to what he said to the king. Nehemiah knew how vital it was to disengage for a while from life's pressures in order to spend time with God and replenish his resources. Everybody needs that kind of spiritual 'space', quiet moments in every day for prayer, meditation and the reading of God's Word. But prayer must never be an excuse for indolence; rising from his knees, this man was better equipped for his everyday work. That essential rhythm of withdrawal and involvement is a vital aspect of effective Christian living. It was characteristic of the ministry of our Lord and is a pattern for all believers.[1]

The narrative describes some dimensions of practical spirituality in the life of Nehemiah.

1. God's servant waits (2:1)

Nehemiah was a man of decisive action, and when he prayed it was natural for him to ask God to provide an early, if not immediate, opportunity for him to speak to the king: *Give your servant success today* (1:11). But as he went from his prayer to daily work in the Persian court, he began to realize that, although *today* was his preferred day, it might not be the right day for making such a huge request. Well over a hundred days came and went as Nehemiah waited for the best moment. Possibly the king had been absent from the palace during those months but it is more likely that, the more Nehemiah prayed, the more he realized that he must patiently wait for the right opportunity. He must guard against hurrying into the

[1] Mt. 14:13–14, 22–25; Lk. 4:42; 5:15–16; 6:12–19; 9:18; 11:1; 21:36–37; 22:39–41, 45–46.

king's presence with a request he had not considered carefully in advance.

The days seemed long and, given his dynamic, extrovert personality, patient waiting would hardly come easily. His alert mind was tumbling with ideas and, with such an immense amount of work to do, he desperately wanted to get on with it. The time he spent with God multiplied those creative thoughts, provided new perspectives, and made him more prepared and composed than he would ever have thought possible. In the quiet place, faith was renewed in a God who knows the best time for everything. Believers constantly need to accept that behind life's frustrations lies a divine purpose; something can be learnt from our most difficult experiences. The apostle Paul discovered that even imprisonments could be used, and saw them not as annoying interruptions but as providential interventions. At Philippi he was severely flogged and put in chains, but he could sing at midnight. Then, even an earthquake was used to bring a prison warder to faith. Later, he wrote to Philippi from another dungeon, affirming that his prison sentence had in three respects 'served to advance the gospel'. It had heightened his sense of privilege in suffering for Christ, pagan soldiers had heard the message, and his fellow-Christians had become more courageous in their witnessing.[2]

Paul would have preferred active engagement in vigorous missionary opportunities but enforced restrictions were part of a greater plan. After all, the early Christian mission had begun not in working but in waiting. For almost six weeks the first Christians did exactly what Jesus had told them to do: 'Do not leave Jerusalem, but wait'.[3] A vast world was waiting to be won but, at that moment, prayerful dependence and obedient listening was a greater responsibility.

Newly converted, the young William Booth was devastated when, at the close of his apprenticeship, it was impossible to get work in Nottingham. He was mystified why the Lord did not answer his persistent prayer for work of any kind. His widowed mother urgently needed his help, but for a full year the prayer was unanswered. It was the greatest trial of a young Christian's faith, but God knew that those twelve months in poverty would later enable him to identify with deprived people in many parts of the world.[4]

Waiting time is not wasted time. Quiet reflection may have provided Nehemiah with fresh thought about how to present his case. Williamson thinks it possible that his reference to the month of Nisan, the beginning of a new year, might be significant. Herodotus preserves the detail that special favours were granted on a Persian monarch's birthday. Perhaps new year was the time for such a

[2] Acts 16:23–34; Phil. 1:12–14, 29–30. [3] Acts 1:4, 12–14.
[4] St John Ervine, *God's Soldier: General William Booth*, vol. 1 (London: Heinemann, 1934), p. 42.

celebration, and Nehemiah realized that the festival was an ideal opportunity to present his appeal. According to the Greek historian, it was held that 'no one who asked a boon that day at the king's board should be denied his request'.[5] It might explain the four-month delay and help to account for the king's expressed surprise that his cupbearer was looking so utterly miserable on a day when everyone else was rejoicing.

2. God's servant trusts (2:2–3)

Looking into such an unhappy face, Artaxerxes asked the wine steward to explain his despondency. Nehemiah's heart missed a beat: *I was very much afraid.* It was totally out of character. His admission literally reads, 'a terrible fear came over me', as if he was unexpectedly gripped by a sudden panic. Some people are naturally fearful, but Nehemiah can hardly be numbered among them. The rest of the book presents a picture of a man who seems totally undaunted in the face of increasing adversity. He copes creatively with a variety of problems, is untroubled by the threats of his enemies, and actively takes the initiative in situations which would be overwhelming for others (2:19–20; 4:1–4, 7–9, 10–15, 19–23; 5:1–13; 6:1–9, 10–14; 13:4–14, 15–22, 23–29).

Fear may have been unusual for Nehemiah, but when the king asked his searching question he was desperately afraid. Most people are fearful about something or other. Natural phobias possess immense power. Some people are afraid of the past, terrified that something sinister will catch up on them. Others are fearful of the present and spend their days imprisoned by crippling fear, fear of the dark, of people, spiders, snakes, water, crowds, confined spaces, open spaces. Others are fearful of the future, its unknown events, possible hardships, inevitable problems, painful insecurity. The terrorizing things are not actually present but form part of a threateningly possible scenario: the fear of illness, poverty, loneliness, insecurity. And then, that inescapable reality, the fear of death.

Paul Tillich has written about humanity's 'three types of anxiety'. The first, characteristic of the ancient world and middle ages, was the fear of death. Then followed the anxiety typical of the Reformation period and later – the fear of guilt. Finally, there is the great twentieth-century phobia – the fear of meaninglessness.[6] Those who receive God's peace have found the answer to life's greatest fears. The early Christians faced ridicule, slander, misrepresentation, hardship, persecution, imprisonment and cruel death in the calm confidence that

[5] *History* 9.110.
[6] Paul Tillich, *The Courage to Be* (London: Nisbet, 1952), pp. 37–59.

they were not alone. Nothing could deflect them from a serene trust which enabled them to look natural fears in the face. Christ had given them the assurance that his peace would always be there, enabling them to put life's problems into perspective, banishing anxiety, marginalizing their adversities, replenishing their resources.

Those three basic fears may not have been absent from Nehemiah's mind. Death was not impossible. Mercurial oriental monarchs were not noted for generous tolerance. Few would be impressed by a sulky face. The wrong word spoken at an inopportune time and he might end on the gallows.

Nehemiah knew something about the fear of guilt. He had spent weeks in prayer, at times weighed down by a sense of sin, his own, those of his family and the wider multitude of his fellow-believers.

Many of our contemporaries ask about the meaning of life, and what is the specific purpose of a particular life. Has it a special place in God's purposes? Are we born merely to eat, drink, sleep, love, work and die? The fear of meaninglessness is not an exclusively twentieth-century phenomenon. Over the months, Nehemiah's questing mind must have ranged widely over such issues. Had that question he had put to his brother Hanani about Jerusalem's welfare originated in the mind of God? Was he meant to do something about it? Was this the reason why he had been entrusted with a privileged responsibility in a Persian court? With such an acute awareness of his people's history, he must have known Esther's experience in that same palace a few decades earlier. He may even have reflected on a famous question born in that crisis and asked himself, 'and who knows whether you have not come to the kingdom for such a time as this?'[7]

Whatever his fears, in the moment of need Nehemiah was given the grace to look up and speak out. *I was very much afraid, but I said ...* We are rarely given the precise resources in advance so that they are stored away like immense, untouched reserves of courage, fortitude, strength and peace. Grace comes in the moment of need. Over the centuries, millions have testified to the truth that in crisis they were enabled to respond to the challenge with a resourcefulness they would scarcely have thought possible. The crisis did not engulf them as they might have feared. It opened new doors and they proved God's sufficiency as never before.

A minister friend of mine once tried to help an elderly believer who, though undisturbed about the idea of death, was fretful about the physical experience of dying. She had asked God to remove the fear but it was still there, robbing her of her former peace. He reminded her that specific resources are given to meet immediate needs. We are not promised a reservoir of blessing given in advance

[7] Est. 4:14 (RSV).

of all life's difficulties; sufficient grace matches present need. 'We are not given dying grace to live by', he told her. She must trust that, as the moment came, peace would come with it. Moreover, she should recognize that it was a futile anxiety. After all, who was to say that she would know anything about the physical experience of dying? She might slip away in her sleep. The Lord often calls his children home suddenly and unexpectedly. They simply close their eyes on earth and open them in heaven.

Nehemiah also proved the abundant sufficiency of immediate grace. He had waited for weeks and now the moment had arrived; he was looking into the clouded face of a bewildered king. The praying months had prepared him for these crucial minutes. He trusted God, and in that moment the courage came. He told the king that it was no longer possible for him to hide his grief. The place where his ancestors were buried had become a desolate waste and fire had ravaged a holy city. The thought of desecrated burial places touched a sensitive chord in the royal mind. It was a wise approach. The Persians revered their ancestors and graves were sacred places. Referring simply to a 'city', Nehemiah made no mention of Jerusalem. Perhaps that was intentional at the start of the conversation, particularly as the king had already pronounced firmly on the subject some years earlier. Artaxerxes asked him exactly what he wanted. Before answering the king, it was essential to speak briefly with Someone else.

3. God's servant prays (2:4–5a)

Then I prayed to the God of heaven, and I answered the king. Nehemiah's prayer is one of the most inspiring prayer experiences in Scripture and a high water mark in the history of prayer. Its essential brevity makes it so compellingly attractive and conjures in the mind a range of emotions. Here is a man who knows how to seek God (1:4; 4:4–5; 5:19; 6:9, 14; 13:14, 22, 29, 31).

It emphasizes *the necessity of prayer*. Although he had prayed at every available opportunity during the past four months, he could not face this critical moment in the conversation without once more looking to God to meet his needs. The destiny of thousands of fellow-Israelites might turn on the way he spoke in the next few minutes. It was far too big a responsibility for him to take on his own. He needed help from beyond.

It describes *the immediacy of prayer*. There is no need for us to get away to a particular place, or wait until we can set aside prolonged time for undistracted reflection. At any moment we can talk to God. There and then, in the presence of a human king, Nehemiah is at the footstool of heaven. François Fénelon advised his readers to 'make good use of chance moments', as when we are waiting for someone, travelling, standing in a queue, for 'at such times it is easy to lift the heart to God and thereby gain fresh strength' for the tasks ahead. Nehemiah would have agreed with the seventeenth-century archbishop's conviction that 'one moment will suffice to place yourself in God's presence, to love and worship him. If you wait for convenient seasons . . . you will run the risk of waiting for ever. The less time one has the more carefully it should be husbanded.'[8]

It illustrates *the naturalness of prayer*. Although Nehemiah had spent hours in prayer over the waiting weeks, to pray again at that crucial moment was the instinctive reaction of a dependent believer. He prayed because it was the most sensible and rational thing to do. He lacked the resources but he knew where they could be found. Abraham Lincoln's testimony has been shared by millions: 'I have been driven many times to my knees by the overwhelming conviction that I had nowhere else to go; my own wisdom and that of all around me seemed insufficient for the day.'

It portrays *the intimacy of prayer*. When in those seconds he *prayed to the God of heaven* it was not a desperate cry to a distant God. He was communing in secret with a caring Father. There was hardly time for words; the sigh became a supplication. Between one breath and another he was in the audience chamber of God, assured that he would not lack anything necessary in his daring venture.

It demonstrates *the confidence of prayer*. He was communing with *the God of heaven*, the God of unique sovereignty, comforting omniscience and limitless resources. Jesus taught his disciples to address their prayers to a Father 'in heaven' and, exemplifying this, he looked to heaven in moments of need.[9]

It proves *the effectiveness of prayer*. The quick petition was immediately answered. The unfailing Lord was at his side. Within seconds, the right and best words were on his lips and, in the same moment, the God of heaven caused generous thoughts to enter Artaxerxes' enquiring mind.

4. God's servant plans (2:5b–8)

Nehemiah had lifted his heart to God; now he must open his mouth to the king. The unhurried prayer-times, frequent meditation and reflection over the past few months now came to rich fruition. He had thought it out carefully. There was nothing remotely haphazard about his utterances. He believed not only in dependent praying but also in deliberate planning. Time and again he had asked the Lord to

---

[8] *The Spiritual Letters of Archbishop Fénelon: Letters to Women*, trans. H. L. Lear (1877), pp. 21–22.   [9] Mt. 6:9; Mk. 6:41; 7:34; Jn. 11:41; 17:1.

guide his thinking as he endeavoured to shape an effective strategy. Ever since he had heard of Jerusalem's troubles, Nehemiah had wanted to help and was eager to offer his best. During the waiting period there was only one skill he could bring to the prospective enterprise: the careful thoughts of an alert and dedicated mind. Later on he would use feet to make the journey, eyes to survey the scene, hands to move the stones, but initially he could only offer heart (*wept*, 1:4) and mind. Now, all that rigorous thinking must become vocal as he shared with the king what he had planned for God.

There are times in life when we are confronted with a challenging opportunity for God but cannot at that moment respond as speedily and wholeheartedly as we would like. Life's other demands make immediate eager participation difficult if not impossible. In the dark days of persecution in late seventeenth-century England, Philip Henry reminded nonconformist believers that when we cannot do what we would, we must do what we can. There were all manner of things which Nehemiah would like to have done during the four-month period of tedious delay, but he did what he could: he prayed, trusted and thought for God, and now he could see how crucial those waiting weeks had been. Because he had given so much time to careful thinking and meticulous planning, he knew exactly how to describe the city's need, answer the king's questions, plan the hazardous journey and obtain the necessary resources.

Nehemiah knew how to describe the city's need. He appealed to the Persian respect for the dead (3, 5) rather than Israelite concern for the living. He spoke first about graves and then about gates. Reference to Jerusalem's severely damaged defences might have produced a quick emotive response from a king who had earlier issued an order preventing a rebuilding enterprise in a city with 'a long history of revolt against kings . . . a place of rebellion and sedition'. Then, he had demanded that such work must cease, 'until I so order'.[10] There was the loophole. Nehemiah had prayed that this might be the moment for the ban to be lifted, but it was an audacious request.

He knew how to answer the king's questions. He might anticipate that Artaxerxes would ask, *How long will your journey take, and when will you get back?* (6). The enquiry was reasonable, and the cupbearer had worked out as accurately as possible how long a project of that kind might take, so he promptly answered the king's question as he *set a time*.

He knew how to plan the hazardous journey. He asked Artaxerxes, *If it pleases the king, may I have letters to the governors of Trans-Euphrates, so that they will provide me with safe conduct*

[10] Ezr. 4:17–23.

until I arrive in Judah? (7). The king alone could help him with two necessities, protection and provision. The long caravan route was particularly dangerous and he would appreciate a military escort.

Everybody is different and there is nothing monochrome about God's servants. Thirteen years earlier Ezra had refused the offer of Persian soldiers to accompany his people on their way back to Judah, believing the 'gracious hand of our God is on everyone who looks to him'.[11] But Nehemiah maintained that *because the gracious hand of God* (8) was upon him, the king granted his request for protection. One man's commitment to God precluded the escort; the other welcomed it. Ezra regarded soldiers as a lack of confidence in God's power; Nehemiah viewed them as evidence of God's superlative goodness.

Christians frequently differ on important issues, and it is a mark of spiritual maturity if they can handle those differences creatively rather than engage in damaging verbal warfare. First-century believers differed on some questions and Paul urged them to 'stop passing judgment on one another'. With such a vast canvas of biblical truth and wide range of Christian experience, we are bound to think differently on occasions. Before we hastily judge other believers or ostracize them, we must make every attempt to understand and love them, and discern what we can learn from them as we 'make every effort to do what leads to peace and to mutual edification'.[12] We must not rigidly stereotype believers into identical patterns of spirituality. The Welsh Puritan, Morgan Llwyd, expressed it well in simple verse:

> Men's faces, voices, differ much
> Saints are not all one size
> Flowers in one garden vary too
> Let none monopolize.[13]

Nehemiah knew how to obtain the necessary resources. He would need timber for walls, towers and gates, as well as for the construction of his own house. It was a well-considered request. Nehemiah had already obtained the name of *Asaph, keeper of the king's forest* (8), so that he knew in advance the precise information necessary for the provision of valuable timber.

5. God's servant testifies (2:9–10)

Nehemiah testifies to the goodness of God in answering his prayers, guiding his mind, directing his speech and meeting his needs: *And*

[11] Ezr. 8:22–23.   [12] Rom. 14:1–23.
[13] Quoted in G. F. Nuttall, *The Welsh Saints 1640–1660* (Cardiff: University of Wales Press, 1966), p. 17.

because the gracious hand of my God was upon me, the king granted my requests (8).

God's servant is convinced that only God could have brought about such a dramatic change in the king's mind and his cupbearer's destiny. The conversation of one Israelite visitor to Susa had initiated a chain of events which was to lead to the complete re-fortification of Jerusalem. Most great enterprises can be traced to insignificant beginnings. When the newly converted gambler Edward Vincent persuaded his reluctant friend Edward Studd to hear D. L. Moody preach, he could never have imagined the remarkable events which would follow. Studd had barely two years to live, but his own dramatically transformed life led directly to the conversion of his three eldest sons. They included C. T. Studd, the outstanding cricketer and, later, missionary pioneer, and Kynaston Studd, who led the young John R. Mott to Christ, issuing in an influential ministry among students and the famous Edinburgh Missionary Conference. And all because the gracious hand of God was upon Edward Vincent.[14]

When the first Babylonian exiles were settling back in Jerusalem, understandably depressed about their limited resources, the prophet Zechariah had urged them not to despise 'the day of small things'.[15] The simple conversation between two brothers in Susa was a small enough thing by human standards but, because *the gracious hand* of a sovereign God was on those two servants, it led directly to a radical change in Jerusalem's history.

Moreover, Nehemiah did not simply reflect on that *gracious hand*; he believed it important to record in writing his profound conviction that everything was due to God's arranging,[16] not human contriving. God's servant had given meticulous thought to his strategy, but all his careful planning could not have led to such a successful project had it not been for the Lord's meticulous timing, constant guidance and overruling provision, so Nehemiah wanted to set that down in his memoirs.

Nehemiah planned everything as carefully as he possibly could, but he affirmed that more than careful organization was necessary if Jerusalem's walls were not to remain a heap of ruins. God must work, and he did; that is why Nehemiah included in his written memoirs the first of many references to his greatest debt. When other people took up his story he did not want this paramount truth to be marginalized: *And because the gracious hand of my God was upon me, the king granted my requests.*

In the firm assurance that God's hand was a generous hand, he

---

[14] John Pollock, *Moody without Sankey* (London: Hodder and Stoughton, 1963), pp. 145–47. [15] Zc. 4:10. [16] See Ps. 118:23.

went to the governors of Trans-Euphrates and gave them the king's letters (9) about safe conduct and the guarantee of necessary resources. Because that hand was a protecting hand, he was able to face not only potential dangers en route but actual dangers in Jerusalem – the sinister and sustained opposition of *Sanballat the Horonite and Tobiah the Ammonite* who, together with others, *were very much disturbed that someone had come to promote the welfare of the Israelites* (10). The hand that strengthened him in Susa was more supportive than ever in Jerusalem.

Nehemiah 2:11–20
3. The servant's strategy

The long journey over, Nehemiah sees Jerusalem for the first time in his life. The change and challenge is humanly overwhelming, but he confronts the fresh scene with a clear strategy. The story portrays exemplary leadership qualities as we see God's servant in action.

1. Replenishing resources (2:11–12)

As he approached Jerusalem, Nehemiah could appreciate why Hanani had been such a despondent messenger when he came to Susa. He too became overwhelmed when he saw the city's shattered walls and useless gates, but at this stage he was not in a hurry to look more closely at the extensive damage. There was a greater priority. He must be at his best before he surveyed the scene. Before embarking on such a major task he gives expression to three personal concerns. We are meant to be at peace with ourselves, encouraged by others, and in harmony with God. Everyone has physical and spiritual needs, and if either is marginalized or ignored we cannot hope to be at our best.

Nehemiah's physical need was rest. The journey of four months would have taken its toll and he began by taking a break. He waited for *three days* (11) before embarking on anything else. He was following Ezra's example, who 'rested three days' when he arrived in Jerusalem.[1] The journey had involved travelling through inhospitable territory at the rate of about nine or ten miles a day, camping at night, and moving off at dawn before the sun's strong rays made travel impossible. A brief period for recuperation was an obvious necessity.

Physically exhausted people are not likely to achieve as much as they desire. Tiredness robs us of essential perspective, multiplies anxiety, makes new opportunities intolerably burdensome and

[1] Ezr. 8:32.

destroys our peace. Elijah was worn out after the physical, emotional and spiritual demands on Mount Carmel and the race to Jezreel had drained all his natural resources. Then, Queen Jezebel threatened to take his life, and it was all too much. Engulfed by fear he ran for safety to a desert hideout. His greatest need was sleep, a good meal and the companionship lovingly provided by an attendant angel.[2]

Jesus emphasized the importance of rest. He needed it, and urged his disciples to find 'space' for relaxation as well as quiet prayer. When he heard about the cruel execution of John the Baptist, he 'withdrew by boat privately to a solitary place'.[3] When his disciples returned from their preaching mission 'and reported to him all that they had done and taught' he knew how much they needed a break. They were so pressed by the needs of so many people 'coming and going that they did not even have a chance to eat'. He quickly identified their greatest need: 'Come with me by yourselves to a quiet place and get some rest.'[4]

Nehemiah's spiritual need was direction from God. Even the valued *few men* (12) he had as colleagues were not told everything about his desires and ambitions. He did not chatter irresponsibly even to people who shared his ideals. *I had not told anyone what my God had put in my heart to do for Jerusalem* (12), and *as yet I had said nothing to the Jews or the priests or nobles or officials or any others who would be doing the work* (16).

Over the eight months of preparation and travel, he became increasingly sensitive to creative thoughts which the Lord fed into his receptive heart and mind. Moreover, God was still speaking to him; the past continuous tense emphasizes the immediacy and continuity of his communion, 'what my God *was prompting* me to do' (NEB). He needed time for further reflection on those imaginative ideas which were to carry the project through to a successful conclusion. Once the work began, innumerable demands would be made upon him. Now it was important to set aside time for God.

These inner reserves of spiritual resourcefulness are indispensable for the servant of God, yet the increasing pressures of contemporary life can crowd out that vital 'space' which we all need for physical rest and spiritual renewal.

2. Assessing need (2:13–16)

Once the rejuvenating rest period was over, it was time for Nehemiah to survey the walls[5] and estimate the likely size of the team and the

---

[2] 1 Ki. 18:46 – 19:9.   [3] Mt. 14:12–13.   [4] Mk. 6:7–13, 30–32.
[5] For an archaeological perspective on Nehemiah's wall, with photographs, see Kathleen M. Kenyon, *Jerusalem: Excavating 3000 Years of History* (London: Thames and Hudson, 1967), pp. 107–111.

materials necessary for such a mammoth task. Sanballat and Tobiah were 'very much disturbed' (2:10) at his mission and they were not the only opponents. These men doubtless had their spies in Jerusalem, and it was important for Nehemiah not to disclose his plans until he had mobilized his physical and material resources. One night, he set off to survey the damaged walls and gates *with a few men* (12) as trusted colleagues. They may have been partners who had travelled with him from Susa or, more likely, reliable locals who knew the terrain and especially those parts of the wall which were almost impassable. A night journey would ensure that Jerusalem's people would not ask too many questions as to why this visitor from Persia was inspecting their desolate city. But it could not be done on his own. He needed trustworthy colleagues, and so do we. We are not meant to go it alone.

The New Testament's descriptive imagery about the church emphasizes interdependence as a vital ingredient in our corporate life. We are limbs in a body which functions on the basis of inter-related co-operation. We are not isolated units but mutually dependent members who are joined together as 'living stones' in a temple which is 'being built'[6] as fellow-believers serve one another for the glory of Christ. At a time when he was embarking on a dangerous exercise, Nehemiah greatly valued the knowledge, experience and integrity of those *few men*. We need one another in the work of Christ.

The moonlight journey with those trusted friends 'is one of the most dramatic scenes in Nehemiah's brilliantly evocative memoirs'.[7] The secret exploration made Nehemiah aware of the extent of the damage and enabled him fully to grasp the opportunities, demands and dangers of his challenging assignment.

It was a *demanding* enterprise. He must look at each section of the wall so that every detail of the repair could be organized expertly and effectively. Whatever we do for God is worthy of our best. Other things perish this side of eternity; everything we attempt for the Lord has enduring value. Paul urged slaves in the first-century churches to tackle their daily work as though they were serving Christ himself.[8]

It was a *hazardous* assignment. Night travel was essential; hidden enemies were all too eager to frustrate Nehemiah's plans for restoration. For this reason he *said nothing* to anyone beyond his colleagues on the small reconnaissance team. Local Persian *officials* were not informed of his intentions and, at this stage, even those *who would be doing the work* (16) with him were kept in the dark. The prospective builders would hear about it once the needs were

---

[6] 1 Cor. 12:12–31; Eph. 2:21–22; 1 Pet. 2:5.   [7] Clines, p. 145.   [8] Col. 3:22–24.

assessed. The careless leakage of information at this early stage might bring the work to the same abrupt end that had wrecked the earlier rebuilding venture. Most work for God thrusts us into the arena of conflict. The enemy is always on the alert, ready to destroy any undertaking which might glorify God and help others. The apostle Paul knew that whenever there is an opportunity for service, the element of opposition is never far away. It will certainly appear in one form or another; the devil will see to that.[9]

It was a *co-operative* venture. Only by surveying the walls and gates could Nehemiah calculate how the work might be divided and what were the likely requirements in terms of personnel and materials. Now was the time to enlist the support of a larger team.

3. Recruiting colleagues (2:17)

In some way not mentioned in the narrative, Nehemiah gathered together a large company of prospective partners. A natural administrator, he soon enlisted the willing help of reliable associates who would accept responsibility for different sections of the work. How a newcomer in an unfamiliar situation was able to muster such an energetic task force is an informative commentary on his leadership skills.

First, Nehemiah identifies with the workers: *Then I said to them, 'You see the trouble we are in'*. Months before it was their trouble (1:2); now it is his trouble as well. He is passionately involved in the city's welfare and feels its need as acutely as though he had been living in the desolate city all his life.

Next, he presents spiritual perspectives. He describes *'the trouble we are in'*. It is not merely that *Jerusalem lies in ruins, and its gates have been burned with fire*. Far more serious than the physical desolation is the spiritual *disgrace*. It is a reproach to the name of God, a matter for scorn and abuse among Jerusalem's pagan neighbours and visitors. The sight of those collapsed walls for well over a century has created the impression in the pagan mind that Israel's God has abandoned his rebellious people and is no longer on their side. So Nehemiah draws the prospective workers' attention to spiritual values and ideals.

Here is a man who is not only ready to work for God but knows exactly why he is doing it. Some church activities are habitually maintained largely because they have been in existence for some time, and the good people who work in them are too busy to evaluate their purpose, motives and aims. Well-established organizations can be perpetuated without examining their precise spiritual aims. Most

[9] 1 Cor. 16:9; 2 Cor. 2:11.

activities could benefit from a healthy evaluation exercise now and again. What is their purpose and how far are they achieving their ambitions? Are they evangelistic, educative or simply social? Could they be done just as effectively by people without a clear faith? If so, in what way do they serve Christ's kingdom? Nehemiah is in no doubt whatever about his objective, and knows exactly why those walls must be rebuilt. It is not simply to defend the city's fortifications and improve its economy. God's Name is at stake in the enterprise, not simply Jerusalem's welfare.

Then, he invites immediate action. Everybody knows exactly what is required, *'Come, let us rebuild the wall of Jerusalem and we will no longer be in disgrace'*, and everyone realizes that the task must begin without further delay. He is making a considerable demand on the dispirited citizens and their fellow-Israelites throughout the region. It will be a highly sacrificial enterprise, for whilst they are working on the walls they cannot be earning their living. How long is it likely to take? How will their families fare in their absence? Who will protect them if they are intimidated by the project's opponents? Before people can respond they need the assurance that, for all his gifts, someone greater than Nehemiah is behind the venture.

4. Inspiring confidence (2:18)

Nehemiah has mentioned the walls but his central theme is the sufficiency of God. His mind dwells on the Lord's greatness as he shares his spiritual ideals with those he wants to work alongside him. They must relate well to one another as fellow-workers, but their greatest need is to be united in the things which matter most – their confidence in, dependence on, and love for God.

Nehemiah believes in the power of persuasive testimony: *I also told them about the gracious hand of my God upon me and what the king had said to me.* Earlier Nehemiah took care to include a reference in his memoirs to the source of his success: 'And because the gracious hand of my God was upon me, the king granted my requests' (9). He was convinced that he had not reached Jerusalem merely because he had been a skilful persuader (3–5), or because the queen was possibly a compliant helper (6), or the king a generous benefactor (7–8), but because God had been a sovereign provider. Furthermore, because the Lord had done that for Nehemiah he knew it might help others if he talked about it. Personal testimony can enrich others by widening their horizons and inspiring their confidence. The psalmist, after celebrating God's mighty acts in history ('Come and see what God has done ... He turned the sea into dry land'), goes on to relate how he has helped in personal experience: 'Come and listen ... let me tell you what he has done for me'.[10]

Nehemiah did precisely that on the day he enlisted his sacrificial workers. The whole chapter is a testimony, a written and vocal affirmation of confidence in a God who hears (4), guides (5), instructs (12) and sustains (20) his people.

Many outstanding Christians were brought to personal faith because someone shared with them the story of their personal experience of Christ. When the sixteenth-century Cambridge priest, Thomas Bilney, was converted through reading Erasmus's Latin version of the New Testament, he sought for an opportunity to share his radiant testimony with the Cambridge scholar, Hugh Latimer, 'desiring him for God's sake to hear his confession'. Latimer naturally imagined he was longing to confess his sins, but Bilney wanted to confess his faith. Bilney's story went straight to Latimer's heart, and yet another great English Reformer received new life in Christ.[11]

Nehemiah's testimony captured those two vital elements in any rich doctrine of God: transcendence and immanence. He acknowledges his transcendence as he worships 'the God of heaven' (4, 20), but his God is not remote and distant. The Lord puts creative thoughts into the minds of his people (12) and his 'gracious hand' is upon them in everyday life (8, 18). Those two attributes of the character of God must never be separated. God's eternal transcendence guards us against irreverence; his immanence and immediate involvement save us from despair. The team can be assured that God is with them but that must never be taken for granted. There is an eternal throne as well as a loving hand. Encouraged by Nehemiah's testimony the people were ready for immediate service: '*Let us start rebuilding.*'

5. Handling opposition (2:19–20)

The builders' opponents have already been identified (10). Now their numbers have increased. *Sanballat the Horonite* and *Tobiah the Ammonite* are joined by *Geshem the Arab*. Earlier, the opponents were 'very much disturbed' (10); now this troublesome trio become highly vocal in their enmity towards Nehemiah and his newly recruited associates. They initiate their opposition campaign the moment the work gets under way. Perhaps a volley of searing verbal insults and sinister insinuations might threaten the project at the start.

[10] Ps. 66:5–6, 16.
[11] Hugh Latimer, *First Sermon on the Lord's Prayer*; R. Demaus, *Hugh Latimer* (1904), pp. 45–46.

First, they derided the efforts of the workers. They *mocked and ridiculed* them (19). The tongue can be a vicious weapon; if we become its victims we must remember that verbal onslaughts have often been part of the enemy's demoralizing tactics. The apostle Paul had to endure a good deal of it. He told the believers at Corinth, where there were numerous antagonists, that he had experienced 'dishonour', been given a 'bad report' and regarded as an impostor, even though he had 'wronged no-one'. People there spurned him as an 'unimpressive' personality with no gifts in speaking.[12] In his evangelistic ministry he was no stranger to mockery and ridicule. His fellow-Jews 'talked abusively' about his preaching at Antioch, and poisoned people's minds in Iconium. He was dismissed as a 'babbler' and 'sneered' at in Athens, received further abuse in Corinth and his message 'publicly maligned' at Ephesus, all preludes to a serious campaign to take his life in Jerusalem.[13] Jesus said that on occasions Christians may have to suffer unjustified insults as when their critics say 'all kinds of evil' against them because of their loyalty to Christ. At such times believers should recall the past ('in the same way they persecuted the prophets'), rejoice in the present (suffering is a privilege), and remember the future ('great is your reward in heaven').[14] Those people who, like Nehemiah and his friends, are *mocked and ridiculed* have been honoured with a place in good company.

They questioned their motives. *What is this you are doing? Are you rebelling against the king?* (19). It was a cutting allegation and one which the more timid workers might hear with dismay. The previous attempt to rebuild had been promptly terminated when Persia's king heard a similar accusation of political disloyalty: 'this . . . is a rebellious city'.[15] Christian workers across the centuries have had to absorb bitter criticism and the imputation of wrong motives. If, on examining our hearts, we know that we treasure no ambition other than the glory of God, it matters little what others may say. When Nehemiah responded to their derision, two things mattered most: the glory of God and the integrity of his workers.

Nehemiah does not stoop to answer their lies. He first exalts the God who has called him to the work. *I answered them by saying, 'The God of heaven will give us success'* (20). He was undisturbed by their fictitious insinuations but he was concerned that God should be magnified in the project. He declared his firm conviction that anything good which came out of their efforts would be entirely due to the generosity of God. His words resonate with persuasive confidence. Whatever the nature of human opposition, God will

[12] 2 Cor. 6:8; 7:2; 10:10.
[13] Acts 13:45; 14:2, 19; 17:18, 32; 18:6; 19:9; 21:31; 22:22.   [14] Mt. 5:11–12.
[15] Ezr. 4:12–16.

bring the work to a successful conclusion but his Name must be magnified from the start.

There may be times when the Lord might use us more evidently if we did not secretly desire personal acclaim. He will not share his glory with another.[16] Eifion Evans preserves a telling story from the mid-nineteenth-century Welsh Revival. Following New Year's Day services, the preacher, David Morgan, was travelling home with an elderly minister who said that, as he had preached, 'so near was the Revivalist to his God that his face shone like that of an angel':

> On the way home I dared not break the silence for miles. Towards midnight I ventured to say, 'Didn't we have blessed meetings Mr. Morgan?'. 'Yes', he replied and, after a pause, added, 'The Lord would give us great things if only he could trust us.' 'What do you mean', I asked. 'If he could trust us not to steal the glory for ourselves'. Then the midnight air rang with his cry at the top of his voice, 'Not unto us, O Lord, not unto us, but unto *Thy* name give glory'.[17]

Nehemiah's other concern was for the integrity of the workers. He told his accusers, *We his servants will start rebuilding, but as for you, you have no share in Jerusalem or any claim or historic right to it* (20). The team could ignore their taunts because the implied disloyalty was a trumped-up charge with no basis in reality. They knew that their consciences were clear before God. But Nehemiah's reply to the indictment explains the reason for the troublesome trio's vilification. From their perspective, Nehemiah's appointment had disrupted the political balance of that region and put Sanballat and Tobiah out of a job as far as Jerusalem and Judah were concerned. Both political and religious considerations account for their opponents' animosity.

From a political perspective, biblical and other evidence suggests that Sanballat's administrative responsibilities for Samaria may have included jurisdiction over the greater Jerusalem area. Now, Nehemiah had arrived in the city with the king's specific authority, and the Samaritan leader was angry that he had been robbed of his former authority over the Israelite people.

The religious issue went deeper. *Sanballat* is a Babylonian name meaning 'Sin [the moon god] has given life' and probably suggests that his ancestors were among those foreign people who settled 'in the towns of Samaria to replace the Israelites' who had been taken to Assyria in the eighth century. These deportees brought their own gods and intermarried with northern Israelites, with the effect that,

---

[16] Is. 42:8.
[17] Eifion Evans, *When He is Come: An Account of the 1858–60 Revival in Wales* (Bala: Evangelical Movement of Wales (1959), p. 57.

in time, 'while these people were worshipping the LORD, they were serving their idols'.[18] It was the spiritual apostasy which troubled Nehemiah, as it had Ezra. We will meet the issue of pluralism later in the book. At this stage it is enough to note that it accounted for Nehemiah's resistance to any idea that these Samaritan people might share in the rebuilding project.

Tobiah was one of Sanballat's close working colleagues, and he too becomes a persistent adversary. His name means 'Yahweh is good', and it is generally held that he was another governor from the region, probably responsible for the oversight of Ammonite territory. He may have been offended by Nehemiah's remarks because of his own (doubtlessly compromised) Israelite roots, possibly arguing that he ought to have been approached about the rebuilding.

Both men were supported by *Geshem*, or Gashmu as he is called later (6:6, margin), an influential Arab who, with his son, 'gained control of a confederation of Arabian tribes and established their rule over a wide territory of North Arabia . . . extending their power to the eastern reaches of Egypt'.[19] Yamauchi suggests that he may have feared that Nehemiah's independent activity 'might interfere with his lucrative trade in myrrh and frankincense'.[20]

Kidner points out that Nehemiah's enemies made the city and its surrounding territory highly vulnerable for, with the increasingly powerful Geshem controlling the southern approaches and an 'already hostile Samaria and Ammon to the north and east, Judah was now virtually encircled, and the war of nerves had begun'.[21] Although the tormenting trio were united in their opposition, their antagonism may have been prompted by slightly different perspectives: Sanballat's political objections, Tobiah's religious sensibilities and Geshem's materialistic interests.

However that may be, Nehemiah had good reason not to associate with them, and their later hostility proves how wise he was to resist their opposition in the early stages. Jerusalem was a 'holy city' (11:1), and those who participated must also be holy, that is, 'set apart' for God's work and 'separated from' anything which might mar their distinctive witness. The holiness theme is prominent in Nehemiah

[18] 2 Ki. 17:24, 29–41.
[19] F. M. Cross, 'Geshem the Arabian, Enemy of Nehemiah', *Biblical Archaeologist* 18 (1955), pp. 46–47.
[20] Yamauchi, p. 691. For further discussion regarding Geshem, see I. Rabinowitz, 'Aramaic Inscriptions of the Fifth Century BCE', *Journal of Near Eastern Studies* 15 (1956), pp. 1–9; W. J. Dumbrell, 'The Tell el-Mashkuta Bowls and the "Kingdom" of Qedar in the Persian Period', *Bulletin of the American Schools of Oriental Research* 203 (1971), pp. 33–44; A. K. Irvine, 'The Arabs and Ethiopians', in D. J. Wiseman (ed.), *Peoples of Old Testament Times*, pp. 292–293; and, for a different view, J. R. Bartlett, 'From Edomites to Nabataeans', *Palestine Exploration Quarterly* 111 (1979), pp. 53–66. [21] Kidner, p. 84.

and will appear again later in his memoirs. It is given rich application in New Testament teaching, where believers are also called to a characteristically different lifestyle modelled on the example of Jesus,[22] actively contributing to the world but not manipulated by it.

The hard work on Jerusalem's walls and gates was a call to spiritual commitment, physical exertion and material sacrifice. It was worthy of their best powers. As a holy people they gave themselves to it with unreserved dedication. It was not a time for dalliance with the enemy; it was a moment for wholehearted dedication to the Lord and in that spirit *they began this good work* (18).

[22] Rom. 12:1–2; 1 Pet. 2:21

Nehemiah 3:1–32
4. The servant's partners

In addition to being an inspiring leader, Nehemiah was also a gifted administrator. His graphic narrative is interspersed with seven lists of names, locations and responsibilities, items from Israel's life, past and present (3:1–32; 7:6–73; 9:38 – 10:27; 11:3–19, 20–36; 12:1–26, 27–47). He knows the importance and value of accurate records. The lists are not a dull recital of forgotten names; they preserve the story of heroic people who played their part in the continuity of the people of God. Not every commentator on this book is impressed by Nehemiah's record-preserving activities. One describes this list in chapter 3 as 'intrusive', another 'a colourless memorandum of assignments'. But the list is neither intrusive nor colourless. It is logical, graphic and relevant.

Nehemiah's first list preserves the names of those workers who left the comfort and security of familiar surroundings to share in Jerusalem's ambitious enterprise. The records may even have formed part of Nehemiah's report to the Persian king. Artaxerxes had guaranteed his safety and authorized the resources, so it was politic to provide a detailed account of the undertaking especially when sinister accusations might once again reach his ears. But, although Persia's king might appreciate the information and Israel's workers value the remembrance, how relevant is the list to a modern reader?

I preached recently at a church which was celebrating three hundred and fifty years of witness in its Lincolnshire market town. Its members had produced some attractive souvenirs to mark the occasion and I was particularly impressed by a colourful tea-towel printed with the signatures of people of all ages who belong to its present congregation. A few of the signatures I recognized, most I did not. Some were people honoured for decades in that church's life, others were young children just beginning their quest for faith. The souvenir is highly meaningful to the present members of that church but, as the decades wear on, the names might become increasingly less familiar. But that does not matter. The signatures may not be recognized but their service will not be forgotten. Worshippers in future generations who look at those names will realize that they are following in the steps of devoted people who loved Christ, maintained the church's witness and served others.

Nehemiah's list is rather like the signatures on that anniversary memento. On a cursory glance it may seem little more than a monotonous collection of names, but a more careful examination of this register of Jerusalem's builders and their specific assignments reveals nine of the ideals, principles and priorities which characterized their work for God.

1. The builders priority

The list tells us where the work began: *Eliashib the high priest and his fellow priests went to work and rebuilt the Sheep Gate. They dedicated it and set its doors in place* (1). It was appropriate that Jerusalem's high priest and his colleagues should set a good example to everyone else. Spiritual leaders are required to do something more than talk. Life's daily example is their most eloquent sermon. Søren Kierkegaard confronted contemporary Danish pastors with this robust challenge:

> Order the parson to be silent on Sundays. What is there left? The essential thing remains: their lives, the daily life with which the parsons preach. Would you, then, get the impression by watching them, that it was Christianity they were preaching?[1]

These Jerusalem priests wanted to be as good as their message, so they committed themselves eagerly to the work and in doing so encouraged the enthusiasm of their neighbours.

That this list should start at *the Sheep Gate* is markedly symbolic. It is saying, 'Put God first'. Close to the wall's north-east corner, this gate provided easy access to the temple, and doubtless took its name from the animals brought through it for sacrifice. This 'Sheep Gate beginning' graphically depicts Christ's mandate to all his followers: 'But seek first his kingdom and his righteousness', believing that other things in life (the total preoccupation of unbelievers) 'will be given to you as well.'[2] The priests *dedicate* or consecrate this first section to the glory of God, and in doing so they exemplify and encourage the commitment of all.

---

[1] Søren Kierkegaard, *The Journals* (Oxford: Oxford University Press, 1938), p. 402.
[2] Mt. 6:33.

2. Their unity

The enthusiastic priests begin the enterprise by setting a good example but they cannot do it on their own. Its eventual success will depend entirely on team work. People from a wide variety of different backgrounds, trades and localities will work together on this shattered wall. Those with experience of building will construct the walls but, before that, numerous unskilled people must clear away the extensive rubble, clean and reshape old stones, and move heavy materials from one place to another. The operation would be doomed to failure if their ranks became disrupted by rivalry or discord. If the task is to be completed they must relate harmoniously with each other and, in its own prosaic way, the list bears witness to their harmony: *Next to him . . . next to them . . . next to him* (3–31) When finished, the rebuilt wall was a testimony to the workers' interdependent partnership.

In the eighteenth century, Charles Wesley put many of Scripture's great themes into matchless verse. Many of the people in the early Methodist societies could barely read, so the hymns were sung more for their educative value than their inspiring melodies. The Wesley brothers knew that their young converts would never develop in spiritual maturity and influence their local communities if they were harassed by disunity. They taught them the inestimable value of one another, encouraging them to sing,

> He bids us build each other up:
> And, gathered into one,
> To our high calling's glorious hope
> We hand in hand go on.

> The gift which He on one bestows,
> We all delight to prove;
> The grace through every vessel flows,
> In purest streams of love.[3]

None of us was meant to live to ourselves. We all need exemplary, supportive and edifying partners. Division is one of the most tragic anomalies in the life of a local church. Jerusalem's new walls were only possible because of co-operative team work.

3. Their individuality

Yet, although these workers served harmoniously together, it did not mean that they were identical stereotypes and boringly monochrome. As Wesley observed in that hymn, we are gifted in

[3] From 'All praise to our redeeming Lord'.

different ways. At least four people in the list have exactly the same name as another person, and the only way of distinguishing them from each other is to mention their family background. Meshullam (4, 6, 30), Malkijah (11, 31), Nehemiah (3:16; 1:1) and Hananiah (8, 30) each have a namesake. Two men building on the walls may have the same name but they are not the same person. They have contrasting personalities, complementary abilities and distinctive gifts. Their unity is essential but their individuality is valued.

The great characters of Scripture illustrate the way God uses different people with varied temperaments to achieve his purposes. God's servants are not all cast in the same mould. In the eighth century BC, when the Lord wanted to address the disobedient people of the northern kingdom, he used two entirely different prophets. Amos travelled there from the south and preached about God's righteousness; he was a shepherd, blunt, rugged and severe. But the Israelites also needed the message of divine love, so God chose a man with a broken marriage, Hosea. The Lord knew how Hosea felt, for he too was the victim of a severed relationship; his people had violated a covenant and gone after other lovers. People with varying gifts can perform complementary tasks.

4. Their unselfishness

The team of workers was drawn from a wide variety of different locations throughout the area. It was not just Jerusalem's citizens who built the wall. People came from eight different places up to a fifteen- or twenty-mile radius. The enterprise could not have been attempted without help from outside. Volunteers came from Jericho (2), Tekoa (5), Gibeon (7), Mizpah (7, 15, 19), Zanoah (13), Beth Hakkerem (14), Beth Zur (16) and Keilah (17, 18). It was of little direct or immediate benefit to them if Jerusalem's walls were repaired. They had their own fields to cultivate, and farms and workshops must be maintained, but they left their homes and families in order to offer themselves for service in the city. If a worker lived in Jerusalem it was an obvious advantage that the walls should be repaired, but not for these people, other than some pride of achievement that in future their main city might be less vulnerable and more likely to prosper. It was work which could benefit others far more than themselves.

Their altruistic partnership is an example which has been followed by the people of God across the centuries. Every week millions of Christians sacrificially donate money for projects they will never see. They are content to give solely because they want to be a blessing to others. Dedicated prayer partners spend hours of their time earnestly praying for some country they will never visit, and intercede for years for missionaries they may not know well and have met only casually years ago. I know of Christian women in a small rural congregation who spend hours every week knitting colourful garments for missionaries to distribute to Third World children. Whilst in Teeside recently I met a man in his eighties who every week washes cars to earn money for TEAR Fund's work among hungry and homeless refugees. These people share eagerly in ventures which bring no personal benefit to them other than the privilege of doing it for the Lord. Those who love Christ have been liberated from the curse of selfishness and find their greatest joy in doing something for others.

5. Their disappointment

But here, as elsewhere in the book, the note of realism is not missing from the story. Nehemiah's impressive list guards us from the notion that everybody in town and country came rushing forward as eager volunteers. Tekoa's leading citizens were well aware of the need but they resolutely refused to help. Other people from that town gave their services freely *but their nobles would not put their shoulders to the work* (5). These nobles (or 'exalted ones')[4] had no intention of dirtying their hands. Numerous Tekoans threw themselves so energetically into the task that after completing one section of the wall (5) they went off to work on another (27), but their *nobles* had no part in it. That phrase *did not put their shoulders to* suggests that it was pride, rather than indolence, which kept them from the work. It is agricultural imagery, describing the 'stiff-necked' ox refusing to be yoked.[5] It was below their dignity to engage in such menial jobs. Nobles from other communities gladly shared in the project (9, 12), but not the aristocrats of Tekoa.

Pride is a cruel enemy. It inflates our self-importance and makes holiness impossible. It views humility as a failing rather than a virtue. It deflects our steps from the way of the cross. It refuses to see Christ as the noblest example and forgets that he poured water into a basin and washed the feet of others: 'I have set you an example that you should do as I have done for you.'[6]

Sadly, we too are likely to find people who do not *put their shoulders* to the Lord's work. Deborah's Song conveys the same note of realism. In time of acute national crisis, she praised God for nobles ready to 'take the lead' and ordinary people who would 'willingly offer themselves', but she too had her frustrations. Four of the tribes stayed comfortably at home at a time when others 'risked their very

[4] The same word is used in 10:29; 2 Ch. 23:20; Je. 14:3.　　[5] Je. 27:11–12.
[6] Jn. 13:1–17.

lives'. There were citizens in Meroz who 'did not come to help the
LORD . . . against the mighty' and earned a bitter curse.[7] Christians
can hardly think of a more scathing criticism: 'They did not come to
help'.

6. Their commitment

In stark contrast to such unresponsive people, the list provides
abundant evidence of men and women who gave themselves devotedly and sacrificially to the venture.

Wholehearted service would certainly be offered by those
Jerusalem citizens who were allocated a section of the wall within
sight of their homes. One man *made repairs opposite his house* (10),
another *opposite his living quarters* (30). Two others *made repairs in
front of their house* (23) whilst a number of priests worked *each in
front of his own house* (28). These people would not be tempted to
do shoddy work. For years to come they would look at their section
of that wall as they went in and out of their homes. They did not
want present work to bring them future embarrassment. They were
determined to bring their best to it. One day every Christian will
give an account of 'the things done while in the body, whether good
or bad'. Paul says that, with such a prospect, committed believers
want to glorify Christ rather than gratify themselves.[8]

Sacrificial service was rendered by men and women who threw
themselves into the enterprise even though they were totally lacking
in experience as builders and labourers. Nehemiah specially mentions citizens who were skilled in other occupations, people not
accustomed to the physical drudgery involved in building construction. Experts must have been at hand who could show priests (1,
28), goldsmiths (8, 31, 32), perfume-makers (8), merchants (32) and
district rulers (9, 12, 14–19) how to build their section of such a
massive wall. And these people were fully prepared to leave their
lucrative professions for an undefined period to engage in gruelling
work which would test their physical resources to the limit.

Over the centuries, the work of Christ's church has been lovingly
maintained by a vast army of women and men who were ready to
do anything which would further God's cause: cleaning, catering,
magazine preparation, flower arranging, building repairs, home
visiting, leaflet distribution and scores of other tasks which will never
be acclaimed this side of heaven, but they have been done for God's
glory and other people's good, and that was reward enough.
Similarly, people from a wide variety of different backgrounds, rich
and poor, women (12) and men united together and sacrificially

---

[7] Jdg. 5:1–2, 15–18, 23.   [8] 2 Cor. 5:9–10.

'worked with all their heart' (4:6). Nehemiah was favoured to have been given such a devoted team.

Without this passage their identity would never be known, but the surviving record is a reminder that individuals matter in the Lord's work. The church across the centuries has been enriched by the unacclaimed ministry of innumerable believers whose primary incentive was to honour God. The nature of their service was of marginal significance when contrasted with its purpose. Those sixteenth-century believers who worked as servants, doing the most menial tasks in Tudor households, were encouraged by Tyndale's exhortation to do it all for God:

> Now thou that ministerest in the kitchen and art but a kitchen page ... knowest that God put thee in that office ... Now if thou compare deed to deed, there is a difference betwixt washing dishes and preaching the Word of God, but as touching to please God, none at all.[9]

7. Their enthusiasm

The people did not merely start the work; they kept at it. We have already seen that some people completed their part of the wall and then went on to work just as enthusiastically on another section. *Meremoth* completed one part (4) and then *repaired another section* (21), and *Meshullam* (4) did the same (31), whilst the men of Tekoa, refusing to be influenced by the bad example of their arrogant nobles, also had two main sections (5, 27) to their credit. Thank God for those who have been eager to go the second mile in God's work.

8. Their privilege

The builders regarded this work not as a gruelling chore but as a priceless opportunity. God had done so much for them and this was their chance to do something entirely for him. Service was a privilege, and specially so for some of the team who had made serious mistakes in the past. Now they had been given an opportunity to demonstrate publicly their renewed devotion and complete surrender. *Malkijah, son of Harim* (11) was one of those men who had married a foreign wife and had been convicted of wrong under Ezra's ministry thirteen years earlier. He had put the matter right, and the building of Jerusalem's wall provided him with an occasion to reaffirm in practical terms his obedience to God and love for his people.

Meremoth (4) was another worker with a sad ancestry. His

---

[9] *The Wicked Mammon*, William Tyndale's Doctrinal Treatises (Parker Society; Cambridge: Cambridge University Press, 1848), pp. 101–102.

grandfather Hakkoz had been excluded from the priesthood because of a mixed marriage, but Meremoth's father Uriah had become a priest and, under Ezra, his son was entrusted with the travellers' silver, gold and the sacred articles.[10] Past failures do not inhibit present grace. Many of Corinth's new Christians came into the church's life from a sordid moral background and the apostle Paul did nothing to hide it. His exposure was not to embarrass them but to exalt the Christ who died for them. Those sexual offenders, alcoholics, thieves and slanderers had been 'washed' by the Lord Jesus and 'sanctified' (or 'set apart') as his transformed witnesses in an alien society.[11]

9. Their reward

Under Nehemiah's inspiring leadership, work on the wall got off to an excellent beginning, but the days ahead were not easy. There were severe hazards and inevitable discouragements, yet as the weeks went by this large team recognized that they were building something which they could dedicate to the glory of God (12:27–43). Their greatest reward was to work together amicably and leave something behind which would outlive their days. In time the workers died but the walls remained. Their 'good work' (2:18) stood the test of time. Jerusalem's walls survived as an honoured monument, not to the builders' fervour but to the Lord's faithfulness. He had inspired their beginning, encouraged their continuance and effected their completion. To succeeding generations those walls were vocal. Their stones 'cried out' with a message evident to all – without God such a visible reality would have remained an unattainable dream.

It is a magnificent thing when a Christian believer can leave something behind in this world which testifies to God's goodness in human life. One of the eight beatitudes in the book of Revelation promises that those who 'die in the Lord' will have this indescribable joy: their earthly 'deeds' which have exalted Christ and enriched others will 'follow them'.[12] They will be effective on earth and unforgotten in heaven. The deeds will 'follow them' on earth, for 'the good they have done does not die with them but will continue to be fruitful to the glory of God'.[13] And they will 'follow them' to glory. Heaven will be rich in surprises as believers discover how eternally significant were their self-effacing deeds. Infinitely superior to Nehemiah's project, their building work is indestructible. No wonder 'each one should be careful how he builds'.[14]

[10] Ezr. 2:59–61; 8:33.   [11] 1 Cor. 6:9–11.   [12] Rev. 14:13.
[13] Philip Edgcumbe Hughes, *The Book of the Revelation* (Leicester: IVP, 1990), p. 164.   [14] 1 Cor. 3:10–14.

Nehemiah 4:1–23
5. The servant's confidence

Once the labourers started work on the building-site, Nehemiah's troubles began in earnest. Earlier tensions were dwarfed by fierce opposition. Optimism and realism are sensitively combined in his dramatic narrative. The team needs not only their leader's vigorous assurance that the God of heaven would give them success (2:20) but also his sensitive compassion, *Don't be afraid* (14).

The essential qualities of leadership are strength and love. Some leaders are persuasive, definite, strong and assertive, and it is unwise to get in their way; they have evident power, but love is in short supply. Others are attractively compassionate, almost to a fault, tolerating anything, fearful lest they 'rock the boat', but sometimes lacking the decisive dynamic that is necessary in effective leadership.[1]

Although by nature a sturdy extrovert, Nehemiah endeavoured to balance strength with love. If his narrative appears to portray a man more powerful than loving, it is largely because the story is set in the arena of sustained hostility. He is fighting for Israel's continuing spiritual existence, but he is not without compassion. He honestly recalls his own experience of intense fear in the palace at Susa (2:2) and can sympathize with the terrified. This leader knows how to come alongside discouraged (10), fearful (11), vulnerable (12) and deprived (5:1–6) people with emotional tenderness as well as moral strength.

Before a few days have gone by, Nehemiah and his colleagues realize that they are in serious trouble. There is opposition outside the ranks (1–9) and depression within (10–23). Yet, however intense, adversity is never a solitary visitor to the soul. Paul believed that trouble enables discerning Christians to unearth hidden treasure.[2]

---

[1] Paul knew the importance of both qualities, Rom. 1:11–12.
[2] 2 Cor. 1:3–11.

Blessings emerge in affliction which are rarely found in periods of ease.

Sorrow is not purposeless if it drives us to God, increases our dependence on him, enhances our sensitivity to the needs of others and makes us more like Jesus. Christ told his followers that they were unlikely to escape trouble[3] and mature believers prefer rather to learn from adversity than bemoan it.

As Nehemiah shares his reaction to the malevolent events of those weeks, his narrative reveals six basic principles which determined his planning, caring, teaching and working in the context of repeated affliction.

1. Conflict is inevitable (4:1–3)

As the work gets under way, the leader is bombarded with trouble from different angles. Initially, trouble comes from outside the ranks; that menacing duo resume the opposition. Sanballat, *angry* and *greatly incensed* about the excellent start made on Jerusalem's walls, *ridiculed* the workers (1) and, before long, his friend Tobiah was *at his side* with further undermining taunts and destructive derision (3). The verbal onslaughts are followed by menacing plots to *fight against Jerusalem and stir up trouble against it* (8). These men know that if they are to wreck the project, damaging words must be supplemented with dangerous weapons.

Then, as if that is not enough, there is trouble from within the ranks. The team is demoralized; the labourers and their families from the surrounding countryside become disheartened in the work and terrorized by the enemy.

The opposition of Nehemiah's enemies intensifies as time goes on. When they first hear why Nehemiah has come to Jerusalem they are 'very much disturbed' (2:10), then mildly amused (2:19) that he has devised such a ridiculously ambitious programme. Once they witness his determination, it is no longer a laughing matter. They begin to impute wrong motives and are intent on bringing him down in the king's eyes (2:19). Now the initial irritation turns to sustained anger and the enemy is *greatly incensed* (1). Sanballat gathers further allies about him and, employing fierce bullying tactics, approaches Jerusalem with a substantial military escort. It is one thing for the builders to hear his taunts but quite another to see his troops. To look up from their work on the walls and see the *army of Samaria* (2) marching towards the city was enough to horrify all but the stoutest members of the team.

The scorn continued as the enemy belittled their qualities (*feeble*

[3] Jn. 15:18–21; 16:1–4, 33; 17:14–16.

Jews), derided their ambitions (*Will they restore their wall?*), mocked their optimism (*Will they offer sacrifices?, i.e.* of thanksgiving and dedication when the wall is rebuilt), lampooned their enthusiasm (*Will they finish it in a day?*), undermined their confidence (*Can they bring the stones back to life?*) and magnified their problems (*those heaps of rubble – burned as they are*).

Tobiah joins in the ridicule, demeaning their efforts. He relieves his annoyance by channelling the bitterness into a sick joke: *What they are building – if even a fox climbed up on it, he would break down their wall of stones* (3). Kathleen Kenyon's archaeological excavations on Nehemiah's walls revealed that they were nine foot thick. Although not as sturdy as the previous wall, it would need more than a few robust foxes to demolish it. Tobiah hoped that his sick humour might cause the builders to cast an apprehensive glance at their hard work and so activate an avalanche of discouragement. Laughter is a choice blessing but it can be a dangerous weapon. If one's laughter produces another's tears, the humour is misplaced.

But Tobiah planned for more than tears. Nehemiah was up against formidable antagonism; his enemies were intent on the total ruination of his imaginative and well-organized undertaking. Anyone working for God can anticipate opposition in some form or other. When the sightless Saul of Tarsus reached Damascus, his initiation into Christian life and experience included a realistic note about 'how much he must suffer' for Christ, and he went on to warn his earliest converts that they too 'must go through many hardships to enter the kingdom of God'.[4] Suffering is the badge of discipleship; taking up the cross authenticates the reality of faith. Yet, however intense the opposition, the believer is not without resources, and they are released in reliant prayer.

2. Prayer is crucial (4:4–9)

The next section of the narrative begins with a personal prayer of Nehemiah on behalf of the people, and ends with corporate prayer by the people.

a. The leader prays

Hear us, O our God, for we are despised. Turn their insults back on their own heads. Give them over as plunder in a land of captivity. Do not cover up their guilt or blot out their sins from your sight, for they have thrown insults in the face of the builders (4–5).

Nehemiah's response to the enemy's assaults is to turn to God.

He prayed *urgently*. Nehemiah's response to this sustained

[4] Acts 9:16; 14:22.

adversity is to hurry into the audience chamber of God. In the presence of his opponents he had declared his conviction that the God of heaven would give success to the builders (2:20) but that must be more than an inspiring rallying cry; heaven's Lord must be sought for earth's needs. His God is acknowledged not only as the source of ultimate success but the Giver of immediate help. In turning to the Lord, Nehemiah knew that there was nowhere else he could go.

He prayed *honestly*. Nehemiah was angry about their ridicule. They had *despised* the workers and poured *insults* on their heads. Nehemiah cannot contain his fury and the exasperation spills out in fervent prayer. He does not need to choose his words carefully. He is in the presence of One who knows the reason for his indignation. There are times when, bewildered and distressed, we cry out in anguish to God, telling him exactly how we feel, as in those experiences when we are pained that he does not seem to answer our prayers or respond to our cry as speedily as we had hoped. It is best to be honest with God. When we are aggrieved, it is better to pray honestly and express our pain in the holy place than harbour resentment and disdain prayer. Moreover, if fierce anger needs to be released it is far better expressed in prayer than in uncontrolled bitterness towards others.

He prayed *passionately*. Nehemiah's prayer is an unbridled expression of turbulent emotions and he cannot conceal his fury. Imprecatory prayers of this kind 'have the shocking immediacy of a scream, to startle us into feeling something of the desperation which produced them'.[5] He has been attacked personally and his motives challenged. Few people can cope with fierce verbal criticism. But, more seriously, his enemies have sinned against God (by opposing his work) and God's people (by maligning their efforts) and Nehemiah does not want their sin to be overlooked: *Do not . . . blot out their sins*.

In the face of his enemies' resolute animosity, it is natural for Nehemiah to speak in this way and, although from our vantage point he would want to pray differently, it is important for us to empathize with him, not criticize him. Christians react to cruelty and injustice in the light of two great biblical events which Nehemiah could not possibly discern as clearly as we can – the death of Christ and the life to come. Commenting on this type of angry prayer in psalmody, Kidner says that to understand such prayers,

> . . . we should have to suspend our consciousness of having a gospel to impart (which affects our attitude to fellow-sinners) and our assurance of a final righting of wrongs (which affects our

[5] Derek Kidner, *Psalms 1–72*, Tyndale Old Testament Commentary (Leicester: IVP, 1973), p. 28.

attitude to present anomalies). Without these certainties, only a cynic could feel no impatience to see justice triumphant and evil men broken.[6]

Nehemiah prayed *realistically*. It would be a mistake to dismiss his vehement prayer as an expression of uncontrolled human indignation. He regards their insults as an offence against God, which indeed they are. They have ridiculed a venture which God inspired and planned. They have not merely reviled God's servants; they have abused God's Name. In calling upon God so passionately, Nehemiah is asking God not to vindicate the workers but to authenticate his truth in the presence of such irreverent and insulting opponents. When God's honour is at stake, it is natural that a man as surrendered and devoted as Nehemiah should be incensed.

The memory of earlier biblical experience may have helped Nehemiah in his moment of crisis. Unexpectedly confronted by Samaria's soldiers, he may even have recalled Hezekiah's prayer at those very walls as Judah's king had sought deliverance from the Assyrian aggressors who had come 'to insult the living God'.[7] His language is markedly reminiscent of the anguished prayers of Jeremiah when he was taunted and persecuted by his threatening neighbours.[8] 'The cry of vengeance is a cry for justice,' comments Holmgren.[9] There is a place for righteous anger.

C. S. Lewis observed that in some circumstances,

the absence of anger is a most alarming symptom and the presence of indignation may be a good one. For if we look at their railings we find they are usually angry not simply because these things have been done to them but because these things are manifestly wrong, are hateful to God as well as to the victim.[10]

Jesus was angry at times. He was angry at the beginning of his ministry when he confronted the loveless legalism of his synagogue opponents and also, at the close of his life, when he witnessed the greedy commercialism of the temple traders.[11] Paul maintained that there is a form of anger which is not sinful: 'In your anger do not sin'. In the right context the anger needs to be expressed. It must not be turned inward and pent up within us; if it is allowed to fester it can damage us. When anger is not handled correctly the offended person can become an offender. That is why the apostle insists that even when those who make us angry do not seek our forgiveness, we must cultivate a forgiving spirit towards them. Sleep ought to

[6] Ibid., p. 26. [7] 2 Ki. 19:14–19. [8] Je. 17:18; 18:21–23.
[9] Holmgren, p. 106.
[10] C. S. Lewis, *Reflections on the Psalms* (London: Geoffrey Bles, 1958), p. 30.
[11] Mk. 3:5; 11:15–17.

bring all anger to the place of rest: 'Do not let the sun go down while you are still angry'.[12]

Nehemiah's prayer is descriptive not prescriptive. In his prayer life Nehemiah needed Jesus just as much as we do. Nehemiah was confident of the 'God of heaven' and, similarly, Jesus told his disciples to pray to their 'Father in heaven'. Christ also taught them and us to 'forgive everyone who sins against us', even to pray for our enemies and those who insult us,[13] though Clines reminds us that 'the Christian magistrate' (to whom, as governor, Nehemiah corresponds) 'may not always be called upon to exercise forgiveness to law-breakers and invaders'.[14]

Nehemiah prayed dependently: *Hear us, O our God.* It is the heart cry of a man in desperate need. The project has reached a crucial stage. The wall has been built to *half its height* and so much dedicated energy has gone into the enterprise, *for the people worked with all their heart* (6). It would be disastrous if, demoralized by Sanballat's ridicule, discouraged by Tobiah's taunts and frightened by Samaria's soldiers, the builders gave up, especially when so much had been accomplished. Only God could save them from discouragement and disaster. That is why Nehemiah prayed. He knew that between his despondent workers and their potential failure were God's abundant resources; immeasurable supplies are released through dependent prayer.

b. The workers pray

Nehemiah's colleagues also sought God in prayer. They, as well as their dependent leader, had every reason to cry to the Lord: *But we prayed to our God and posted a guard day and night to meet this threat* (9). The earnest petition of leader and people continue to teach us about prayer – its necessity, naturalness, partnership and comfort.

These people believed in *the necessity of prayer*. The enemies united as they laid destructive plots to overthrow the work. Sanballat from the north, Tobiah and the Ammonites from the east, the Arabs from the south and the Ashdodites from the west meant that Jerusalem was virtually encircled by vicious enemies, fiercely intent on damaging the cause. *They all plotted together to come and fight against Jerusalem and stir up trouble against it. But we prayed . . .* (8–9).

There is something here about *the naturalness of prayer*. Under serious threat and in extreme adversity it was the most logical thing for them to do. There was so much that they were unable to do. They could not forget the ridicule, dismiss the danger, ignore the plots or scatter the soldiers, but they could pray, and pray they did.

---

[12] Eph. 4:26.   [13] Mt. 6:9; Lk. 11:4; Mt. 5:11, 43–44.   [14] Clines, p. 160.

It was natural for them to do so, for in prayer they were affirming their faith, sharing their anxieties, acknowledging their weakness and confessing their need.

This threatened team of builders believed in *the partnership of prayer*: 'We prayed to our God' – expressing their unity and corporate reliance. Like their building work, their praying was a further corporate activity in which they could help one another.

Jerusalem's builders valued *the comfort of prayer*. They described their Lord as *our* God, the God of infinite wisdom (he knew what to do), compassionate care (he wanted to help them), limitless power (nothing daunted him), and available resources – everything they needed was there for the asking. No wonder they prayed.

3. Discouragement is understandable (4:10–12)

The realism of Scripture is one of its many attractive features. These Old Testament stories were 'written to teach us', so that through the endurance which God inspires and 'the encouragement of the Scriptures we might have hope'.[15] The Bible does not confront us with an idealistic portraiture of life. Imagine this story of Nehemiah's ambitious enterprise totally without problems or difficulties. It would dishearten us rather than inspire us, for it would be describing a world totally different from our own. Life is tough at times and, however much we pray, its trouble can increase rather than decrease. Prayer is not a convenient device for removing life's problems but a loving God's provision for coping with them. Nehemiah describes his five-fold problem at this crucial stage of the project.

a. The extent of the discouragement

Jerusalem's workers had more than enough to cope with, surrounded by enemies and threatened with disaster, and now there is additional trouble. The *people in Judah,* men and women from the surrounding towns and villages, came to Nehemiah describing not only the depressing working conditions in the city but grieved also about the dangers to which their families were exposed in the countryside. Jerusalem's workers are not the only people in danger. The enemies have threatened to attack the homes of those Judeans whose menfolk were away from home working on the city walls. Nehemiah's problems are far from localized; they have spread from the city to the wider life of the Judean community.

[15] Rom. 15:4–5.

b. The exhaustion of the workers

Meanwhile, the people in Judah said, 'The strength of the labourers is giving out' (10). That expression *giving out* comes from a verb meaning 'to stumble' or 'totter' as in Isaiah's exposure, 'Jerusalem staggers, Judah is falling'.[16] It is a vivid picture of an exhausted labourer, reeling under the heavy load he is trying to carry. They had been working for several weeks and, under the pressure of external opposition, the initial enthusiasm was beginning to wane. It is always easier to begin a work for God than continue it. Perseverance is a rich and rare quality, especially when we feel physically tired and spent. Anyone seriously committed to the work of Christ can sympathize with these sighing people.

In time of acute depression, the prophet Elijah felt it impossible to carry on: 'I have had enough, LORD.' His trouble doubtless had its roots in physical and nervous exhaustion. Depression always distorts reality; it throws everything out of perspective. He wished he might die, but God's angel began by providing the worn-out prophet with essential food and refreshing sleep. How badly he needed it, because as soon as he had eaten the meal he went off to sleep again. Only when he had eaten a further meal was he encouraged to continue his journey.[17] The Lord knows our needs ('the journey is too much for you', he said to Elijah), and does not want us to put excessive pressure on our physical and emotional resources. We were never meant to push ourselves to the extreme limit of our natural energies. Our strength must be replenished with adequate rest and good food. That is one of the reasons why God included a weekly rest day in the covenant he made with his people. We were never designed to live without restorative relaxation. His prescribed lifestyle, embodied in the Ten Commandments, focused on the inter-related elements of honouring God, loving others and caring for ourselves.

c. The immensity of the enterprise

When the labourers began, it seemed such an exciting thing to be doing, but as the weeks went by they became increasingly overwhelmed by the daunting practicalities. Huge stones and a seemingly vast amount of debris had to be cleared away (2:14) before they could continue the extensive building operation. The Babylonian armies had ruined Jerusalem's walls and damaged the many houses attached to them: *there is so much rubble that we cannot rebuild the wall* (10).

That doleful *we cannot* has destroyed many an imaginative

[16] Is. 3:8.   [17] 1 Ki. 19:3–9.

Christian objective. It has been said that in the history of the church, pessimism has always been a greater problem than atheism. On the threshold of Canaan the fearful travellers said they could not possibly enter the new land. They concentrated on their weakness rather than God's strength. Nehemiah had to persuade his rubble rousers not to make the same mistake. The labourers' strength might well be giving out but God's power was available, sufficient and inexhaustible.

d. The aggression of the opponents.

This was yet another intimidating dimension of their trouble. People in both urban and rural contexts were paralysed with fear when new threats came from their enemies. The hostility of the opponents was directed both at the city's builders and at their homes in the Judean countryside.

First, the builders were demoralized by the threat of a surprise attack as they worked on the walls: *Also our enemies said, 'Before they know it or see us, we will be right there among them and will kill them and put an end to the work'* (11). The strenuous effort involved in removing vast piles of rubble and carrying it outside the city was hard and difficult enough. Now they are told that they will be slaughtered whilst doing it.

Secondly, people in other parts of the province were in equal danger. The women of Judah, whose husbands had left home to work on the walls, were terror-stricken. *Then the Jews who lived near them came and told us ten times over, 'Wherever you turn, they will attack us'* (12). The Hebrew here in verse 12 can be translated as a plea from the Judeans urging their husbands to return home. In view of the actual danger to which the builders were exposed in the city and the potential danger their wives and children might be in if their homes were unprotected, they were in effect saying, 'You must return to us', that is, to save yourselves and to defend us. Alternatively, it may be that the Judeans were urging their fellow-countrymen to abandon work on the walls simply because, in the light of physical exhaustion, practical problems (extensive rubble) and hostile opponents, they considered it an unattainable enterprise.

e. The fear of the participants

In the light of all these troubles, fear was a major difficulty. Some of *the Jews who lived near* Nehemiah's enemies were constantly harassed by fresh threats and increasing intimidation. Their hostile neighbours robbed them of peace, and fear spread quickly among the harrassed people. The dedicated leader knew that, in addition to earnest prayer, the situation called for radical action. The crisis underlined the crucial importance of a united team.

4. Unity is essential (4:13–20)

Keenly aware of such intense discouragement, Nehemiah devised a strategy to meet the immediate crisis.

First, he mobilized his team by making sure that the most vulnerable parts of the wall were protected by appointed guards. As an emergency measure he *stationed some of the people behind the lowest points of the wall at the exposed places, posting them by families, with their swords, spears and bows* (13). Members of extended families knew each other well enough to allocate respective duties effectively, and the presence of their women and children close at hand was a constant reminder that they were not simply fighting for the city's walls but for the family's and community's future. Posting these emergency troops at *the lowest points of the wall* ensured that the menacing enemy could see that Jerusalem's militia was a force to be reckoned with.

Secondly, Nehemiah considered his options. It was a time for some kind of public assembly but first he *looked things over.* He was not a man for hasty, ill-considered actions. Before he did anything else he went to see how the emergency troops were getting on. Christ's work is sometimes spoilt because things are done hurriedly and without careful consideration of the likely consequences. Mark tells that when Jesus arrived in Jerusalem at the beginning of that last eventful week of his public ministry, he went to the temple and 'looked around at everything, but since it was already late, he went out to Bethany with the Twelve'.[18] He saw merchants' tables and the money-changers' booths, but it was not the right time to overturn those tables and address those who were so blatantly misusing the temple. Although he was profoundly disturbed by what he saw, he was in full control of his emotions. It was a time to think but not to act. Action was best delayed to the following day when there would be a more opportune occasion for the exposure of their sins. Only after he had *looked things over* did Nehemiah summon together *the nobles, the officials and the rest of the people* (14a).

Thirdly, Nehemiah shared his faith. He *stood up* in a public assembly and urged the people, *'Don't be afraid of them. Remember the Lord, who is great and awesome, and fight for your brothers, your sons and your daughters, your wives and your homes'* (14b).

Their leader knew what it was to be overcome with terror (2:2). He could enter sympathetically into the fears of his colleagues, but

[18] Mk. 11:11.

he also believed that fear is conquered by reflecting on the sufficiency of God: *Remember the Lord.* Nehemiah uses the words of his opening prayer (1:5), when he first heard of Jerusalem's plight. Now he is leading the venture in the city he reminds himself and his contemporaries of the uniqueness, power (*great*) and holiness (*awesome*) of God. The Lord had promised to meet the needs of his people, however serious their adversities, and would not go back on his word. Their circumstances had changed, the work was more difficult and the enemy more active, but the Lord was exactly the same. They must *remember* God. We are astonished that Nehemiah could even suggest that they might forget God but, in time of crisis, they could – and so can we. In his last letter before execution, Paul urged his colleague Timothy to 'Remember Jesus Christ'.[19] Did the apostle really imagine that this dedicated young minister could ever forget Jesus, the source of his life, the secret of his strength and the substance of his preaching? But when trouble comes, Scripture's great realities can be temporarily displaced by anxious thoughts. Believers often need that timely reminder.

Fourthly, Nehemiah announced his plans. The highly visible emergency protection force had alerted the enemy to their efficient organization and military strength. The plot for the surprise attack had been foiled. Nehemiah believed it was now safe for the builders to return to their allocated work-areas on the walls. The leader made sure that, from now on, the entire work force was permanently and efficiently protected so he divided his team into builders and soldiers: *From that day on, half of my men did the work, while the other half were equipped with spears, shields, bows and armour* (16). Even the labourers who carried rubble away from the city were supplied with armour and *did their work with one hand and held a weapon in the other* (17). Each of the builders was equipped with *his sword at his side as he worked* (18).

To ensure that builders, labourers and residents were aware of approaching danger, their leader devised a temporary warning system. A trumpeter stayed by Nehemiah's side so that the troops could be quickly gathered together at the place of most urgent need: *Whenever you hear the sound of the trumpet, join us there.* Nehemiah thought of everything.

5. Sacrifice is inescapable (4:21–23)

But, although Nehemiah made careful plans to meet every possible emergency, his organizing ability would have been useless without the radical sacrificial involvement of both leader and people. The

[19] 2 Tim. 2:8.

work continued throughout every available moment of the entire day, *from the first light of dawn till the stars came out* (21). Normal siesta times were ignored because every worker knew that the wall was not required merely to enhance Jerusalem's architecture or beautify its physical appearance; those well-fortified defences and strong gates were vital for future security. People who lived in nearby villages no longer went home to sleep, but stayed within the city's slowly rising walls so that they could serve *as guards by night and workmen by day* (22). Nehemiah, his brothers and his personal escort set a choice example to the rest of the workers. They even slept in their clothes so that they were fully dressed and ready at the moment of attack.

The story of Christ's church across the centuries is a chronicle of exemplary heroism and sacrificial service. Many of the outstanding personalities of Christian history had to cope with immense hardship of one kind or another. They too proved that there was no service without suffering. Their remarkable achievements are well known but their inward conflicts and adversities are easily forgotten: John Calvin, teaching, writing and preaching despite repeated attacks of the quartan fever, tuberculosis, renal colic, chest infections, gout, nephritis (one is hardly surprised that he confessed to occasional 'impatience fever'); Richard Baxter, expounding Scripture, encouraging friends by supportive letters, writing books, 'a pen in God's hand' though scarcely free from pain on any day throughout his life; John Wesley and George Whitefield, uplifting Christ and winning souls though both saddened by unhappy marriages; Charles Haddon Spurgeon preaching, sometimes at his best, when he was in the dark valley of depression; Tom Barnardo doing everything humanly possible for the orphan children of London whilst being cruelly slandered by a man who ought to have known better. All these people derived their inspiration from Scripture, recalled that all its great characters experienced some form of pain and recognized that following Christ involves costly living at some point or another in life. In time of intense persecution, John Bunyan reminded his contemporaries of inevitable sacrifice: the believer 'that is resolved for Heaven, if Satan cannot win him by flatteries, he will endeavour to weaken him by discouragements.' And again, 'there is no man that goeth to Heaven but he must go by the Cross; the Cross is the standing way-mark, by which all they that go to Glory must pass by.'[20]

---

[20] John Bunyan, *The Heavenly Footman*, in *Miscellaneous Works*, vol. 5, ed. Graham Midgely (Oxford: Clarendon, 1986), pp. 158–159.

6. God is invincible

Leader and people, builders and soldiers, parents and children all knew that, in the face of evident opposition, the success of the enterprise was dependent on the God who inspired its beginning. The narrative of chapter 4, with its recurrent problems and imminent dangers, is deliberately interspersed with affirmations of faith and confidence in 'the God of heaven' (1:5; 2:20). The story of adversity becomes a testimony to the abundant sufficiency of God. Nehemiah renews their confidence in the Lord.

Their God, he points out, is *unique* (4, 9). He enjoys a personal relationship with his people. With buoyant confidence they address him as *our God* (4, 9). He is the God who treasures his people because he is bound to them in covenant love.

God is *attentive*. Nehemiah can turn to God in crisis and know that he will be heard (1). Moreover, it was not simply the leader who prayed, but the people as well: *But we prayed to our God* (9).

He is *righteous*. Those who deliberately maligned God's people would find that their insults would come *back on their own heads* (4) for that was exactly what Scripture warned about those who deliberately offended God and his people.[21]

He is *powerful*. He is the *great* God (14) of the Israelite people who had repeatedly enabled them to achieve humanly impossible things because of his invincible omnipotence.

He is *holy*. Those who hurl their reproaches at God's people are insulting the truly *awesome* God (14) to whom those people belong. He cherishes them and to hold them in contempt is to revile the God who makes them what they are.

He is *sovereign*. He not only strengthens the Israelite soldiers as they stand poised for action on Jerusalem's walls but he also works behind the enemy lines. He frustrates the plots of Israel's enemies (15) and reduces their vindictive plans to mere human vapourings.

He is *unfailing*. In time of extreme crisis, Nehemiah can assure his team, *Our God will fight for us* (20). He is not in the slightest doubt that the Lord he has told them to remember (14) is unchanging and dependable. He cannot disappoint or fail them.

With such confidence and commitment, Nehemiah and his colleagues continued to build despite verbal assault, psychological pressure, physical danger, natural discouragement, crippling fear and extreme danger. They were enabled to continue not because they gloried in a robust faith but because they trusted in a reliable God. It is clear from this passage that there were times when the people's trust and heroism was frail ('strength is giving out . . . we cannot

[21] Ps. 94; Dt. 32:40–43; Rom. 12:19.

rebuild') but Nehemiah's confident words reverberated throughout the entire community, *Our God will fight for us.* The leader knew that his people must work hard but, in the last analysis, the success would not depend on their sustained exertion but on God's assured strength.

When Nehemiah assured his partners, *Our God shall fight for us,* they knew that, although exertion is necessary, dependence on the Lord is rewarded.

The reader of this chapter in Nehemiah's memoirs cannot fail to be impressed by the transforming effect in society of one committed believer. God uses him not just as a resourceful leader but as salt and light [22] in his community. Without the radical impact of his robust and attractive confidence in God, the enterprise which began so successfully could have ended in crippling disappointment. Seriously undermined by constant ridicule and contempt (1–3), then overwhelmed by fear (8, 14), despondency (10) and insecurity (11–12), at least some of his contemporaries abandoned work on the wall (15). God turned it all around because he used a dedicated believer who was in the right place at the right time.

Contemporary Western society lacks public figures of excellence to look up to and is in urgent need of good role models. Politicians lacking firm ethical principles and churchmen with a compromised message have little of significance to contribute to a post-Christian culture. In the modern world, novelists, dramatists and film-makers vividly depict sordid lifestyles but rarely question them. Nations bereft of spiritual and moral exemplars are in perilous danger. In our contemporary leadership vacuum, the media's passion is simply to 'reflect society' not elevate it. A former professor at the London School of Economics says, influenced by secularism, we 'have been liberated to follow our impulses' so that 'anything fixed is to be rejected as a barrier to the one grand and impossible project of building a life in which everyone enjoys the perfect satisfaction of needs.'[23] It is an unattainable goal, and those who pursue it are doomed to frustration. Personal satisfaction is a by-product which can only be obtained by embracing two greater priorities: honouring God and loving our neighbour.

Mid-fifth-century Jerusalem was privileged to have at the centre of its life a communicator with integrity and passion. He urged his contemporaries to 'Remember the Lord who is great and awesome' (14) and not allow subtle, alien and corrupting influences to undermine their faith and sabotage their values. In the previous century, Jerusalem had damaging leaders 'within her like a roaring

[22] Mt. 5:13–16.
[23] Kenneth Minogue, *The Silencing of Society* (Altrincham: The Social Affairs Unit, 1997), pp. 44, 47.

lion tearing its prey'. Religious officialdom taught 'that there is no difference between the unclean and the clean' so that God was 'profaned among them'. In such moral and spiritual degeneracy God looked 'for a man among them who would build up the wall and stand before me in the gap on behalf of the land . . . but I found none'.[24] What was missing in Ezekiel's day was evident in Nehemiah's. His confident faith, resilient courage, sacrificial work and consistent lifestyle turned a situation of potential breakdown into enduring testimony.

[24] Ezk. 22:25–30; *cf.* Ps. 106:23.

Nehemiah 5:1–19
6. The servant's compassion

The next section of Nehemiah's memoirs illustrate his resourceful leadership qualities in dealing with a totally different issue in Judah. In each of the preceding chapters he confronts a different problem. In chapter 1, God's servant copes with a personal problem: the news of Jerusalem's plight, his consequent destiny, and willingness to accept responsibility for the reconstruction of the city's walls. Chapter 2 presents a political problem: how can a palace official convince Persia's king to release him for such an assignment? Chapter 3 depicts the administrative and material problem of building the walls and the disappointment of some influential people's non-involvement in the project (3:5). Chapter 4 deals with the physical problem of imminent attack and the psychological problem of discouragement within the team. Chapter 5 exposes a serious economic and social problem, which Nehemiah must handle firmly, speedily and compassionately if the work is to be finished and the community is to prosper.

The narrative now provides us with some hitherto undisclosed information. When Nehemiah left the palace at Susa it was not merely as an influential Israelite with permission to rebuild Jerusalem's walls but as the king's appointed 'governor' of Judah (14). His imperial authority accounts for the apparent ease with which he convened special meetings to discuss major aspects of the work (2:16–18; 4:14; 5:7–13) and helps to explain the hostility of his enemies, people who had doubtless benefited from the community's earlier lack of decisive local leadership. Responsibility for Judean affairs had probably been in the hands of Sanballat as the nearest official governor, and he would hardly have welcomed (2:10) the intrusion into his domain of a new, well-organized and altruistic leader like Nehemiah.

The scene changes dramatically from Jerusalem's wall to Judah's urgent economic needs. To his work as building-site manager

Nehemiah adds new skills as an imaginative and effective social worker. The story describes Nehemiah facing a new problem, finding a solution and behaving in an exemplary fashion.

1. Nehemiah's problem (5:1–5)

The builders had given themselves sacrificially to an exacting task, and their main work was gradually coming to an end. Once the huge gates had been set in place (6:1), the assignment would be complete. However, for some time the exhausted workers had been labouring under severe economic difficulties and, with increasing pressure from distressed homes, they could hold out no longer. Both *the men and their wives raised a great outcry* of complaint against *their Jewish brothers* (1) concerning some alarming acts of greed which had resulted in widespread poverty and injustice. Several factors had combined to produce a situation in which many families had been reduced to destitution and despair.

We have already seen that, in order to build the wall, the team of builders and labourers had been recruited from a wide area. Many of Judah's towns and villages supplied men and women for the arduous tasks of clearing rubble, cleaning and re-shaping the large stones, and skilfully replacing them along the walls in forty different sections. To undertake this work, the people had taken a step of faith. They had left their normal trades, crafts and professions, farms and smallholdings, for a period of two months, and the sacrifice was now beginning to cut deeper into home and family life. With the leading bread-winner away from home, many large families (2) were without food.

Although in that kind of hand-to-mouth economy eight weeks away from work would inevitably create serious difficulties, Judah's economic hardship was not simply due to the events of the past couple of months. The region had been through a period of *famine* and food supplies had become scarce. Greedy merchants used the opportunity to inflate the price of grain, and some people had been compelled to mortgage their fields, vineyards and homes to raise money to feed their hungry families (3).

Moreover, the Persian king's taxes on their fields and vineyards had been increased to meet rising imperial expenditure, and as a result many people had found it impossible to meet these additional burdens. One of the demoralizing aspects of Persian rule in this period 'was the draining away of local resources from the provinces to finance the imperial court, the building of magnificent palaces and the interminable succession of campaigns of pacification or conquest'.[1] Mention of *the king's tax* in the ears of the governor was sure to gain attention and create concern. Nehemiah would certainly need to support the collection of these dues, normally payable on the amount of produce obtained from the *fields and vineyards* (4).

To make matters worse, having parted with their fields, some of these destitute families were in such dire straits financially that they had been compelled to sell some of their family members into slavery. The practice was common enough in the ancient near-east but the Mosaic law provided for the complete restoration of every slave's freedom after a period of six years' service.[2] The law also insisted that debtors should be released from all financial liability in every seventh year,[3] a provision which had probably suffered neglect in this period (10:31) just as the slave-law had in their earlier history.[4]

Some Israelite moneylenders made capital out of this economic hardship and increased the anguish by demanding exorbitant interest rates, a practice condemned by God's Word.[5] Ezekiel had earlier described the exacting of 'excessive interest' and making 'unjust gain from your neighbours' as one of Jerusalem's 'detestable practices'.[6] Yet despite that condemnation and its threatened consequence, here they were in the next century repeating one of the offences which had led them into exile. To meet the cruel demands of greedy moneylenders, borrowers had been forced either to sell themselves or their *sons and daughters to slavery* (5) despite the fact that the Mosaic law expressly prohibited the charging of interest on loans made to fellow-Israelites.[7] Such blatant indifference to the teaching of God's Word was a sin which could not be overlooked.

2. Nehemiah's solution (5:6–13)

When Nehemiah heard about such inhumane conduct and widespread poverty, he did three things: he made a considered personal response to the grievance, arranged a specific public occasion to discuss the issue, and produced an irrefutable case for putting the matter right.

First, Nehemiah made a balanced personal response to the grievance. On hearing the people's *outcry and these charges* of greed, inconsistent conduct, heartless behaviour and injustice, Nehemiah

---

[1] Blenkinsopp, p. 307; *cf.* Frye, *The Heritage of Persia,* pp. 112–114. The Persians collected vast sums of money from taxes. When Alexander the Great entered Susa in the following century, he found about 270 tons of coined gold and about 1,200 tons of silver stored up as bullion (Yamauchi, p. 707).
[2] Ex. 21:2–6; Lv. 25:38–55; Dt. 15:12–18.   [3] Dt. 15:1–11.   [4] Je. 34:8–16.
[5] Pr. 28:8; Ezk. 18:8, 10–13, 14–17.   [6] Ezk. 22:2, 12.
[7] Ex. 22:25; Lv. 25:35–37; Dt. 23:19–20; Ps. 15:5.

became *very angry* (6). Yet, once again, we see a leader in perfect control of the situation. Although emotionally stirred by what he had seen and heard, he refuses to act merely on the level of intense anguish: 'I mastered my feelings' (NEB). Anger is an appropriate but not a sufficient response. Emotional distress was followed by intellectual reflection which in turn led to practical action.

Confronted by a tense, difficult and widespread problem, Nehemiah says he *pondered* the situation in his *mind* and, only then, *accused the nobles and officials* (7). His response is at three levels: emotional, intellectual and volitional. The heart is moved (*very angry*), the mind is engaged (*I pondered them*) and the will is motivated (*and then accused*). When good people in our world hear of cruelty, oppression and discrimination, they are frequently moved by what they see on television news bulletins and read in their newspapers and may become *very angry* at such appalling neglect and brutality but, all too often, the response stays on that level of the merely emotional and then, often under the pressure of 'compassion fatigue', vapourizes into thin air. The heart has been moved but nothing more.

The mind must be stirred so that we become informed about the situation, whether it be of refugees, the hungry, homeless, sick, oppressed or the scores of other tragic needs in the contemporary world. Only as we become more aware of the extent of human need are we likely to make a specific response and do something about these huge global injustices of our time. We thank God that many of our contemporaries are not content simply to view hardship on their television screens, but that they then go on to offer their services to agencies like TEAR Fund or a missionary society, either for a short-term enterprise or summer vacation project. The emotional response is followed by an intellectual inquiry which issues in particular work on behalf of needy people.

Secondly, Nehemiah arranges a specific public occasion to discuss the issue. Even with the authority of the imperial court behind him, the governor knows that he cannot possibly rectify this grim situation on his own. He sensitively hears the oppressed, boldly addresses the offenders and wisely convenes a meeting. It would not be enough privately to accuse *the nobles and officials* of alarming wrong. The whole community must be brought together, so that deprived families can voice their complaints directly to these rapacious citizens: *So I called together a large meeting to deal with them* (7). He knew that it would not do merely to obtain a quick verbal agreement with the individual offenders. They could stand arguing with him for hours if their precious money was at stake. They must be brought face to face with the problem and not merely rely on Nehemiah's information about the heartbreaking poverty of many

Judean homes. Convening *a large meeting* assured deprived people that something was about to be done, and at the same time convinced the avaricious offenders that the governor could not be ignored. The convening of the *large meeting* frequently played a significant part in the spiritual and moral development of God's people following Ezra's return,[8] and this was certainly the right moment for another one. It is a reminder of the importance and usefulness of a public meeting on crucial humanitarian, social and community issues, to share information, influence public opinion, enlist support and mobilize effective action. Without such united and well-organized propaganda, good intentions can be dissipated and imaginative ideas evaporate into thin air.

Thirdly, Nehemiah produced an irrefutable case for putting the matter right. What he had to say at the meeting was crucial, and the governor uses his fine mind to marshal eight facts to present a persuasive and well-integrated argument for rectifying such monstrous injustice.

a. The appeal to conscience (5:8)

The appalling situation was all the more distressing in that, prior to Nehemiah's return, some impoverished people had been forced to sell themselves or their children as slaves to Gentile homes but, wherever possible, they had been generously *bought back* (8) by their fellow-countrymen. Now, without houses and lands and in deeper poverty still, many were compelled to return to slavery, this time in Israelite homes, enslaved by people who belonged to the same community of faith. Surely the offenders' consciences are disturbed that the abundant generosity of those Israelites who had bought them back from Gentiles had been overshadowed by the appalling greed of their new masters. These Jewish slave-owners were probably guilty of robbing their slaves of their 'seventh year' freedom promised by the law of Moses. The introduction of a specific promise to observe the 'seventh year' provisions, and to 'cancel all debts', in Nehemiah's later act of covenant renewal (10:31) suggests that the new agreement was regularizing a feature of the Mosaic law which had been marginalized or ignored in Judah.

b. The appeal to love (5:8)

One of the most alarming aspects of this cruelty was that the offenders had ignored the special relationship which every Israelite believer had with others united by the same covenant. These deprived

[8] Ezr. 10:5, 7–8; Ne. 2:17–18; 8:1–10:39; 13:1–3.

neighbours were their *Jewish brothers* and they are accused of selling their *brothers*.

That dimension of unique intra-personal relationships was a marked feature of the covenant. They enjoyed a special relationship, not only with God but with one another, and Nehemiah's repeated use of *brothers* is meant to confront them with another aspect of their covenant obligation which they had either overlooked or ignored. The laws of Moses about generosity towards debtors and kindness to others repeatedly emphasize the nature of that 'brotherly' relationship. The impoverished person is a 'poor brother' or a 'needy brother'.[9] Such people belong to the same family of faith and ought to be loved, not robbed.

These *brothers* who had been condemned to slavery in Israelite homes were worse off than their compatriots in exile. Before returning to their homeland, they did at least have the privilege and security of living together as united families. Now the greed of fellow-Israelites was destroying family unity. Nehemiah's words opened the eyes of the offenders to their markedly incongruous behaviour, touched their consciences, and robbed them of any attempt to justify their conduct: *They kept quiet, because they could find nothing to say.*

c. The appeal to morality (5:9a)

Building on the conscience and compassion argument, Nehemiah then appeals to their moral sensitivity: *So I continued, 'What you are doing is not right.'* His exposure was not merely designed to make them feel uncomfortable about their rapacious lifestyles, but to confront them with essential moral obligations in a good and just society. People who want to enjoy the benefits and advantages of community life cannot live selfishly and totally heedless of others. They are not isolated hermits, largely indifferent to the needs of other human beings, but have chosen to live interdependent lives within structured communities, recognizing that such a pattern of living brings companionship, convenience and security. But community life not only offers privileges it also makes demands. The Ten Commandments provided the Israelite people with a pattern of community care as well as spiritual responsibility. By severing the links between slaves and their families, these materialistic citizens were making it impossible for them to 'honour' their parents in any meaningful way. They had stolen the freedom of their poverty-stricken employees, and covetousness was certainly at the root of all these social evils. It offended the law of basic human morality and Nehemiah appeals to it, *'Shouldn't you ...?'*

[9] Dt. 15:1–11; 22:1–4; 24:14–15.

The governor chooses his words with care because he believes that, although greedy, they are capable of moral persuasion. As Kidner says, 'There is invitation as well as reproach in his *Ought you not . . .?* [RSV] or more simply "Will you not . . .?"'[10] Nehemiah pleads with the offenders on the basis of fundamental ethical principles which are at the root of any secure and well-ordered society.

Contemporary society prefers relativism to absolutes in its choice of moral options. People do what they want rather than what they ought. '*Shouldn't you . . .?*' (or RSV's '*Ought you not . . .?*') are unacceptable moral interrogations; people prefer what is palatable to what is obligatory. But Nehemiah knew that his community's social future could only be built on the sure foundation of sound ethical standards. That involved the recognition that our fellow-humans are made in the image of God,[11] and that we have a responsibility to determine our moral values from what we know of God's nature and what we read in God's Word.

d. The appeal to theology (5:9b)

'*Shouldn't you walk in the fear of our God?*' Nehemiah now appeals to their knowledge of God's character. As Israelite people, committed to a covenant relationship with God, do they not want to acknowledge his uniqueness, reverence his holiness, receive his mercy, reflect his love, pursue his will, and obey his Word? In their callous treatment of others these greedy Israelites had failed to display these qualities. The Hebrew people knew that doctrine must not be divorced from life; belief and behaviour are the inseparable components of authentic faith. It was basic to the Israelite understanding of God that his children were expected to live like him, being holy as he is holy, merciful as he is merciful and righteous as he is righteous.[12] Those who failed to do so were not only passively ignoring God's Word but actively dishonouring his person. For centuries, Israel's wise men had taught their communities that he 'who oppresses the poor shows contempt for their Maker, but whoever is kind to the needy honours God.'[13] Nobody could possibly plead ignorance of such a basic concept and covenant condition. They knew it, but had neglected to do it.

e. The appeal to Scripture (5:9b)

It is possible that Nehemiah may have wanted to remind his contemporaries of a specific passage of Old Testament teaching. The language he uses and the remedy he suggests are strikingly

---

[10] Kidner, p. 96.   [11] Gn. 1:26–27.   [12] Lv. 11:44–45.   [13] Pr. 14:31; 17:5.

reminiscent of the Lord's commands regarding the year of Jubilee. He may have been saying that in view of the desperate condition of Israel's poor, this would surely be an opportune time to show the same generosity to the poor as to aliens during the fiftieth year. In their studied indifference to local penury, these avaricious money-makers were not even treating their fellow-Israelite paupers as generously as the law expected them to deal with deprived aliens.

The governor pleads with them to *let the exacting of usury stop! Give back to them immediately their fields, vineyards, olive groves and houses, and also the usury you are charging them* (10b–11). Nehemiah's reference to *the fear of God* in this context may deliberately recall the specific teaching about the poor in Leviticus 25:

> If one of your countrymen becomes poor and is unable to support himself among you, help him as you would an alien or a temporary resident, so that he can continue to live among you. Do not take interest of any kind from him, but *fear your God* . . . You must not lend him money at interest or sell him food at a profit. I am the LORD your God . . . If one of your countrymen becomes poor among you and sells himself to you, do not make him work as a slave. He is to be treated as a hired worker . . . Do not rule over them ruthlessly, but *fear your God*.[14]

God had spoken clearly in his Word about their practical responsibility to care for deprived people in local communities, but they had disregarded the message.

f. The appeal to testimony (5:9c)

Moreover, the inconsistent conduct of the offenders not only dishonoured God and ignored Scripture; it nullified their witness to the unbelieving world. The offenders must rectify this evident social injustice for only in this way could they *avoid the reproach of our Gentile enemies.* Israel had been entrusted with a unique testimony to the nations. They were not only to declare what God is like but manifest those qualities in their lives. That was the theological and moral basis of the covenant God had made with them, an agreement embodied in the Ten Commandments. It was both a visual as well as a verbal testimony. If their pagan neighbours saw them behaving cruelly towards their own people, how could they possibly be persuaded of the uniqueness and reality of Israel's distinctive faith? Who would believe that Israel's God was kind, merciful and compassionate when his worshippers were cruel, merciless and mean towards the people he loves?

---

[14] Lv. 25:35–43, and see the repetitive 'fear your God' in 25:17, 36, 43.

Consistent testimony is a central biblical theme and figures prominently in New Testament teaching about the Christian life. Jesus taught his followers that an exemplary lifestyle is not only a crucial element in personal faith but an effective instrument in winning converts and refining society, prompting others to magnify the God who makes such conduct possible.[15] First-century Christians knew that their witness in the world must be as eloquent in their daily behaviour as in their verbal testimony.[16] People with consistently attractive Christian lives not only make faith visible and credible but challenge the unbelief of their contemporaries. Edgar Wallace, a prolific writer of thrillers for an earlier generation, was influenced by the Christian living of a Methodist friend, J. B. Hellier. He said, 'I believe that much of the good which is within me came because I knew him. He is an everlasting barrier between me and atheism.'[17]

Conversely, these rapacious Israelite slave-owners and moneylenders would make their distinctive message a *reproach* in the eyes of their *Gentile enemies*. Inconsistent lifestyles seriously damage the effectiveness of Christian witness. W. E. Sangster used to pose the searching question: 'Are some people outside the Church of Jesus Christ because I am inside?'[18]

g. The appeal to experience (5:10)

Nehemiah does not deal with the situation as a detached observer. He is also involved personally in what is happening and tells the offenders, *I and my brothers and my men are also lending the people money and grain. But let the exacting of usury stop!* There are two possibilities here. Nehemiah may be either confessing a mistake or offering an example.

He may be confessing a mistake. It is possible that as local governor and a man of some substance, Nehemiah too had loaned money and grain to needy people, even expecting some payment of interest. In that case, he is here confessing his own neglect of God's Word regarding the exacting of interest from his own people. As a government official his financial affairs may have been the responsibility of others, but he has realized that he too is implicated in the offence. As McConville says, Nehemiah 'does not hide the fact that he too has been lending. Since everything here depends on motive, however, we need attribute nothing unworthy to him. His

---

[15] Mt. 5:13–16.
[16] Phil. 1:11; 2:14–16; Tit. 2:9–10; 1 Pet. 2:12–15; 1 Jn. 3:10–15; 4:19–21.
[17] Margaret Lane, *Edgar Wallace* (London: Hamish Hamilton, 1964), p. 68.
[18] W. E. Sangster, *A Spiritual Check-up* (London: Epworth, 1952) [unpaginated pamphlet].

preaching is therefore backed up by practice and it is costly.'[19] After all, there is nothing in Scripture to suggest that Nehemiah or any other biblical character, apart from Christ, is sinless. It is an attractive thought that a man of this calibre, yet capable of such an error, was honest enough to confess it. The difficulty about such an interpretation is that he could hardly have been *very angry* (6) about practices of which he too was guilty, and the later verses in this chapter describe the outstanding generosity (14–18) of a man who would hardly have looked for interest from seriously deprived people.

More likely, Nehemiah is offering an example. He is saying that he, his brothers and colleagues have loaned money to fellow-Israelites but totally without interest, and he is urging others to do the same. Generously following the Jubilee-year pattern, they ought to release the property they have taken as security against loans and also return the interest they had exacted. The *hundredth part of the money, grain, new wines and oil* is probably, as Kidner suggests, 'in monthly terms (*i.e.* 12 per cent per annum)'.[20]

h. The appeal to commitment (5:11–13)

The governor's demand that the situation be rectified without delay, *Give back to them immediately their fields . . . and also the usury you are charging them,* meets with a prompt response: *We will do as you say.* He believed in the necessity of specific, immediate, irrevocable and public resolution so he *summoned the priests* as the religious officials, ordering them to attend a public oath-taking ceremony to ensure that these nobles will *do what they had promised.* It was not a time for tentative suggestions or vague promises. Once the oaths had been taken, Nehemiah's use of priestly witnesses is followed by prophetic practice: *I also shook out the folds of my robe and said, 'In this way may God shake out of his house and possessions every man who does not keep this promise. So may such a man be shaken out and emptied'* (13).

It was like an act of 'prophetic symbolism', one of those stark visual aids which sometimes accompanied the prophetic word. Their purpose was not merely to illustrate truth and make the prophet's sayings more memorable. To the eastern mind the sign was inseparable from the event it portrayed. It almost initiated the action it described. When the eighth-century residents of Jerusalem saw Isaiah walking through its streets 'stripped and barefoot' like a

[19] McConville, p. 101.
[20] Kidner, p. 97.

captive, they would not dismiss the prophet's behaviour as bizarre or alarmist. People would shudder because, behaving like that, he was setting the dreaded judgment process in motion. Later, when Jeremiah lifted an earthenware jar and hurled it to the ground, the onlookers would be horrified as they saw the shattered pieces flying in all directions: 'I will smash this nation and this city just as this potter's jar is smashed and cannot be repaired.'[21]

Similarly, Judea's greedy nobles would not regard the shaking of Nehemiah's robe as an eccentric public act intended merely to drive the point home. It was a visible as well as audible public warning that if they did not *keep this promise* they would certainly become as destitute as the poorest man or woman in Judea, *shaken out and emptied*, robbed of property and possessions.

Nehemiah was determined that the enormity of this social sin should be recognized for what it was, a blatant act of rebellion against God's person, Word and people. By what the offenders did (attended the *large meeting*), said (oaths), saw (Nehemiah's shaken robe) and heard (*the whole assembly said 'Amen'*, 13b), they would be held to those firm promises, made in the presence of others, to put these things right without delay. The whole assembly *praised the Lord* that such a dire situation had been rectified and those who took the oaths *did as they had promised*.

3. Nehemiah's example (5:14–19)

In describing Nehemiah's own lifestyle in this period, the memoirs relate how he behaved, first negatively (what he did not do to impoverish others) and then positively (what he did do to help others). He says that during the twelve years he served as *governor in the land of Judah*, he had been motivated by two biblical principles.

a. Reverence for God (5:15)

Before he contemplated what was profitable for himself, he considered what was pleasing to God. *Earlier governors* had repeatedly *placed a heavy burden on the people and took forty shekels of silver from them in addition to food and wine. Their assistants also lorded it over the people. But out of reverence for God I did not act like that.*

In Nehemiah's thinking *reverence for God* was not merely a deferential posture in public worship (8:6). It had a practical consequence in everyday life. For this governor it meant honouring God's name, obeying God's word and loving God's people. It was

[21] Is. 20:1–4; Je. 19:1–2, 10–11.

because he feared God that he did not take their food (14), grasp their money, drink their wine or abuse their subservience: *Their assistants also lorded it over the people* (15b). The fear of God increased his respect for other people made in the image of God, and it was a controlling spiritual principle in Nehemiah's life. He worshipped a God who was 'awesome' (1:5; 4:14) and, like others, he found 'delight in revering' God's name (1:11). That reverential fear determined his conduct (5:9, 15) and became a decisive principle in judging the character of others (7:2).

Nehemiah had immense spiritual confidence (4:20: 'Our God will fight for us'), but the assurance did not make him brash and presumptuous. Believers do not always find it easy to achieve the delicate balance between confidence and dependence, certainty and reverence. It is possible to take the Lord for granted. Samson was helped through many difficulties but repeatedly presumed upon God. Then the awful day came when he did it once too often: "'I'll go out as before and shake myself free." But he did not know that the LORD had left him.' King Uzziah was alarmingly presumptuous. He 'was greatly helped until he became powerful. But . . . his pride led to his downfall' and he came under the judgment of a holy God. No wonder his contemporary, the prophet Isaiah, was overwhelmed by a vision of God's holiness and confessed his sin.[22] The Lord Jesus is the believer's constant example of 'reverent submission' to a 'Holy Father' and a 'Righteous Father'.[23] Christians are assured of life's necessary spiritual resources, but these are given in response to submissiveness and reliance.[24]

b. Compassion for others (5:17–18)

After explaining that, in contrast to his predecessors in office, he had not lived extravagantly, the governor goes on to show how he did live. He had lived generously, by providing meals for others, and considerately, by not taking food from others: *I never demanded the food allocated to the governor, because the demands were heavy on these people* (18). Instead of exacting large monetary payments from local people to meet his hospitality account, he had fed officials and visitors out of his own salary (17) and an *abundant supply* of food and wine was made available on a daily basis for feeding others. These heavy costs were usually met by the local governor's (as opposed to the imperial) taxes, but Nehemiah refused to put this extra burden on the shoulders of an already destitute community. Nehemiah hopes that his own example of generosity and thoughtfulness will be taken up by other affluent people in the province. Like

[22] Jdg. 16:20; 2 Ch. 26:15–21; Is. 6:1–5. [23] Heb. 5:7; Jn. 17:11, 25.
[24] Col. 3:22; Heb. 12:28.

himself, other wealthy people had the same opportunity to do good with their money rather than squander it upon themselves.

The early Christian churches were left in no doubt about their responsibilities to the poor. In the subsistence economy of first-century society, the vast majority of people were living on the bread-line. It was an economy in which equilibrium, not growth, was the normal expectation. It is reliably estimated that for ninety-eight per cent of the population basic necessities were in short supply.[25] The apostle Paul (who hardly belonged to the affluent two per cent) did not exaggerate when he said he had 'often gone without food' and made several references to his experience of extreme hunger.[26] Yet in such a deprived economic context, Christian believers were reminded of their responsibility to people worse off than themselves.[27] It demonstrated their love for God as well as for the people he created and treasured.

Before leaving the memoir's description of Nehemiah's campaign for human rights and social justice, we ought to observe three attitudes to money in this chapter. It describes those who need it, idolize it and share it.

First, these deprived people were in desperate need of help. Normal agricultural labour diverted to an essential but demanding building scheme, together with famine, high taxation, poverty, debt and slavery, had combined to produce widespread anguish in Judah, and many families were without essential supplies of food. Sadly, the story is not peculiar to the history of antiquity. Millions of our contemporaries are in poverty, and vast numbers are without adequate supplies of food and drink, shelter and security. Living in this global village, Christians cannot possibly be indifferent to millions of men, women and children in this world who also say through their tears, *in order for us to eat and stay alive, we must get grain* (2). In every year, the Third World has to repay the West three times more in debt payments than it receives in humanitarian aid.

Some sacrificial giving to the work of Christian and other relief agencies, an intelligent understanding of and appropriate campaigning for a compassionate approach to the international debt issue, prayerful intercession for relief workers in such desperate conditions, all these and more must play some part in the contemporary Christian's response to such enormous and scandalous deprivation.

Secondly, the offenders in this chapter had made a god of money. They had forgotten that, though it is one of life's evident necessities,

---

[25] Bruce Malina, *The New Testament World: Insights from Cultural Anthropology* (London: SCM, 1981), pp. 72–73, 82–85; Frances M. Young and David F. Ford, *Meaning and Truth in 2 Corinthians* (London: SPCK, 1987), p. 172.

[26] 2 Cor. 11:27; 6:5; 1 Cor. 4:11; Phil. 4:12.   [27] Jas. 1:27; 2:14–17; 1 Jn. 3:17–18.

it is not one of life's greatest priorities. Those who devote their lives to acquiring it are rarely content. Its ruthless pursuit becomes an insatiable lust. There are two things which every person needs to remember about money: it cannot satisfy, and it will not last. The healthiest bank balance does not guarantee happiness and it has no significance whatever beyond the grave. When the actor and filmstar Wilfrid Hyde White died at the age of 87, one obituary included his sad confession that he had been too materialistic: 'I've owned 12 horses, seven Rolls Royce's, and I've had mistresses in Paris, London and New York – and it never made me happy.'[28] Christians need money as much as anybody else, but they refuse to idolize it. It is a commodity to use, not a god to be worshipped.

Thirdly, Nehemiah is an excellent example of a believer who put his money to good use. He tried to help others in need by *lending the people money and grain* (10). He knew of officials who were guilty of alarming exploitation and spent their lives eagerly grasping every coin which might come their way but, *out of reverence for God*, Nehemiah *did not act like that* (15). Instead, he met out of his own pocket the heavy costs of necessary hospitality, refusing to tax his poverty-stricken contemporaries, *because the demands were heavy on these people* (18). He was not perfect, but in his reverence for God, obedience to Scripture and love for others, he is a model of practical and generous social care.

[28] Obituary, 'The Daily Telegraph', 8 May 1991

Nehemiah 6:1–19
7. The servant's protection

Nehemiah has not seen the last of his opponents. He has coped magnificently with varied problems – personal, political, pastoral, administrative and social. Now, his united team has *rebuilt the wall and not a gap was left in it*. All that remains is to *set the doors in the gates* (1) – but he is soon confronted with fresh troubles. They are part of the enemy's design to shatter him as he puts the final touches to a highly successful operation. The memoirs now record details of four distinct plots made against God's servant at a crucial time in the enterprise.

1. A plot to kidnap him (6:1–4)

The opponents saw that there was little hope of destroying Nehemiah's work but there was still time to bring him down personally. By now they realized that he had not just come to Jerusalem to tackle an important building assignment. He was determined to establish the community as well as secure the city. He was not simply a works manager. God had raised up an influential spiritual leader. So his enemies set their hearts on destroying him, and the only way to get at such a well-protected citizen was to lure him from his colleagues and on to enemy territory. Once kidnapped, they could easily dispose of him. In order to satisfy the Persian king, a plausible story could be easily fabricated attributing his death to the sudden attack of robbers.

Nehemiah tells us, *Sanballat and Geshem sent me this message: 'Come, let us meet together in one of the villages on the plain of Ono'* (2). The suggested location for the meeting, about halfway between Samaria and Jerusalem, would have lured the governor into the borders of the hostile territories of Ashdod and Samaria. It would have taken him a full day to get there and, allowing a further day for the discussion and another for the return meant that, at this crucial stage, he would be away from his work for half a week. It was neither the right time nor place for a regional consultation, especially when Nehemiah knew that they were up to no good. The invitation appeared innocent but was a thinly disguised death sentence: *But they were scheming to harm me.* The governor was discerning, resolute and inflexible.

He was discerning. He was a man of prayer and unlikely to receive an invitation of this sort without taking it into God's presence. The Lord put into his heart what he might do for Jerusalem's security (2:12) and his own safety. Over the months, he had been called (1:11), strengthened (2:2), equipped (2:4–9), encouraged (4:6), protected (4:15) and guided (5:1–13) by 'the God of heaven' (2:20). Now he was being warned by the Lord that this consultation idea was nothing but artful and highly dangerous bluff. The time Nehemiah spent with God made him sensitive to divine guidance and warning. He was prompted by God to refuse the invitation, knowing that his enemies were set on his destruction.

Throughout the centuries, Christians have been grateful to God not only for sensitive promptings as to what they might do but clear warnings about what should be avoided. The gift of discernment is a choice spiritual quality, urgently necessary when apparently reasonable ideas harbour the seeds of potential disaster. In the first century, John told his readers that they must not merely accept things which have an appearance of being helpful or useful; evil may be lurking under the guise of the good. They are to 'test the spirits to see whether they are from God'.[1]

Nehemiah was resolute. He knew that the Ono suggestion was disastrous and said so. The governor was a man of decided principles. He knew exactly what he believed about the situation and responded to the request with firm conviction. Some of his contemporaries might well accuse him of being intractable, unforgiving, uncooperative, self-opinionated and the rest, but, once Nehemiah was convinced of the right action, nothing would deter him from defending and maintaining his views. We live in a culture in which intolerance is regarded as society's greatest enemy, yet many of our contemporaries will not tolerate people with firm moral and spiritual convictions. Men and women with clear views and uncompromising standards about sexual behaviour, marriage, alcoholism, drug abuse and pro-life issues, such as abortion and euthanasia, are dismissed as bigots and prudes who ought not to be tolerated. A world without strong moral foundations needs the witness of believers with informed conviction as well as unlimited compassion.

Nehemiah was inflexible. He not only had the conviction but kept

[1] 1 Jn. 4:1.

101

to it, though frequently urged to reconsider his initial response. His enemies entertained high hopes that their kidnapping scheme might well succeed if only they had the patience to absorb the occasional rebuttal. To their first approach Nehemiah *sent messengers to them with this reply: 'I am carrying on a great project and cannot go down. Why should the work stop while I leave it and go down to you?'* (3). But they refused to take 'No' for an answer: *Four times they sent me the same message, and each time I gave them the same answer* (4). It is one thing to have a conviction; it is quite another to stand by it. Nehemiah refused to be manipulated. Once he had discerned the danger and expressed his response, nothing would move him. Both church and society in the modern world need people with that same uncompromising determination to honour God and remain true to their principles, however persistent the calumny and however great the cost.

2. A plot to malign him (6:5–9)

When Nehemiah refused the invitation for the fourth time, Sanballat knew that he must change his tactics. The suggestion about a meeting in a village on the Ono plain was repeated a fifth time, but on this occasion the messenger also carried an open letter, suggesting an agenda for the proposed conference. This *unsealed letter* was virtually public property; anybody the messenger encountered was free to read it. It accused the governor of dishonourable intentions and corrupt motives in building the wall and seriously questioned his integrity as a leader: *It is reported among the nations – and Geshem says it is true – that you and the Jews are plotting to revolt, and therefore you are building the wall. Moreover, according to these reports you are about to become their king and have even appointed prophets to make this proclamation about you in Jerusalem: 'There is a king in Judah!' Now this report will get back to the king; so come, let us confer together.*

It was a subtle and treacherous ploy. The accusation that he was organizing a revolt, however untrue, could issue in his immediate recall to Susa. Sanballat and his menacing colleagues had only to make that kind of report to the Persian authorities and the damage was done. 'There's no smoke without fire.' Even though Nehemiah was not remotely guilty of such charges, it was a huge temptation to talk with them, bring everything out into the open, assert his innocence, trace the source of the scandal, demand that the unjust accusation be withdrawn and so on. They knew that a man of honour would hate the thought of libellous statements circulating in an open letter. But Nehemiah had the wisdom to discern that their allegations had no basis in fact and, far from being *reported among the nations,* had been voiced by nobody but themselves.

Once again, this spiritually alert leader knows exactly how to respond to an accusation of that sort: *I sent them this reply: 'Nothing like what you are saying is happening; you are just making it up out of your head.' They were all trying to frighten us . . . But I prayed* (8–9).

It is not easy to handle unjust accusations. The problem is as old as time itself, and Scripture offers some helpful insights. If some damaging smear has been made on our character and we are assaulted by slander we must realize that, although painful, the experience can be educative, teaching us something about ourselves, Scripture and God.

First, perhaps there is something we can learn about ourselves, even from unkind words about us. We need honestly to examine our hearts to see if there is any truth whatever in the accusation. It may be ill-intended, but that does not mean that there may not be a grain of truth in the cruel thing that has been said. We need to pray with the psalmist, 'O LORD my God, if I have done this and there is guilt on my hands – if I have done evil'. . . 'Search me, O God, and know my heart . . . See if there is any offensive way in me'.[2]

Secondly, there is something we can learn from Scripture. The Bible offers us clear guidelines about our response to unkind and untruthful things which may be said against us. God's Word forbids retaliation which only multiplies the sin, and we must not attempt to take any kind of revenge.[3] We are to intercede for those who 'falsely say all kinds of evil' against us because of our allegiance to Christ.[4] We are also to pray for ourselves, especially for patience to absorb falsehoods either in silence (like Jesus before his accusers)[5] or with temperate speech, knowing that 'a gentle answer turns away wrath' and that 'a patient man . . . who controls his temper' is better 'than one who takes a city'.[6] If our consciences are clear, it is often best not to attempt to justify ourselves. Given time and patience, many of the worst accusations are often seen for what they are and discredit those who have perpetrated them.

Thirdly, however sad the circumstances, there is always something we can learn about God. Psalm 7 tells us that when David was troubled about allegations made against him by a Benjamite named Cush, he discovered in his emotional pain that God was his refuge (1–2), judge (3–9) and shield (10–17). In the light of these great truths he determined to shelter (1–2), search (his own heart, 3), trust (11)

---

[2] Ps. 7:3–4; 139:23–24   [3] Rom. 12:17–21.   [4] Mt. 5:11.   [5] Mk. 14:61.
[6] Pr. 15:1; 16:32.

and praise (17), knowing that God alone can bring good out of evil. David proved that the trouble caused by a slanderer 'recoils on himself; his violence comes down on his own head' (16). Those who trust God leave him to do his own work and ask him for the strength, patience and love to cope with such a highly unpleasant form of adversity. In this particular trouble, Nehemiah found his strength in realism, prayer and Scripture.

He was realistic, knowing that verbal assault of this kind was inevitable. It was part of the enemy's intimidation campaign, *They were all trying to frighten us, thinking, 'Their hands will get too weak for the work, and it will not be completed'* (9). There was bound to be opposition to such a worthwhile enterprise, and Nehemiah realized that a resourceful leader learns to take it in his stride. He refused to be either belittled, deflected or embittered by it.

Nehemiah was helped as he prayed, *Now strengthen my hands.* The enemy longed for their hands to be discouraged, so Nehemiah pleaded for strong ones and, as he prayed, the strength came as well as the discernment, reliance and confidence he needed.

Nehemiah was helped as he reflected on Scripture. The enemy had organized this intimidating verbal warfare with the express purpose of weakening the hands of the workers and, as Nehemiah prays, it is possible that the words 'weak hands' remind him of Isaiah's words about an earlier trial: 'Strengthen the feeble hands, steady the knees that give way; say to those with fearful hearts, "Be strong, do not fear; your God will come, he will come with vengeance; with divine retribution he will come to save you."'[7]

Fear is a recurrent theme in Nehemiah's memoirs and it is prominent in this chapter. Three of its four sections contain variations of the Hebrew word for 'frighten' (*yārē*; 9, 13, 14, 19). In a terrorizing context the governor may well have found comfort in Isaiah's message. People who walk the way of holiness have found an answer to fearful hearts, feeble hands and weak knees.

3. A plot to intimidate him (6:10–14)

The attacks became more malevolent as time went by. That is often the way with adversity. The first Christians were not shielded from trouble, and it seemed to get worse with every passing month. They were first ridiculed, then imprisoned, then threatened, then flogged, then killed.[8] Nehemiah's troubles became more sinister in form and more menacing in intensity. He visited a friend, one of Jerusalem's prophets, and had every reason to feel safe with a professed man of

[7] Is. 35:3–4.   [8] Acts 2:13; 4:3, 17–21; 5:40; 7:57–60; 12:2.

God. Possibly he wanted to share his problems and be assured of a godly man's support during such intense opposition. But the old friend became a new enemy. Nehemiah called on *Shemaiah* at a time when the prophet was *shut in at his home* (10). The phrase is ambiguous, but possibly means that he had confined himself to his home pretending that he too was afraid of Nehemiah's opponents, or that he 'had shut himself up as a symbolic action to indicate that his own life was in danger and to suggest that both must flee to the temple'.[9] This would have created in Nehemiah a sense of fellow-feeling and may even account for Nehemiah's original purpose in visiting him, to encourage and support him as a godly prophet under pressure from the enemy. But it was all a specious trick. Shemaiah had been paid to initiate this next destructive plot. *He said, 'Let us meet in the house of God, inside the temple, and let us close the temple doors, because men are coming to kill you – by night they are coming to kill you'* (10).

It was another attempt to destroy Nehemiah's character. The plan to do so on the grounds that he was a subversive revolutionary had failed miserably. The governor had seen right through it, exposed the lie, and treated it with the contempt it deserved. When they could not accuse him of being a political rebel, they tried to make him a religious transgressor. Nehemiah was not a priest, and here was this false prophet suggesting that he should go into the temple as a victim seeking asylum, misusing God's house, and violating the temple's prohibitions which forbade access to the holy places by anyone other than priests. The prophet's suggestion about closing the temple doors suggests that Shemaiah intended either to lure the governor into an area reserved exclusively for priests or, with the doors closed, at least say that Nehemiah had violated the holiness rules. Robbed of witnesses, Nehemiah's denial of a prophet's word would count for nothing.

Once more, Nehemiah was sensitive to danger and *realised that God had not sent him, but that he had prophesied against me because Tobiah and Sanballat had hired him. He had been hired to intimidate me so that I would commit a sin by doing this, and then they would give me a bad name to discredit me* (13).

Nehemiah's moral integrity was above reproach and his conduct in Jerusalem had been impeccable. If they could not kill him, they knew that the most damaging thing they could do against a man of honour was to defame his character. Although Jerusalem's governor was well endowed with material possessions, he believed that a 'good name is more desirable than great riches'.[10] He realized that this plot to vilify him before his family, friends and colleagues was aimed at

---

[9] Yamauchi, p. 714.   [10] Pr. 22:1.

destroying his influence in Jerusalem. The enemy knew that Nehemiah was not likely to end his commitment to his people once the walls had been rebuilt. The time he had spent with them made him aware of other aspects of their moral and spiritual life in urgent need of renewal, and his heart was set on a greater task than the reconstruction of broken walls. The enemy did not want such a good work to begin, and the best way to halt the reformation was to degrade the reformer. The plan aimed at destroying his character, using fear as their primary instrument.

There is a note of urgency in Shemaiah's voice: *by night they are coming to kill you.* But Nehemiah had confidence in a God who is sovereign (1:5; 2:4, 20), wise (2:12), powerful (4:14, 20), merciful (9:17), compassionate (9:19), generous (9:20, 25) and patient (9:30), a Lord determined to deliver his trusting servant from the worst of dangers.

Once again, help is mediated through prayer (14). He gradually makes the discovery that Shemaiah is not the only prophet who is working against him. A prophetess named Noadiah and additional male prophets have also been manipulated by the governor's enemies and have voiced this relentless intimidation campaign. They have mobilized a destructive assault on Nehemiah but he responds, not by attacking them, but by seeking God (14). He is determined that the righteous God shall be the judge, not Jerusalem's governor. The Lord knows their hearts, their unworthy allegiance, corrupt motives and damaging intentions, and he will deal with them all, Sanballat, Tobiah, Geshem, Shemaiah, Nodiah *and the rest of the prophets* in sovereign justice. They imagine they are devising imminent destruction for him; in reality, they are preparing a grim destiny for themselves.

4. A plot to undermine him (6:15–19)

Despite these repeated and concerted attempts at Nehemiah's downfall, the project was brought to a highly successful conclusion. *So the wall was completed on the twenty-fifth of Elul, in fifty-two days. When all our enemies heard about this, all the surrounding nations were afraid and lost their self-confidence, because they realised that this work had been done with the help of our God.*

From his first discreet enquiries and midnight exploration of the broken walls, Nehemiah knew that there would be opponents, and the work should begin without delay. That meant the rebuilding programme had been undertaken during the hot summer months between late July and mid-September, when hard relentless work of that character must have been desperately exhausting. But now it was done and, for centuries, even when that particular wall had been replaced, the project would remain as a unique tribute to its leader's vision, his colleagues' tenacity and, most of all, the Lord's help. Here was yet another testimony to the providence and protection of God.

Nehemiah's memoirs are a magnificent commentary on the persuasive effectiveness of human testimony. Throughout the enterprise, Nehemiah was determined to acknowledge either in speech or writing the source of their strength. He began by testifying in writing that all great projects for God begin in the place of honest, reflective and reliant prayer (1:4–11). He then testified that it was because 'the gracious hand' of God was upon him that he obtained permission to leave Persia with authority, protection and provisions (2:8). Once in Jerusalem, he testified to the prospective builders about the miracle of that 'gracious hand' (2:18), and he continued to testify not only to sympathetic believers but to unbelieving scoffers as well: 'The God of heaven will give us success' (2:19–20).

He testified compassionately, when morale was low, 'Don't be afraid . . . Remember the Lord' (4:14). He testified gratefully, placing on record his indebtedness to God's sovereign power in frustrating the evil designs of the enemy (4:15). He testified confidently as the beleaguered team divided into builders and soldiers: 'Our God will fight for us' (4:20).

To his wealthy but loveless contemporaries he testified perceptively: 'Shouldn't you walk in the fear of our God to avoid the reproach of our Gentile enemies?' (5:9). In writing, he testified humbly, that 'out of reverence for God' he 'did not act like that' (5:15). When troubles began to mount daily, he testified dependently about a God who would strengthen his hands (6:9) and now, with the walls rebuilt, he testifies adoringly that even his enemies acknowledge that *this work has been done with the help of our God* (16).

But the troubles continue and are not limited to Nehemiah's opening months in Jerusalem. The introductory phrase, *Also in those days* (17), looks beyond the eight-week building project and carries the sense of 'furthermore, throughout that period'.[11] This time the narrative describes a more subtle form of intimidation than we have seen so far. With obvious pain the governor realizes that many of Jerusalem's prophets were opposed to him (14). He goes on to discover that many among Judah's nobility had also joined their ranks, for *the nobles of Judah were sending many letters to Tobiah, and replies from Tobiah kept coming to them. For many in Judah were under oath to him . . . Moreover, they kept reporting to me his good deeds and then telling him what I said. And Tobiah sent letters to intimidate me* (17–19).

[11] Williamson (1985), p. 261

This was possibly the worst affliction of all. If the enemy can be precisely identified, then the source of the trouble is evident and one can take suitable precautions. But the sinister dimension of the latest attack is that the determined opponent has so furtively infiltrated the ranks of the region's nobility that it is now virtually impossible to distinguish enemy from friend. The most innocent conversation is likely to be repeated to a destructive adversary and its words twisted and distorted beyond recognition. With the help of Judah's nobles, Tobiah is constantly receiving fresh material which he can wield for his vicious designs. He has masterminded this plan of underground espionage by using two (probably related) means – one commercial, the other marital.

First, knowing the weakness of Judah's nobles for money, he has established firm trading alliances with them: *For many in Judah were under oath to him.* Nehemiah must have wondered whoever he could trust. Some of his erstwhile friends were Tobiah's business partners and, despite their knowledge of Tobiah's earlier harmful tactics, they had 'sworn allegiance to him'[12] and therefore did their utmost to present the enemy in the best possible light. Now that they were making money out of their relationship, they soon forgot his recent determination to eliminate them (4:8).

The enemy has changed his tactics from a thorough-going frontal attack to a persistently subversive underground campaign. Judah's postmen did well out of it! The nobles sent *many letters to Tobiah, and replies from Tobiah kept coming to them.* How subtly the enemy works. With what skill can he distort the facts and obliterate the memory. Now that the materialistic nobles are raking in handsome sums of money out of Tobiah's trading projects, they are no longer worried that at one time he had ruthlessly schemed for Israel's destruction (4:11).

People with a single eye to monetary gain rarely look elsewhere for help. They seldom reflect on yesterday's blessings, today's temptations and tomorrow's insecurity. Money buys little that matters. We leave all our possessions this side of eternity. Then, what will matter most is not how wealthy we have been on earth but how rich we are in heaven. Jesus issued a warning relevant in every culture, continent and century, 'Watch out! Be on your guard against all kinds of greed; a man's life does not consist in the abundance of his possessions'.[13]

Tobiah's other manoeuvre in his sinister offensive was to secure favour through marriage alliances: *he was son-in-law to Shecaniah ... and his son Jehohanan had married the daughter of*

[12] *Ibid.*   [13] Lk. 12:15–21.

Meshullam (18). Here is Nehemiah's first direct reference to one of Judah's greatest problems – the temptation to marry either an unbeliever or half-believer. Under pressure of personal aggrandizement, financial advantage, business interest or social preferment, many people were lured into marriage with someone either outside Israel's faith (an act prohibited by the Mosaic law) or (as was probably the case with the Tobiah entourage) with a partner who did not profess an uncompromising allegiance to Israel's covenant obligations. Such half-hearted believers were merely nominal Israelites, outwardly glorying in the advantages of their faith but unprepared to meet its demands.

Tobiah made sure that he had strong links with Israel's nobility through the most intimate of all human relationships. The nation's spiritual priorities would not in the future be under the scrutiny of great prophetic and priestly leaders. The days of those famous exemplars were gradually drawing to a close. Zerubbabel, Haggai, Zechariah, Malachi, Esther, Ezra, Nehemiah were among the last of Israel's celebrated leaders until, at last, the greatest of all appeared among them.

In the years ahead, Israel's spiritual destiny was to depend on devout families rather than renowned leaders. It was no accident of circumstance; it had always been part of the divine intention. The word was not to be the prerogative of prophets or priests, not on professional lips but within sincere hearts, and especially those who treasured the truth within families: 'These commandments that I give you today are to be upon your hearts. Impress them on your children. Talk about them when you sit at home ... When your son asks you, "What is the meaning of the stipulations ... the LORD our God has commanded you?" tell him ...'.[14] That ideal of family unity, security and testimony depended essentially on obedience to God's warning word about unsuitable, let alone prohibited, marriages. Sadly, on such a fundamental issue many potentially good people in Israel fell.

Like Ezra before him,[15] Nehemiah was to face the problem in its most acute form when those who taught the law in such matters failed to keep it (13:23–30). When there is a chasm between what people preach and what they do, untold disasters are sure to follow. It is a sobering story, but the Bible does not encourage naïve and groundless optimism. Its dramatic narratives and searching teaching constantly remind us that only those who do what God has said are guaranteed what he will give.

In conclusion, we should note that two main lessons dominate this chapter: the enemy's subtlety and the Lord's sufficiency.

[14] Dt. 6:6–7, 20–21; Je. 31:33–34.   [15] Ezr. 9:1–4.

The enemy is subtle. Behind these various attacks on God's servant there stands a far more sinister enemy than Sanballat and Tobiah. These men are merely pawns in the devil's manipulative campaign to frustrate God's work. Nobody can escape his sinister advances. Even the perfect ministry of the Lord Jesus was initiated by a period of severe testing in which the devil did his utmost to deflect Christ from his unique mission. The devil met Jesus in the wilderness with temptations similar to those encountered by Nehemiah and his contemporaries. They were temptations to please himself (bread from those stones which lay in the sand), parade himself (ruling over the nations in return for allegiance to the enemy), and prove himself (leaping from the temple pinnacle) rather than accepting that what God had said ('You are my Son, whom I love') is true.[16]

They are temptations markedly similar to those which lurked at every street corner in fifth-century Jerusalem, and they are just as powerful and persuasive in the contemporary world: temptations to materialism (get bread), hedonism (please yourself) and secularism (ignore God). The lust for money by hired prophets and avaricious nobles, the lust for pleasure (even at the cost of disobedience) by those who ignored God's will about marriage, and the lust for power by the governor's enemies, are sick evidence of the devil's work, and he is active still.

The tactics change as they did in this chapter's account of Nehemiah's testings. Here we can see the enemy as cunning (1–3), luring a good man on to dangerous ground,[17] persistent (4) as a 'roaring lion' constantly on the prowl 'looking for someone to devour',[18] untruthful (5–8) like 'the father of lies',[19] versatile (10–14), constantly changing his tactics,[20] undeterred (17–19), always stumbling across clever fools who do not know they are being used[21] – but, thank God, frustrated when believers pray (9), and when they leave their daunting disappointments in God's hands (14) as they trust him both for strength (9) and wisdom (12).

This chapter's second great lesson is that the Lord is sufficient. Throughout this section of the memoirs one adversity has followed hard on the heels of another. 'When sorrows come, they come not single spies, But in battalions.'[22] Life is like that, and Nehemiah's story has been preserved in Scripture to demonstrate how we too, faced with multiplied testing, can handle such pressures creatively.

Threatened by imminent persecution, the Christians of Asia Minor were assured that life's multichrome troubles, 'all kinds [poikilois] of trials', are matched by 'grace in its various [poikiles]

---

[16] Lk. 3:22; 4:1–13.   [17] Lk. 22:31–32, 54–62.   [18] 1 Pet. 5:8.   [19] Jn. 8:44.
[20] 2 Cor. 2:11; 11:14–15.   [21] Lk. 22:2–6.   [22] Hamlet, IV, v.

forms'.[23] Whatever the suffering, it is always accompanied by sufficient strength. As James says, 'he gives us more grace'.[24] The prologue to John's Gospel puts it superbly, 'From the fulness of his grace we have all received one blessing after another.'[25] Grace is the ground on which fresh grace is constantly provided or, as B. F. Westcott once put it, 'Each blessing appropriated became the foundation of a greater blessing.'[26] That word 'fulness' (*pleroma*) was part of the ancient world's nautical vocabulary; it described the ship's complement. Before leaving port the vessel was carefully checked to ensure that there was an adequate crew and that the cargo included sufficient food, drink, medical supplies, spare cloth to replace torn sails, ropes, in fact everything necessary for its journey.[27] That was the ship's complement or completeness. John's Gospel began by assuring its Christian readers that, however great the pressures of life, all their needs would be met out of the abundant completeness and inexhaustible sufficiency of Christ.

[23] 1 Pet. 1:6; 4:10.　　[24] Jas. 4:6.　　[25] Jn. 1:16.

[26] B. F. Westcott, *The Gospel according to St John* (1894), p. 14.

[27] Xenophon, *Hellenica* 1.6.16; 1.6.24, of a ship's complete crew, *cf.* the second-century (AD) Lucian, *Vera Historia* II, 37, 38; *cf.* J. B. Lightfoot, *St Paul's Epistles to the Colossians and Philemon* (Macmillan, 1927), pp. 256–257.

Nehemiah 7:1–73
8. The servant's convictions

After the wall had been rebuilt (1), Nehemiah's work was far from finished, so he tackled his other assignments with the same commitment and persistence which he had brought to the building operation. In this next chapter we are provided with another of his lists, one almost identical to that in Ezra 2, but there is something more here than a convenient archive from Israel's past. The opening sentences and the list itself provide us with a number of insights into Nehemiah's leadership style, and they are strikingly relevant in our albeit different world.

The completion of the wall was a magnificent and memorable achievement and one in which Nehemiah was uniquely used. For the Christian, the desire to be 'used' by God is surely one of life's greatest ambitions. In the mid-nineteenth century two missionaries sailed from England to work among the cannibals of Fiji, James Calvert and John Hunt. These two evangelical ministers worked from different theological perspectives. Hunt was a Wesleyan following the teaching of Arminius, whilst Calvert was a staunch Calvinist. Although the two men were not in agreement on some important doctrinal issues, they shared one great passion in common – holiness of life. They knew that in a pagan environment there is little point in theological orthodoxy which is not matched by an appropriate lifestyle. Their work was set in a grim context. Hunt says that on many days he had to choose between having his shutters open to get some air in the stifling heat or closing them because he was nauseated by the stench of human bodies cooking in the village cauldron. In order to keep themselves sane in such an uncongenial setting, they wrote regularly to each other about their favourite theme of sanctification, correspondence which was subsequently published. In one of the earliest letters,[1] Hunt shares

---

[1] John Hunt, *Entire Sanctification . . . in Letters to a Friend* (1853), p. 3.

with Calvert the longing that they might 'escape the curse of a useless life'.

Nehemiah certainly avoided the curse of leading a useless life, and this chapter helps to explain why he was used so effectively as a leader. He treasured a number of firm convictions which determined the nature of his life and work for God. Ten principles of an effective leader emerge in the surprising context of an Israelite archive.

1. Honour spiritual priorities (7:1)

With the wall complete and the city's gates set in place, the governor made some important appointments. The *gatekeepers and the singers and the Levites* were assigned to their specific responsibilities. The brief detail focuses on three issues close to Nehemiah's heart and vital to the community's physical, spiritual and intellectual development.

Their *physical* need was protection. Israel's *gatekeepers* may have been originally assigned to specific duties as temple doorkeepers or stewards, but it is clear (3) that the governor realized how important it was to widen these responsibilities to include the regular supervision of the city's main entrances. There were distinct physical hazards. Hopefully, the recently fortified (and, later, newly populated) city would gradually develop a thriving economy; marauding bandits and armies could soon have designs on a community not noted for a strong military presence. The gatekeepers may also have served as guards or watchmen, familiar sentries in eastern cities.[2]

It is clear from Nehemiah's later narrative that gatekeepers were also entrusted with moral responsibilities (13:22). When on a return visit to Jerusalem the governor found alarming instances of Sabbath-breaking, he gave precise instructions, first to his own servants, then to the Levite gatekeepers, that the city's doors be firmly bolted so that pagan traders could not enter the city to sell their goods on a holy day of rest and worship.

Contemporary communities would benefit from dedicated gatekeepers, men and women with alert ethical principles, concerned to protect the young, elderly and vulnerable in a society with declining values – a society with far too many people who, ignoring the casualties, have become sadly indifferent to lowering standards. The modern world needs moral watchdogs, people who will endeavour to guard our cities and communities from destructive influences, such as pornography, deviant sexual practice, child abuse, drug

---

[2] 2 Sa. 13:34; 18:24–27; Ps. 127:1; Is. 21:11–12; Je. 31:6; Ezk. 33:2–7.

abuse, solvent abuse, teenage alcoholism, abortion, euthanasia and other moral perils to which our nation and others are increasingly exposed. Thank God for moral gatekeepers who keep a compassionate and careful watch to minimize the extent to which innocent people can be damaged, who keep a careful eye on local traps and dangers, undertake careful research, make informed protests, contact Members of Parliament regarding unhelpful aspects of legislation, and give practical assistance in the local community to help people who are victims of these and other perils.

Their *spiritual* need was worship. Nehemiah appointed *singers* to lead the community in its adoration of God. For the past two months the building of the city's walls and its attendant social problems had necessarily concentrated attention on material, physical and economic issues, but the appointment of *singers* reminded Nehemiah's contemporaries that there is more to life than work and money. Their greatest priority was to ensure that God was at the heart of their personal, local and national life. The governor gave precedence to the maintenance of temple worship. Human beings were made not just to please themselves and serve others, but to honour God. Those who deny this essential dimension of life cannot hope to please God and live a balanced, influential and satisfying life. We were made for communion with God,[3] and when we deny that spiritual dimension to our lives and deliberately cut ourselves off from God, we become weakened and imperilled by spiritual suffocation. We are not living as God intended and things cannot possibly go right.

Millions of people of our generation deny the importance of spiritual values. The majority of our contemporaries in the Western world prefer to live without God. Biblical truth is arrogantly dismissed as an irrelevant aspect of remote antiquity. In secular contexts Christianity's authority is challenged, its values derided, its convictions disdained and its followers ridiculed. Moreover, the scepticism is not restricted to the Western Christian tradition nor to the United Kingdom alone. In his 1990 Reith Lectures, the Chief Rabbi told us that the 'majority of Jews are highly secularized' and quoted a survey in the United States which revealed that only 17 per cent regarded 'religious observance' as the quality 'considered most important to their Jewish identity'. Another survey among American Jews showed that almost two thirds *disagreed* with the statement that 'To be a good Jew one must believe in God'.[4]

[3] Gn. 1:26–27.
[4] Jonathan Sacks, *The Persistence of Faith: Religion, Morality and Society in a Secular Age* (London: Weidenfeld and Nicolson, 1991), p. 7, citing Nathan Glazer, 'American Jewry or American Judaism', in Seymour Martin Lipsett (ed.), *American Pluralism and the Jewish Community* (New Brunswick: Transaction Publishers, 1990), p. 35.

In his day, Nehemiah was alert to the gradual infiltration of secularist ideas and vigorously opposed measures which endangered Israel's spiritual values. He did everything possible to ensure that the people worshipped God regularly and acceptably and that spiritual ideals were kept uppermost in their community. When people went to the temple, their minds were lifted above those mundane issues which had dominated their minds throughout another week. As they worshipped together, they could reflect on the meaning of life, the confidence of faith, the assurance of forgiveness, the primacy of love, the guarantee of strength, the horizons of hope – treasures not available for purchase in Jerusalem's market places but, in the temple, their reality was confirmed. That is why the worship of God was Israel's highest ideal. Without it they were reduced to the values of the godless. Nehemiah appointed the temple's *singers* so that the praise of their generous and unfailing God might have the highest possible priority within Israel's community life.

Their *intellectual* need was teaching. Nehemiah knew that there was more to faith than singing. If the heart is to be inspired in worship then the mind must be informed. Faith must be grounded in spiritual certainties, and somebody must be responsible for communicating those great unchanging truths. So Nehemiah made sure that *Levites were appointed* to function as Israel's teachers and pastors, and to convey to the people the great realities of their faith.

The Levites' role in Israel had been dignified with a long history. The presence and function of the tribe of Levi was a constant reminder to other Israelities of the centrality of spiritual issues in a society where a complete tribe was set apart for God's work and witness in the community. The priests were chosen from that tribe alone, and other members of the tribe shared in supportive ministries in the wilderness tabernacle, temple and throughout the scattered Israelite communities. It is possible that, during the exile, with no temple to serve, these supportive assignments may have been marginalized, leaving the major responsibility in the hands of the priests alone. When Ezra prepared to leave for his homeland, he 'checked among the people and priests' and 'found no Levites there', so he made arrangements for both Levites and temple servants to join the returning exiles to meet the new spiritual responsibilities which lay before them.[5]

Whatever their role in the past, Levites of this post-exilic period appear to have shared a pastoral, educative and exemplary function, such as that described by Malachi.[6] When Ezra read God's Word to the Jerusalem congregation, the Levites served as interpreters and

[5] Ezr. 8:15–20.   [6] Mal. 2:4–7.

exponents of Scripture (8:7–8). Nehemiah knew that every community within his province needed a teacher who would share the truth of God's Word and relate it to the issues of contemporary life. In a relativist and pluralistic age like ours, one of our greatest needs is for preachers, teachers and homegroup leaders who will faithfully communicate the eternal truths of Scripture, and share them in a manner which will demonstrate their unique authority, crucial importance, contemporary relevance and timeless appeal.

Nehemiah's appointment of *the gatekeepers and the singers and the Levites* testified to the governor's priorities for body, spirit and mind. The people needed physical and moral protection, inspiring worship and effective teaching.

2. Value reliable partners (7:2)

Aware of the need of trustworthy colleagues, Nehemiah says that he then made two further appointments, which extended the leadership base in the city: *I put in charge of Jerusalem my brother Hanani, along with Hananiah the commander of the citadel, because he was a man of integrity and feared God more than most men do.*

The governor mentions two essential qualities for his co-leaders – reliability and reverence. At a time when it was difficult for Nehemiah to distinguish friend from foe (6:10, 17–19), it was vital to have dependable partners in the work of supervising Jerusalem's community life. The gatekeepers would need someone to administer and oversee their duties and, in view of serious threats made in the past (4:11–12, 16–23; 6:10), effective military cover was necessary for the future.

Reliability was crucial. The building work had been undertaken by people who were not easily deflected from their assignment, however tough the hazards (4:19–23). The greater task of renewing Jerusalem's moral and spiritual life demanded leaders of similar integrity who would be utterly faithful to their governor. This was particularly vital when both prophets (6:10–14) and priests (13:4–9, 28) were capable of being manipulated by the enemy in the interests of monetary gain.

Reverence for God was the other requirement for leadership. The two qualities are interrelated in that those who genuinely honour God can be trusted by others. These two leaders put God first in their lives. Hananiah was a military commander in charge of Jerusalem's citadel. He was used to issuing commands to his soldiers, but he knew that he must first receive his orders from the Lord. Nobody in Hananiah's life mattered more than God. Every day he surrendered his life afresh in worship, obedience and trust. Fearing God *more than most men do* was a rich testimony to the exemplary spirituality of these unsung heroes who were Nehemiah's dependable colleagues during his governship.

3. Recognize specific dangers (7:3)

Hanani and Hananiah were made responsible for the security of Jerusalem's citizens because Nehemiah recognized that the earlier attacks could easily be resumed. Newly fortified walls were no guarantee against future onslaughts. The enemy was ruthless and determined, and everything possible would be done to undermine Nehemiah's leadership, so the governor made two provisions, first about the gates and then about the guards.

Nehemiah's orders that Jerusalem's gates were not to be opened *until the sun is hot* probably ought to be translated 'while the sun is hot', *i.e.* 'during the heat of the day' (NEB), in the siesta period when in the extreme heat most people would be resting. This explains the governor's order that *While the gatekeepers are still on duty, make them shut the doors and bar them*. Nehemiah envisaged the possibility of a daytime attack.

The governor then issued instructions about the guards. The two newly appointed leaders were to ensure that some of Jerusalem's citizens accepted responsibility as sentinels at fixed positions around the city walls, usually close to their own homes.

As a gifted leader, Nehemiah knew that he had to be a step ahead of the enemy and make provision for the safety of his people. That is still an important dimension of leadership responsibility. Jesus warned Peter of the enemy's intentions, and the apostles Paul and Peter urged the early Christian people constantly to be alert to the devil's destructive schemes. When John wrote his letters from Patmos to specific churches in Asia Minor, he was putting all Christians on their guard against Satan's insidious snares – religious, doctrinal and moral.[7] In times like ours, when pluralism, hedonism, materialism and relativism shape contemporary values, gates and guards are as necessary in the church as in Nehemiah's Jerusalem.

4. Encourage strategic planning (7:4)

The governor knew that Jerusalem could never become a thriving city until it increased the number of its permanent residents. For decades it had hardly been a suitable place to bring up a family, and Judah's more rural settings had offered far more by way of stable community life and security, as well as land for cultivation,

---

[7] Lk. 22:31; 2 Cor. 2:11; 1 Pet. 5:8–9.

but now things were different. The newly constructed walls and gates were impressive and protective, and *the city was large and spacious but there were few people in it, and the houses had not yet been rebuilt.*

Nehemiah began to make arrangements for repopulating Jerusalem and obtained access to the records of those people who had returned to Judah over eighty years earlier, led by Zerubbabel and his colleagues. The governor knew how important it was to think ahead. A major exercise like repopulating a city could not be achieved as easily and speedily as the rebuilding of Jerusalem's walls. Far too much was involved. He was no longer organizing a temporary work force. He was expecting people to uproot themselves from familiar surroundings in order to live in a totally different social environment. Most of them would be moving from small rural communities, where they knew everybody, to an urban context; it meant forsaking neighbours and friends of long standing. It was not an easy thing, either to plan or carry into effect, but he knew it was vital if the city was to prosper economically and develop socially.

It is important for us not to miss what this passage may be saying to us about urban ministry. The principles underlying this chapter have a direct application to leadership in the church, but the narrative itself is describing a repopulation scheme and naturally directs our attention to one of the major social issues of our time – the problems and opportunities of urban expansion. Although it is naturally impossible to compare relatively small fifth-century Jerusalem with a modern city, its social and economic environment was markedly different from rural Judah, and a move from one community to the other would make inevitable demands. In our own day, it is estimated that by the year 2,000, about half of our world's six billion people will be living in cities, and that within another fifty years over seven billion people will populate nine hundred cities of more than a million inhabitants.

The world's cities are being populated at an alarming rate, especially in Africa, Asia and Latin America. At one time London was the world's largest city; now it no longer has a place in the top twenty. Urban problems are widespread and unprecedented – overcrowding, disease, unemployment, lack of basic services such as power, water, sanitation. Yet, these cities have been described as 'places of hope, creativity, energy and choice' and as magnets which 'attract a bewildering range of people and lifestyles, languages, cultures and faiths'. One vicar of an inner-city parish in Manchester has a local primary school in which the children speak thirty-two mother tongues.[8] The late twentieth-century world has come to the city. The church's global vision is being focused into a strategic urban challenge.

Nehemiah's plan to ensure that people came to live in a developing fifth-century city says something to us in a society faced with immense urban development. We have already seen that Jerusalem's governor was concerned about the exploitation of the poor, and he campaigned vigorously for his people's physical welfare, family security, social environment and economic well-being, as well as for their spiritual commitment. The book's closing chapter shows us that, in the face of increasing secularism, materialism and pluralism, Nehemiah insisted on spiritual priorities, adequate rest and relaxation in a heavily dominated commercial environment, as well as on family stability. Nehemiah was a governor who both feared God and loved people, priorities which ensured that social concerns never became marginal issues.

When the apostle Paul embarked on his great missionary journeys, he visited many of the great cities of the ancient world – Jerusalem, Ephesus, Athens, Corinth, Rome – and encouraged believers in those cities to continue his imaginative initiatives in evangelism. For him, it usually began by establishing links with God-fearing people who had yet to hear the clear presentation of the gospel. It involved hiring rooms where lectures and discussions could take place in a non-threatening atmosphere. It encouraged the visitation of people in their homes, as well as using opportunities to contact citizens outdoors in city streets, squares and market places. Paul went to meet people where they were, and his creative evangelistic mission provides us with relevant models for urban ministry in the contemporary world. Inspired by this energetic apostolic example, many of the great City Missions and inner-city churches have maintained their witness alongside compassionate social outreach. Their continuing ministry is described in a growing literature about contemporary urban mission.[9]

For many of Nehemiah's contemporaries, the move to Jerusalem was possibly the greatest sacrificial act of their lives but, as we shall see later (11:1–2), there were people who volunteered to do it because they believed in the importance of the city, its spiritual opportunity,

---

[8] For these statistics, insights and references, I am indebted to Michael Eastman, 'Faith in the City?' in the Scripture Union Bible Reading notes *Encounter with God* (Oct–Dec 1996), pp. 53–60.

[9] *E.g.* R. Bakke, *The Urban Christian* (Bromley: MARC Europe, 1987); M. Eastman (ed.), *Ten Inner City Churches* (Bromley: MARC, 1988); R. Joslin, *Urban Harvest* (Welwyn: Evangelical Press, 1982); C. Marchant, *Signs in the City* (London: Hodder and Stoughton, 1985); S. Murray, *City Vision: A biblical view* (London: Daybreak, 1990); D. Sheppard, *Built as a City* (London: Hodder and Stoughton, 2nd ed. 1974); *Staying in the City: Faith in the City Ten Years on* (London: Church House Publishing, 1995).

physical security, social stability and economic future. Their vision and venture is matched by those evangelical Christians of our own time who refuse to leave the city without its servants and witnesses, people who are ready to devote their energies to evangelistic opportunities, pastoral care, practical social concern, and the just pursuit of human rights in the great urban communities of our world.

5. Seek divine guidance (7:5a)

But the idea of meeting Jerusalem's spiritual, social and economic needs by repopulation did not originate in the mind of Nehemiah. The governor insists that the initiative was with the Lord: *my God put it into my heart to assemble the nobles, the officials and the common people for registration by families*. The plan to establish and prosper Jerusalem was in the heart of God long before it was communicated to the mind of Nehemiah. This important detail reminds us of a crucial spiritual principle. Many rich opportunities for service are available to Christians in any and every generation, but it is impossible to respond to the challenge of them all. We must wait upon God for clear direction about precisely what he wants us to do. Our energies and resources must be directed to those places where he wants us to be, and that can only be discerned as we spend regular time in God's presence.

Before the first Christians went out into the world, they were told to stay at Jerusalem. As they waited upon God they were given a vision (winning the world), a strategy (to start where they were, Jerusalem), a programme (nearby Judea, then hostile Samaria and on to the unknown 'ends of the earth') an unchanging promise ('you will receive power') and an indwelling friend ('when the Holy Spirit comes on you').[10]

The mission started in the city. Jesus told them that that was where the witnessing must begin, among those who had mocked, scorned, dismissed, denied or rejected Christ: 'repentance and forgiveness of sins will be preached in his name to all nations, *beginning at Jerusalem*'.[11] At that time Jerusalem was surely the worst city in the world, the place where its citizens had crucified God's Son. The determined rejection of Jesus is the most serious sin of all; beside it, other sins pale into relative insignificance. It is that sin, not others, which will take the impenitent to judgment and a lost eternity. When Jesus said that his disciples were to announce the good news to Jerusalem's murderers, blasphemers, liars, mockers and cowards, he was saying that forgiveness is for the worst; pardon is for all.

Those men might have preferred to begin their ministry in a place

[10] Acts 1:8; Mt. 28:18–20.   [11] Lk. 24:47.

where they were not known, where it was more safe to proclaim the truth, where they might not be imprisoned, flogged, even killed, as some were in Jerusalem.[12] But they knew they must obey their orders. If Jesus has said that the mission was to begin in that heart-less and Christ-rejecting city, then it must. They had to do what their Redeemer wanted, and that continuing sensitivity to divine direction was communicated to the many who joined them in their mission. The apostle had many strategic cities yet to evangelize in various parts of Asia Minor, but the Holy Spirit firmly closed some doors Paul would otherwise have entered eagerly, and opened others which might only have appealed to him later.[13] God put it into his heart to enter Europe, and so he crossed over into another continent under the Spirit's orders. Effective Christian leadership requires something far more than initiative, resilience, resourcefulness and creative imagination. It demands submissive, total and resolute obedience.

6. Utilize available help (7:5b)

In his desire to respond to divine prompting regarding the repopulation of the city, the governor *found the genealogical record of those who had been first to return*. In that archive he *found written there* a list of *the people of the province who came up from the captivity of the exiles whom Nebuchadnezzar king of Babylon had taken captive*.

A list of names follows which, with occasional variants, also appears in Ezra 2 at the point where that book describes the first return, encouraged by Cyrus in 538 BC under the leadership of Zerubbabel and Jeshua.

Although Nehemiah was doing something new, repopulating the city, it did not deter him from making full use of something old. The list of returnees was immensely valuable as a record of Israel's families (6–25) who had come back to the land under Zerrubbabel in 538 BC and the places where they settled on their return (26–38). He did not dismiss the past as something of little or no significance. Nehemiah took something which belonged essentially to the past and made it serve the needs of the present and future. History was important to him, because it was a living story which related how truths and values had been sacrificially transmitted. It described the heroism of dedicated personalities and the continuity of their faith. It was not a dead thing, locked away in irrecoverable antiquity. It was a living process of godly succession and he was part of it.

The people mentioned in his list could have told their own story

---

[12] Acts 4:1–3; 5:17–18, 40–42; 7:54–60; 12:1–5.   [13] Acts 16:6–10, *cf*. 8:26–29.

of indebtedness to God and his faithfulness to them through several generations. For the people who lived in Judah in the time of Nehemiah, it preserved the memory of their fathers and grandfathers, people who had served God in a variety of different ministries across the decades (39–60). It was a story of men and women in the previous century who were prepared to leave the relative security of their comfortable lives in another country to return to a 'homeland' they had never seen and to a new and challenging pattern of living. These people had been willing to uproot themselves from secure and familiar surroundings in Babylon to follow God's call to a more precarious and vulnerable existence in a land and capital city which had been ravished by the enemy and left destitute and neglected. They were making a new exodus and, like Abraham, Joseph, Moses and Joshua before them, had committed themselves to a venture of faith, dependence and obedience. The list was more than a catalogue of obscure names; its brief mention of Israel's families was a compressed narrative of the courage, love and loyalty of men and women who at God's bidding went out not knowing exactly where they were going.

It did not merely provide Nehemiah with the data he required and later acted upon (11:1–2) in his repopulation plan; the archive was a contemporary incentive to those who lived in Judah's countryside to come and live in Jerusalem and follow in the footsteps of sacrificial forefathers who were prepared to venture into the unknown.

The message of the past and the study of church history is in grave danger of being marginalized in today's world. It no longer figures prominently in courses of ministerial training, and in programmes of theological and religious studies. Fascination with the present makes some people impatient about the past: 'We must face the problems of our world, not retreat into theirs.' But the Israelite people had better perspectives on life. They did not dismiss the past and hurl it behind them as something they were eager to forget. The past stretched out in front of them. They could not discern exactly where they were going but they could clearly see where they had been. That story inspired them to face the future and enabled them to discern from their past the loving purposes of God, how clearly they had been guided, how miraculously they had been helped, how unfailingly they had been sustained, how undeservedly they had been used.

Richard Baxter took delight in the story and teaching of fellow Christians from earlier periods of history and wrote about 'the profitable and pleasant company and help at all times' he had derived from their writings: 'I have dwelt among the shining lights, which the learned and wise and holy men of all ages have set up and left to illuminate this world.'[14] In the same century, George Herbert urged his fellow-clergy to read books by believers from other centuries. No nation has all the resources it needs and no century has all the graces: 'God in all ages has had his servants' and 'as one country does not bear all things that there may be a commerce, so neither has God opened, or will open, all to one, that there may be a traffic in knowledge between the servants of God for the planting of love and humility'.[15] If we seriously suggest that we have nothing to learn from our fellow-Christians in the past, we disregard their love (in taking the trouble to write for us), despise their gifts and endanger our humility. Nobody has a monopoly of God's grace. When we reflect on the great saints of earlier centuries, we need to remember that we have not left them behind in an antiquated past. They are ahead of us in the resplendent glory.

7. Identify complementary gifts (7:6–60)

Nehemiah's list does not only provide us with the names and locations of the returning exiles. It describes the various forms of service in which many of these devout people were engaged throughout the decades as priests (39–42), Levites (43), singers (44), gatekeepers (45), temple servants (46–56), initially designated by King David 'to assist the Levites',[16] and the descendants of Solomon's servants (57–60), originally appointed by David's son to supplement the work of the temple servants by performing menial tasks around the spacious building and its precincts.

This wide variety of people represented different gifts which across the centuries had been brought to the service of God. It reached back to the time of Moses and the institution of the priesthood, and on to the establishment of the kingdom under David and Solomon and the later story of God's people, through good and ill, prosperity and adversity, both in their homeland and away from it, right down to their resettlement in sixth-century Judah.

It was a reminder to Nehemiah and his contemporaries that people bring a variety of gifts to the Lord's work. During his governorship he had relied on all these people and, in addition, had benefited from the ministry of labourers, builders, gatekeepers, soldiers, teachers, administrators, caterers and servants, and there were still other work opportunities for God's servants in the developing life of this new community. The multicoloured grace of God has equipped his people with a variety of choice gifts, and all believers are personally equipped in one way or another. Our responsibility before God is

[14] Richard Baxter, *Dying Thoughts* (1683), pp. 223–224.
[15] George Herbert, *A Priest to the Temple* or *The Country Parson* (1652), chapter 4.
[16] Ezr. 8:20.

to discern, develop and use our gifts for the enrichment of others and for his glory alone.[17] We all need to hear the personal exhortation at the close of one of Paul's prison letters when he told his friend Archippus, 'See to it that you complete the work [*diakonian*, *i.e.* ministry, service] you have received in the Lord'.[18]

It is the Christian leader's responsibility to identify potentially gifted people within the life of a congregation, to be alert to these emerging gifts, encourage their development, and make possible the exercise of those gifts for the benefit of others. There can be little doubt that the secret of Nehemiah's ministry in Jerusalem was team work of a very high order. His autobiographical narrative presents us with a model of interdependent ministry, highly motivated and sacrificially exercised towards precise objectives and God-glorifying ends.

8. Obey biblical teaching (7:61–65)

The list identifies over six hundred people who returned but *could not show that their families were descended from Israel* (61). A number of priests who were similarly without clearly defined Israelite ancestry are mentioned because *they were excluded from the priesthood as unclean* (64). This is the first direct reference in Nehemiah's memoirs to an issue which became crucially important in Judah: the emergence of pluralism in a nation surrounded by pagan neighbours with other religious allegiances. The desire to maintain a 'pure' priesthood was, as we shall see later, not prompted by a cruel desire for 'ethnic cleansing' but by a passion to obey their covenant obligation not to worship other gods. It was an issue tackled resolutely and essentially by Ezra thirteen or fourteen years earlier, and was a necessary precaution against the infiltration of syncretistic ideas which had bedevilled Israel's history in the past and in part led to the judgment of the Babylonian exile. People from other faiths who wished to commit themselves unreservedly to the worship of the only true God were permitted to do so,[19] but there was no room for compromising alliances with other religions. The rigorism here is not designed to preserve a pure race but to protect a pure faith within a community of believing people who would later welcome God's Son, the world's Saviour and Israel's Messiah.[20]

Those who married partners with other religious allegiances, different spiritual principles and alien moral standards, endangered the continuity of Israel's faith. Nehemiah had later experience of the damage which could be done to the preservation and proclamation

---

[17] Rom. 12:4–8; 1 Cor. 12:4–11; 1 Pet. 4:10–11.   [18] Col. 4:17.
[19] Ex. 12:48; Nu. 15:14–16; Ru. 1:16; 2:12.   [20] Acts 13:32; Rom. 9:4–5.

of that faith within families (13:23–24). We shall see later how important it was for him to insist that his contemporaries obeyed the guidelines of Scripture regarding their loyalty to God, restricting marriage to partners who gladly acknowledged his exclusive claim upon their lives.

9. Encourage generous giving (7:66–73)

The important spiritual issues of marriage and generosity to the Lord's work are two topics which not only emerge later in Nehemiah's story (10:30, 32–39; 13:10–13, 23–29) but appear together in the final sentences of his book (13:30–31). Both are practical expressions of the believer's obedience to Scripture. Those who love God's Word will not neglect God's work. The generous amounts given by the returning exiles to the Lord's work remind us that, although our best gift is ourselves,[21] it is important not to neglect our responsibility in the regular giving of our money. These few sentences preserve an account of sacrificial and exemplary giving.

First, the giving was sacrificial. These newly returned exiles had yet to establish themselves in their homes, farms and businesses. The money they gave had been earned as a result of hard work in Babylon, and they might well have held back until they saw how their financial situation developed and stabilized once their life in a new land was back to normal. But they did not reason like that. They put God first, believing that, if they honoured him, he would care for them.[22]

Moreover, the giving was exemplary. To Ezra's original list Nehemiah adds a note about his own giving. He wants to set a good example by giving a thousand drachmas of gold, as well as gifts in kind like bowls and garments for the use of the priests. He knows how wrong it would be for a leader to expect from others that which he had not already done himself. Generous giving can inspire others to loosen their purse strings; it is a practical testimony to a believer's gratitude as well as an expression of love, obedience and trust that the Lord will meet our needs.

10. Exercise responsible stewardship

Looking back over this chapter, we can see that, as a good leader, Nehemiah was aware of the unique privilege God had given him in leading Israel's life at that time. The prayers which are frequently interspersed through his narrative demonstrate that he had a keen sense not only of personal responsibility but also of ultimate accountability. He had only one life to live. He was a dedicated

[21] 2 Cor. 8:5; Rom. 12:1–2.   [22] 1 Sa. 2:30; 15:22; Mt. 6:33; Phil. 4:19.

layman, not a formal religious official, an ordinary man with extraordinary gifts. He *found* this *genealogical record* (5) from Israel's past and used it to inspire her present and future needs. In his hands, this century-old archive testifies afresh to the governor's priorities in the exercise of his stewardship. He believed passionately not only in the physical security, social welfare and economic stability of the city but also in those qualities and ambitions without which no spiritually minded community can possibly survive, let alone develop: the adoration of God, the communication of truth (1), the encouragement of integrity, the need for reverence (2), the quest for guidance (5), the privilege of service, the multiplicity of gifts (39–60), the pursuit of holiness (61–65) and the grace of generosity (70–73). There is more to this archive than a list of forgotten names; it is a declaration of a godly community's spiritual commitment.

B. Reforming the community (8:1 – 13:31)

Nehemiah 8:1–18
9. 'Bring out the Book'

We have already seen that Nehemiah's ambition was not simply to reconstruct the city's defences but to revitalize a spiritual community. Writing in the same century as Nehemiah, the Greek historian Thucydides made the point that it is the people not the walls that make a city.[1] The spiritual, moral and social contribution of committed men and women is of greater importance than strong bulwarks, but Jerusalem's governor soon discovered that reforming a community is a more exacting task than restoring its walls. He believed that the people living within the newly fortified city and their neighbours in the surrounding towns and villages had a right to spiritual prosperity as well as physical security.

As soon as the building work came to an end, an unusual event took place which was to prove dramatically influential in the spiritual life of God's people. The work was finished during the late summer month of Elul (6:15), and the next month, Tishri, marked the beginning of the year. The first day of this *seventh month* was a public holiday known as the Feast of Trumpets.[2] So, only a few days after the completion of the rebuilding project, hundreds of men, women and children gathered in Jerusalem for a new year celebration in which God's written Word played a central part. An outdoor public meeting was devoted entirely to hearing the reading and interpretation of Scripture.

1. God's Word valued (8:1–8)

The distinctive characteristics of this meeting for biblical exposition are strikingly relevant in our late twentieth-century world. Western materialistic culture has become increasingly indifferent to the Bible. The latest statistics suggest that in England and Wales the number of regular churchgoers who read the Bible on a daily basis is declining

---

[1] *History of the Peloponnesian War* VII.77.   [2] Lv. 23:23–25; Nu. 29:1.

year by year. Of the 700 people interviewed in connection with a recent survey, only 15% were committed to day-by-day Bible reading. Another 15% stated that they never read any version of the Bible outside a church service. Almost 40% indicated that they read the Bible at home only once a year or less.[3] Committed Christians who neglect the privilege and discipline of daily Bible reading are severing their links with vital spiritual resources. God speaks uniquely to us through his Word, and if we close our ears to this daily conversation we cannot hope to develop into mature believers. Those who attended this Jerusalem Bible study meeting led by Ezra and Nehemiah have important things to say to us. They were wholehearted Bible students.

a. The people were single-minded

Although these people were from different homes within Jerusalem's walls and beyond, they were driven by a common desire to hear the Word of God uniquely recorded in Scripture. They assembled *as one man* (1) in that large public square. However diverse their individual likes and dislikes, this common desire to listen to the message of Scripture took precedence over everything else. In our own times, Christians are frequently divided on a wide variety of issues. They take a different stance, sometimes markedly so, on matters concerning ministry, ordination, baptism, the Lord's Supper, divine healing, ecumenical involvement, patterns of worship, their concept of the church, the work of the Holy Spirit, charismatic gifts and the second coming of Christ. Nobody wants to pretend that matters of this nature are of marginal importance, but to isolate our distinctive ideas is to marginalize the vast store of biblical truths which unite us.

In the end of the day, we may not explain every biblical verse in exactly the same way, but a common desire to honour, apply and obey God's Word will draw us closer together rather than separate us sharply from one another. It is part of the devil's strategy to magnify our differences and minimize those immense Spirit-inspired doctrines which honour God, exalt Christ and enrich our witness. A passion to study these central themes of Scripture ought to draw God's people closer to one another. An insatiable appetite for the faithful and relevant interpretation of Scripture is a powerful unifying force within the life of God's people.

[3] Bible Society Survey, conducted by Research Surveys of Great Britain, September 1995.

b. The people were enthusiastic

The most remarkable feature about the demand for Scripture at this outdoor meeting was that it appears to have been initiated by the people rather than their leaders. *They told Ezra the scribe to bring out the Book of the Law of Moses* (1). They craved for God's Word as hungry people long for food. This passionate quest for biblical truth is something more than mere human desire; it is a gift from God. Throughout biblical and Christian history, one of the characteristics of genuine revival has been the sovereign initiative of God in giving men and women a longing for spiritual things. It is not artificially promoted by religious leaders but initiated by God himself. The people yearn for God's truth and cannot have enough of it. As the psalmist said, it is 'sweeter than honey' to their taste, a lamp for their feet, the joy of their hearts, and infinitely more valuable than gold; they long for it as a person short of oxygen gasps for breath.[4] It was that kind of craving which drove this vast crowd of people into the square by Jerusalem's Water Gate to hear the public reading of Scripture.

c. The people were attentive

Once they came together, nothing was going to distract them from the immense blessing they could receive from God's Word. Every eye was fixed on the *high wooden platform* which had been specially constructed in the city square (4). From there, Ezra and his colleagues were both visible and audible, and the eager listeners hung on every word: *All the people listened attentively* (literally 'the ears of all the people [were]') *to the Book of the Law* (3). This Jerusalem congregation clearly expected God to speak directly through the Word he had given to Moses centuries before. There was a vitality and urgency about their listening. Our daily reading of Scripture will only be of minimal worth if it becomes a mere habit, undertaken hurriedly, mechanically, or half-heartedly. If we are to derive help from it, this life-imparting exercise takes time. Throughout history, Christian devotional writers have frequently emphasized the importance of meditation as one means of quietly, patiently and sensitively imbibing the message of a Scripture passage. We need to allow time for it to penetrate the mind, stir the heart and direct the will.

Similarly, merely listening to the public exposition of Scripture may not achieve what it might if we do not give our deepest attention to what we have heard. Calvin used the illustration that merely to listen is to be like a warrior whose splendid but unused armour is

---

[4] Ps. 119:103, 105, 111, 127, 131.

hung up and allowed to go rusty. Christian preaching must be eagerly received and constantly applied. In the Reformer's words, the Christian must allow its message to become 'deeply fixed in his own heart'. Calvin said that we must make the preached message our own so that by meditation it becomes 'enclosed within the deepest recesses' of the human mind.[5]

d. The people were responsive

From the beginning of their meeting, this eager congregation recognized that they were not listening to the words of Ezra but to the voice of God. What Moses had reverently and reliably written centuries before was God's unique Word to them so, when Ezra *opened the book* (5), the people, convinced of its authority, rose to their feet. It was an outward expression of their immense reverence for the message of Scripture, a practice still maintained in synagogues and by some churches when the congregation rises for the reading of a biblical passage.

Moreover, they made a vocal as well as a physical response. Ezra gave thanks to God for the book in his hand and, as he *praised the LORD, the great God*, the congregation *lifted their hands and responded* by adding their *Amen* (6) to the words of the preacher. They made their own affirmation of commitment and loyalty audible by saying, 'Yes, may it be so'. Ezra could lead them in worship, but his words would remain as a solitary expression of his personal devotion unless the people identified themselves with what he was saying on their behalf.

In this meeting, the people made no distinction between the exposition of Scripture and the offering of worship. Exposition and adoration belonged together, each flowing naturally into the other. 'Worship' has become a 'buzz word' in the contemporary evangelical vocabulary but its meaning is in danger of being narrowly restricted to that aspect of our praise which is expressed in singing. Yet we adore God as much by faithful exposition as by wholehearted singing. One must not be detached from the other. Just as the hearing of the Word can degenerate into arid intellectualism or mere conventional listening, so the vigorous singing of songs and hymns can become meaningless repetition not necessarily related to heart and mind. Neither listening nor singing is immune from the danger of distraction, insincerity and half-heartedness. At Ezra's meeting, their reading from the book led directly to the opening of their hearts

[5] *Commentary on the Book of Psalms* (Edinburgh, 1845), vol. 1, p. 325 (Ps. 19:11), and vol. 5, p. 43 (Ps. 119:166); for Calvin's teaching on the importance of meditation in the Christian life, see Ronald S. Wallace, *Calvin's Doctrine of the Christian Life* (Edinburgh: Oliver and Boyd, 1959), pp. 218–225.

and mouths in praise and penitence. Lively, relevant, biblical exposition ought to promote genuine adoration, just as inspired singing can create a longing for more of the truth we have been exalting. Neither must be allowed to become an end in itself.

e. The people were submissive

The Jerusalem worshippers not only rose to their feet but fell to their knees. *Then they bowed down and worshipped the LORD with their faces to the ground* (6). Recognizing that by his Word the living God was present among them, they had no greater desire than to fall before him humbly, gratefully and adoringly. Seeking his face meant covering their own. It was the kneeling posture of a suppliant in desperate need of help, an indebted beggar gratefully acknowledging an undeserved gift, a servant who waits obediently in the presence of a beloved master.

The people honoured the uniqueness of *the Book ... which the LORD had commanded for Israel* (1); it was natural to stand, and then to kneel before the God who was communicating with them directly through his Word. We do not worship the Book, but we adore the God of the Book who addresses us uniquely through it. Calvin made the point that we 'owe to the Scripture the same reverence as we owe to God since it has its only source in Him'. Moreover, we need to come to the Bible submissively, not solely because the Lord is its unique source but because he is its only effective interpreter: 'Let us therefore remember that it should be embraced with the greatest reverence and, since by our own strength we could never aspire to such heights, let us humbly ask God to make it possible for us by the spirit of revelation.'[6] Those who recognize this book's origin constantly acknowledge their dependence on the Holy Spirit who communicated it in the first place.

f. The people were teachable

These people knew that the word of God given to Moses was not only applicable to the people to whom it was originally given. God's Word is always contemporary and relevant. Every part of it has something appropriately meaningful for every generation. We may not always have the patience or discernment to identify that message, but that does not mean that it is not there. At this Jerusalem outdoor meeting the Levites were the appointed interpreters of

---

[6] John Calvin, *Second Epistle of Paul the Apostle to the Corinthians and the Epistles to Timothy, Titus and Philemon*, trans. T. A. Smail (Edinburgh: Oliver and Boyd, 1964), p. 330 (2 Tim. 3:16), and p. 229 (1 Tim. 3:8–10); see also Ronald S. Wallace, *Calvin's Doctrine of the Word and Sacraments* (Edinburgh: Oliver and Boyd, 1953), pp. 102–106.

God's unique Word. They gathered the congregation into smaller groups, *making it clear and giving the meaning so that the people could understand what was being read* (8). Their work may indicate either that they were linguistic translators, or that they were biblical interpreters.

The Old Testament Scriptures were written in Hebrew and the Levites may have translated Scripture into the everyday language of Aramaic, certainly a later feature of synagogue worship. People all over the world have the right to read or hear the message of the Bible in their own language, yet 350 million people in today's world have no Christian Scriptures in their own tongue. In the late twentieth century there are still over 4,000 languages without any copy of Scripture, and out of over two thousand languages and dialects translated only 349 have a complete Bible.[7] Yao, for example, is spoken by 2 million people in Malawi, Mozambique and Tanzania and, although they have had a New Testament for over a hundred years, the only part of the Old Testament at present available to them is the book of Psalms. Such people cannot read these Nehemiah stories for themselves. The fact that we can do so ought to have a twofold effect in our lives: gratitude and generosity. We will surely be thankful that we can read this Scripture passage without a translator, and we can resolve to share in Bible translation work somewhere in the world by regular giving.

Doubtless, as the people gathered in smaller groups, the Levites also served as biblical interpreters, *making it clear* (8) by explaining how the passage related to the issues of their own day. This aspect of the Levites' ministry was done so effectively that, within a short time, people's consciences were smitten and they could not help shedding tears.

We cannot be certain which part of the Pentateuch Ezra read to the people that day, but the magnificent interpretation of the Law in Deuteronomy, given to Moses as the Israelites were about to enter their new land, may well have formed a central feature in the exposition. It would certainly have been relevant as Jerusalem's citizens and their neighbours faced the challenge of a better quality of spiritual life within their newly fortified community.

The relevant application of Scripture is of paramount importance. It is not a book which simply describes life in the world of antiquity; it is a message for today, vibrant with meaningful up-to-date application in late twentieth-century society. Perhaps the *application* of Scripture is the hardest aspect of both personal Bible study and Christian preaching but, in both cases, personal reader and public

---

[7] *Bible Translations: Update and Background* (1996), Bible Society, Swindon.

preacher must struggle hard to bridge the gap between what we have read and what we must do.[8]

2. God's Word applied (8:9–12)

The people's response to the interpretation and application of Scripture at this huge outdoor meeting was evident and immediate. Whenever God's Word is relevantly applied, the implications are wide reaching.

a. Scripture exposes our sins

The first sign that God's Word was reaching the hearts and informing the minds of these people was that they began to grieve about their failures. This unique book had touched their consciences, heightening their awareness of ways in which they had disobeyed, dishonoured or ignored God. The seventeenth-century preacher, William Bridge, used a biblical illustration popular among the Reformers and Puritans when he described the Bible as a 'looking glass'. Using a mirror, we see three things: the material glass, the reflection of our own image, and also that of the things around us in the room. As we see the glass itself, we are reminded that Scripture is God's testimony to his own nature. 'There is God seen especially, and Christ seen', says Bridge, but 'there also you see yourself, and your own dirty face; there also you see the creatures that are in the room with you, and their emptiness, the emptiness of men, and of all comforts and relations.'[9] Without the mirror we would have no vision of ourselves. The people wept because what they heard in the reading of Scripture condemned their lifestyle. But they would not have had an awareness of their sinfulness unless they had first been confronted with the mirror of Scripture's revelation of the majesty of God. The bright light of his holiness revealed their impurity, his faithfulness challenged their disloyalty, and his compassion their selfishness.

Moreover, seeing themselves exposed in the mirror of God's Word, the people became distressed concerning the universality and consequences of human sin. Everybody present was guilty. In one way or another they had all fallen 'short of the glory of God'; that made the offence so tragically universal, deeply serious and inescapably personal. Sin was the root, and sins were the fruit of their transgression. In their case, the particular offence may have been their blatant disregard of what God had declared in his Word about the danger of spiritual compromise by marrying partners with totally

---

[8] Jack Kuhatschek, *Taking the Guesswork out of Applying the Bible* (Leicester: IVP, 1990).   [9] Jas. 1:23–25; William Bridge, *Works* (1845), vol. 1, p. 411.

incompatible religious allegiances, an issue necessarily prominent in the ministries of Malachi, Ezra and Nehemiah. The threatened outcome of such arrogant disobedience was God's judgment upon them. They had broken their covenant promise of exclusive love and total loyalty, and Scripture's sombre repeated warnings must have descended upon them that morning like the relentless blows of a hammer.[10]

Yet, despite the seriousness of their sin, the people were urged to dry their tears. Scripture not only condemns sin; it proclaims the remedy. The Levites urged the congregation, *Do not mourn or weep* (9). Within ten days this new year holiday would be followed by the Day of Atonement. On that annual public declaration of God's mercy, all 'the uncleanness and rebellion of the Israelites' would be fully, immediately and irrevocably pardoned, 'whatever their sins have been'. On that day, the atoning sacrifice was offered; the scapegoat would 'carry on itself all their sins to a solitary place'. The people were confronted with a visible sign as well as a verbal assurance: 'Then, before the LORD, you will be clean from all your sins.'[11]

Each year, that Levitical scapegoat anticipated a greater atonement by far. The day came when, on that first Good Friday, God's Son carried our sins to the cross in his sinless body. By that unique sacrifice, those who repent and believe are eternally forgiven. They too hear the reassuring word, *Do not grieve, for the joy of the LORD is your strength* (10). Theirs is the joy of prayer heard, God's promise fulfilled, sins cleansed and strength renewed.[12]

b. Scripture widens our horizons

Scripture not only makes us aware of our own failures, it also opens our eyes to the needs of others. The people were not to indulge in grovelling introspection when there was a world out there needing the assurance of forgiveness and love. It was a day of rejoicing, a time to celebrate God's mercy to them and his compassion for all. The holiday was to be marked by festival meals to which families and communities should invite their neighbours, and the best of food must be sent to those people who lacked the basic necessities of life. Readings from Deuteronomy would certainly have convinced them that God was concerned about the poor, widows, fatherless, orphan and alien, in fact anyone who had *nothing prepared* (10) for this celebration meal.[13]

In this global village, our neighbours are as near as our television

[10] Rom. 3:23; Ex. 34:16; Dt. 4:24–27; 7:3–4; 23:2–6; Ezr. 9:1–2, 10–12; 10:1–2, 10–11; Ne. 10:30; 13:23–29.   [11] Lv. 16:16, 20–22, 29–30, 34.
[12] 1 Jn. 1:7–9; Ps. 32:5; 51:1–7, 10–12; Is. 55:6–7.
[13] Dt. 14:28–29; 15:1–11; 24:10–22; 26:12.

screens, where we are forcefully reminded of utter deprivation and obscene poverty in other parts of the world. The latest TEAR Fund statistics tell us that 1,000 million people will go to bed hungry tonight. Those who read Scripture or listen to its faithful exposition cannot ignore the cry of the destitute. James taught his readers that Scripture's most searching test is not what we know but what we do about it. The person who 'looks intently' into that mirror realizes that it is vital to 'look after orphans and widows in their distress' as well as 'to keep oneself from being polluted by the world'.[14]

It is a sad reflection on the limitation (even perversity) of the human mind that Christians who sometimes differ widely on their attitude to the Bible polarize their interests in a manner this passage of Scripture does not encourage. The evangelical rightly emphasizes the priority of faith and personal commitment to Christ issuing in forgiveness, reconciliation and assurance of eternal life. Those who interpret the Bible from a liberal or radical perspective are sometimes embarrassed by this 'personal conversion' dimension and prefer to focus on the Christian's community responsibilities. Many of them have an enviable record of social concern expressed in care for the homeless and hungry in their own localities as well as in the Third World. But the dichotomy between personal experience and practical compassion is not permissible for any Christian who takes Scripture seriously. The 'personal salvation' emphasis is not a *cul de sac* of individualistic experience; it is an open road to loving service in a world where God wants us to be, in Luther's words, a 'Christ' to our neighbour:

> Hence, as our heavenly Father has in Christ freely come to our aid, we also ought freely to help our neighbour through our body and its works, and each one should become as it were a Christ to the other . . . that is, that we may be truly Christians.[15]

Paul's famous body imagery never suggests that the hands and feet are exclusively restricted to ministry within the narrow confines of the church. We are to 'do good to all people', especially (but not exclusively) to 'those who belong to the family of believers'.[16] The Christian is sent beyond the believing community to a world which in many places has yet to see Christ compassionately at work through the sacrificial lives of his people.

---

[14] Jas. 1:25–27.
[15] Martin Luther, *On the Freedom of a Christian*, in *Luther's Works* vol. 31 ed. H. J. Grimm (Philadelphia: Muhlenberg Press, 1957), pp. 367–368.
[16] Gal. 6:10.

c. Scripture guarantees our resources

Through the explanation of Scripture, this congregation was assured of specific help from God. The people had sent some of the best gifts of food to their deprived neighbours, but Nehemiah reminds them that they have received from God gifts which money could not buy: *Do not grieve, for the joy of the LORD is your strength* (10). His words focus on three immense resources for the believer: peace, joy, and strength.

The people are urged, first, to quieten their distressed minds: *The Levites calmed all the people, saying, 'Be still ...'* (11). However great their sins, they could be completely forgiven and be at peace in their hearts. Paul told his friends at Rome that 'we have peace with God through our Lord Jesus Christ'. He assured the Philippian Christians that God's peace was watching over their lives like a soldier on guard, protecting their hearts and that, however great their problems, the 'God of peace' was with them in it all. More important than all else, Jesus himself bequeathed his peace to his disciples. He had no material possessions to leave to his followers but, before departing, gave them the assurance of an abiding peace. When our conscience accuses us, he reminds us that his death procured our complete cleansing and whispers his reassuring word in our hearts, *Be still*.[17]

The people's joy in life was not to be found in ideal circumstances, material prosperity or social popularity but in the Lord. Their joy is derived from the knowledge of who he is, what he does, what he says and what he gives. They constantly reflect on the joy of discerning the Lord's nature (as compassionate, holy, just, merciful, righteous, generous), of observing the Lord's deeds (in Scripture, history and experience), of claiming the Lord's promises (as in this particular verse), and of receiving the Lord's resources, such as the forgiveness, peace, security and joy described or implied throughout this passage.

That joy is the source of constantly renewed strength. The guarantee of such comprehensive resources fortifies their lives and provides the dynamic for daily living. That word 'strength' was used by the Hebrew people to describe a fortress or well-protected stronghold. When they are in trouble, God's people know of the place of their secure refuge: it is in the Lord himself, his character, works, Word and gifts.

Joy is a recurrent theme in this chapter (10, 12, 17). This congregation discovered that joy was to be found in acknowledging God's greatness (6), appreciating God's Word (8–9, 12) and helping God's people (10–12). Joy is a rare commodity in the contemporary world.

---

[17] Rom. 5:1; Phil. 4:7, 9; Jn. 14:27; 16:33; 20:19, 21, 26; 1 Jn. 1:9.

A recent Gallup survey conducted for *The Daily Telegraph* indicated that 'British people are filled with unprecedented gloom about virtually every aspect of life. They are far more despondent than a generation ago about standards of health, knowledge, honesty and behaviour.' On the eight subjects on which Gallup sought views, pessimists outnumbered the optimists in every case. Possibly the most striking single finding is the one concerning 'peace of mind'. Nearly three-quarters of the people believed that their contemporaries have less peace of mind than in the past.[18]

The Israelites who assembled for their morning Bible Reading at Water Gate square have crucial things to share with our dispirited contemporaries. They are saying that peace, joy and strength are in the Lord alone, and the experience of God's people throughout biblical and Christian history repeatedly confirms that their testimony is true.

3. God's Word shared (8:13-18)

The day following this huge meeting, the heads of families gathered with Jerusalem's spiritual leaders for further study of God's Word. Their reading on the second day reminded them that halfway through this seventh month they were to celebrate the Feast of Tabernacles.[19] Scriptural teaching concerning this week of celebration was to be communicated by the heads of families to everybody else in the country. They were to *proclaim this word and spread it throughout their towns and in Jerusalem* (15). During the forthcoming festival, God's Word was not only to be declared orally but enacted visually so that, by hearing and seeing, people would recall what he had done for them. The Feast of Tabernacles directed God's people to three great themes.

a. Thanksgiving for the past

This festival was their annual reminder of God's protection and provision centuries earlier as their forefathers travelled through the wilderness on their journey from Egypt to Canaan. During those long years, they lived in *booths*, simple tents made from leaves and branches, as they made their way through a dangerous desert. Natural hazards, wild animals and marauding enemies were a constant threat to their safety, but through it all the Lord had brought them safely to the land he had promised to give them. Amid the

---

[18] *The Daily Telegraph*, 3 June 1996.
[19] Lv. 23:33–43; Nu. 29:12–39; Dt. 16:13–17. The occasion described in Ne. 8 vividly recalls the teaching in Dt. 31:9–13.

pressure of new challenges, it was all too easy to forget what he had already done for them, not just in the wilderness but since they had settled in their own country. Even now, some of them did not have a proper home in Jerusalem (7:4), but at this festival they confessed that their confidence was in the Lord, not in walls and buildings. Sovereignly he had guided them, generously he had fed them, and powerfully he had protected them; such abundant and evident mercy must never be forgotten.

Tabernacles was an annual reminder of their immense indebtedness to God. In the inevitable pressures of late twentieth-century life, we too can be so concerned about what we want God to do that we forget what he has already done for us. Like Samuel, we too can testify, 'Thus far has the LORD helped us'.[20] Each day we need deliberately to recall the Lord's goodness to us, possibly noting down specific instances of his promised help. Forgetfulness is at the root of a great deal of discontent. Obsessed with what we need, we ignore what we have.

b. Witness in the present

Another aspect of Tabernacles and the other annual festivals was their impressive witnessing value. Once they settled in the land, the Israelite people did not live in detached, insular communities. Their towns and villages were visited by merchants and travellers. In Nehemiah's time, we know that traders from the northern coastal country of Tyre established a permanent base in Jerusalem for the sale of fish and other commodities (13:16). The Feast of Tabernacles would take any community's visitors by surprise. As local people went to live in these homemade tents for an entire week, people who knew little of their history and culture would naturally ask what was happening during this week's holiday and, intrigued by the event, enquire why they were living outside their own homes for this period of national celebration. It was a magnificent opportunity for them to *proclaim this word and spread it* (15) to visitors, strangers and aliens as well as to their own children and young people. It was a remarkably vivid teaching-aid for people who knew the importance of passing on to this and the next generation the truths which God had entrusted to them.

c. Confidence in the future

This feast of 'booths' also spoke convincingly to the discerning Israelites about their perspective on life and their consequent pattern of behaviour. It told them that, not just during their past history, but

[20] 1 Sa. 7:12.

in present experience, they were a pilgrim people. Occurring at this particular time, the feast may have been 'a sobering reminder of impermanence against a *false* trust in walls'.[21] Like their great forefather, Abraham, they 'lived in tents, as did Isaac and Jacob', but they were 'looking forward to the city with foundations whose architect and builder is God'. Even when Abraham reached Canaan, he still lived 'like a stranger in a foreign land' because he and all the Israelite people were 'longing for a better country – a heavenly one' and God had prepared that city for them in eternity.[22] Christians also look beyond this world to that home, for which God is constantly preparing them. That does not cause them to opt out of their present responsibilities; far from it. Their stance as 'aliens and strangers' in this life creates a sense of urgency as well as perspective.[23]

However enriching or disappointing their present experience, Christians know that ultimate satisfaction is reserved for the future which Christ has promised them. It has been said that people who have something beyond will never be weary. In late twentieth-century secularist society, Christians witness to the fact that life in this world is not the sum total of all that God has in store for believers. The best is yet to be.

In a moving exposition of what this feast of Sukkoth still means to Jewish people, Jonathan Sacks says that 'the tabernacle in all its vulnerability symbolises faith: the faith of a people who set out long ago on a risk-laden journey across a desert of space and time with no more protection than the sheltering divine presence.' The Chief Rabbi reflects,

> Sitting in the *sukkah* underneath its canopy of leaves I often think of my ancestors and their wanderings across Europe in search of safety, and I begin to understand how faith was their only home. It was fragile, chillingly exposed to the storms of prejudice and hate. But it proved stronger than empires. Their faith has survived.[24]

Three outstanding aspects of Christian commitment – worship, witness and heaven – are brilliantly captured in this Israelite festival, and though we do not, like our Jewish friends, publicly celebrate this autumn feast, we must treasure its truths. Its message is for people of all countries and cultures. In Nehemiah's day these temporary 'booths' were erected in four different areas of witnessing

---

[21] McConville, p. 119.   [22] Heb. 11:9–10, 14–16; 13:14.
[23] 2 Cor. 5:5; Heb. 11:13; 1 Pet. 1:1; 2:11.
[24] Jonathan Sacks, *Faith in the Future* (London: Darton, Longman and Todd, 1995), pp. 150–151.

opportunity (16). They were constructed *on their own roofs* (family life), *in their courtyards*, where they welcomed guests (social life), *in the courts of the house of God* (religious life), and *in the square by the Water Gate*, where people sold their produce (business life). At home, in the neighbourhood, at worship and at work they were to testify to these great unchanging realities of God's faithfulness in the past, generosity in the present and provision for the future. People with such firm and grateful assurance are persuasive witnesses.

Nehemiah 9:1–37
10. Discovering more about God

During the seventh month, these Israelite people celebrated three important aspects of their relationship with God: worship (the Festival of Trumpets, with its offerings to the Lord), forgiveness (the Day of Atonement) and trust (the week-long Feast of Tabernacles). The day after Nehemiah and his contemporaries had dismantled their 'booths', they met again for another public assembly marked by confession (1–2), adoration (3–5), reflection (6–37) and commitment (38).

They devoted this twenty-fourth day of the month to fasting, penitence, meditation and prayer and, once again, God's Word was given special prominence. The detailed prayer of Nehemiah 9 develops naturally from the preceding chapter. Nehemiah 8 focuses on God's Word to them; now the people respond with their words to him, words of genuine sorrow about their sins and of grateful remembrance of God's grace. Their six-hour service was likewise divided into two parts. First, they listened to God's Word, and then responded to its message by confessing their sins and by worshipping the God whose nature and promise guaranteed their pardon.

This vital two-way relationship is inspired and encouraged throughout Scripture. Listening to God (Bible reading) and responding to him (prayer) are twin aspects of every believer's experience. There can be no spiritual growth or development in Christian maturity without the regular cultivation of this dual privilege and discipline. For Nehemiah's contemporaries, the biblical message was like a revealing mirror which exposed their disobedience and disloyalty, and the moving prayer in chapter 9 demonstrates the radical impact of God's Word in their lives. The divine prohibition of mixed marriages had been wilfully ignored not only by the people but also by the priests, men who surely knew why God had forbidden alliances of that kind. Ezra's earlier ministry had denounced the moral carelessness of Israel's religious leaders, men who should have set an example to their fellow-Israelites.[1]

The serious and attentive reading of Scripture, whether privately or publicly, will create its own response. God's Word drives us into the presence of the One of whom it so uniquely, eloquently and relevantly speaks, and we will emerge from his presence as Christians who have been challenged, convicted, pardoned, taught and inspired by listening to his Word. Every encounter with God in the pages of Scripture reveals something more of his nature, deeds, purpose, promises and resources, and these discoveries then need to be directed into responsive conversations with the God who has spoken to us through the Bible.

The chapter preserves one of Scripture's most detailed prayers of confession,[2] in the double sense of confession of sin to God and of faith in God. As the people are led in prayer by the Levites, their vision of God is enlarged. The exposition of God's nature and character which emerges in this chapter is rich in teaching, challenge and encouragement. It stimulates the mind, searches the heart and directs the will. The knowledge of God is portrayed in this chapter in six basic ways.

1. Revealed in Scripture

Israel's years in exile had driven back to Scripture those Levites who compiled this magnificent prayer. They had the alertness of mind and sensitivity of spirit to acknowledge that the decades in Babylon were the consequence of serious failure to obey God's Word in the past. The best among them were eager to listen more carefully to what God had said in earlier days. These teachers were not mere book-worms, students of distant antiquity with a merely intellectual knowledge of what God had said. They had absorbed this dynamic message, taken it to their hearts and memorized its great words and timeless themes. It had spoken dramatically to them, had transformed their own lives, and was woven into the fabric of their personal experience.

Their prayer is a brilliant mosaic of biblical quotations, recollections, images and phrases. The devout Levites who led the penitent citizens in this act of confession knew Scripture by heart, and they channelled its rich vocabulary into believing prayer. The prayer's memorable language owes a big debt to patriarchs, prophets, priests and psalmists, and accurately expresses the people's disappointment with themselves and their confidence in God.

[1] Ezr. 9:1–2.
[2] Similar confessional passages which reflect on national transgression are found elsewhere in the Old Testament, *e.g.* Jos. 24; Ezr. 9; Pss. 78, 105, 106; Dan. 9.

There is scarcely a sentence in the prayer which does not display this debt.[3] It is a superb example of using the Bible in our prayers. The Bible is given to us not only so that we can learn about God's nature and will, but also to inspire our conversation as we talk with him. There are times in all our lives when we cannot fully articulate how we feel and what we want to say to him. Moreover, none of us imagines that our stumbling words are good enough when we confess our sins, express our gratitude or seek his help. But, provided we use these great biblical words sincerely and not repetitiously, there can hardly be a better vehicle than Scripture itself to convey what we really feel. Uniquely inspired by God's Spirit, these believers in biblical times spoke deeply from the heart, and their prayers were heard and answered. We cannot hope to find better words to express exactly what we feel when we converse with God.

When this Jerusalem congregation prayed, therefore, they made their predecessors' words their own. They had grieved God as generations had before them and, just as their forefathers had experienced God's merciful compassion, so would they. The language itself identified them with those who had gone before and reminded them of the Lord's unchanging faithfulness.

As we read this sincere prayer, we overhear the Levites recalling the precise words which God had already given them in Scripture. Exact phrases from the past are on their lips as they seek God's cleansing. Consider a few examples. They recall God's power as the pursuing Egyptians were *hurled . . . like a stone into mighty waters* (11),[4] and his reliable promise as, *with uplifted hand* (15),[5] he committed himself to fulfilling his Word. They rejoiced in God's nature as *a forgiving God, gracious and compassionate, slow to anger and abounding in love* (17),[6] and grieved that his loving words contrasted so sharply with the disloyal, blasphemous words of the wilderness idolators who stood before their offensive idol and said, *This is your god, who brought you up out of Egypt* (18).[7] They remembered the gift of God's *good Spirit* (20),[8] the teacher of a privileged people, *as numerous as the stars in the sky* (23).[9] On entering the land, they were given its *cities . . . houses . . . wells . . . vineyards and olive groves* (25; the order of words directly follows Deuteronomy 6:11); no wonder they *revelled*, literally 'luxuriated',[10] in the Lord's *great goodness*.

Yet, these unique people had put God's law *behind their backs*

---

[3] For detailed examination of biblical quotations and allusions in this passage, see Myers pp. 167–169 and Clines pp. 193–197.   [4] Ex. 15: 5, 10.

[5] Ex. 6:8; Nu. 14:30; Ezk. 20:5; 47:14.

[6] Ex. 34:6; Ps. 86:15; 103:8; 145:8; Joel 2:13; Joh. 4:2.   [7] Ex. 32: 4, 8.

[8] Ps. 143:10.   [9] Gn. 22:17; 26:4; Ex. 32:13; Dt. 1:10; 10:22; 28:62; 1 Ch. 27:23.

[10] Ryle, p. 261.

(26).[11] In his corrective love, God *handed them over* to their enemies (27, 30),[12] but *from heaven* he heard their cry for help (27).[13] Because of his *great compassion* (19, 28, 31)[14] and *great mercy* (31),[15] he gave them *deliverers* (27)[16] who *rescued them from the hand of their enemies* (27),[17] though earlier he had *abandoned* them (28).[18] But, despite these gracious deliverances, his people persistently *paid no attention* (30) to the prophetic word.[19]

Although they had failed him, their God had proved himself to be *great, mighty and awesome* (32).[20] He always *keeps his covenant of love* (32)[21] and stood by them even in the midst of *the hardship* that, throughout history, had *come upon* them (32).[22] Israel has been persistently rebellious in rejecting God's commands and *the warnings* he *gave them* (34).[23] Now they are back in the land he *gave our forefathers* (36),[24] they are still suffering, for ruling powers are taking their *harvest* (37).[25]

This chapter's use of earlier Scripture is a reminder that we are not likely to have a big vision of God if we do not spend time with the magnificent book he has given to us.

2. Confirmed in history

History was always important to God's people. From the literary perspective alone, we should be grateful that when, inspired by God's Spirit, they set down in writing the story of God's mighty deeds, they were making a unique contribution to the recorded history of the ancient world. Paul Johnson makes the point that, 'fascinated by their past from very early times', the Israelites were 'the first to create consequential, substantial and interpretative history':

> They knew they were a special people who had not simply evolved from an unrecorded past but had been brought into existence, for certain definite purposes, by a specific series of divine acts . . . No other people has ever shown, particularly at that remote time, so strong a compulsion to explore their origins.[26]

[11] Ps. 50; 17; Ezk. 23:35.
[12] Jdg. 2:14; 6:1; 13:1; 2 Ch. 28:5; 36:17; Ezr. 5:12; Ps. 78:61–62; Je. 32:3–4, 24–25, 43; La. 1:14; 2:7; Ezk. 23:9; 31:11; 39:23.   [13] 2 Ch. 6:21, 23, 25, 30, 33.
[14] Jdg. 2:18; Ps. 119:156.   [15] Dn. 9:18.   [16] Jdg. 3:9, 15; 2 Ki. 13:5.
[17] Jdg. 2:16, 18; 8:34; 10:12; 13:5.
[18] Jdg. 6:13; 2 Ch. 12:5; Is. 2:6; 54:7; Je. 7:29; La. 2:7; Mi. 5:3.   [19] Zc. 1:4.
[20] Dt. 10:17; Dn. 9:4.   [21] Dt. 7:9; 1 Ki. 8:23; 2 Ch. 6:14; Dn. 9:4.
[22] Ex. 18:8; Nu. 20:14.   [23] 2 Ki. 17:15.   [24] Dt. 6:23; 8:1; 19:8; 2 Ch. 6:31.
[25] 1 Sa. 8:11, 14–17.
[26] Paul Johnson, *A History of the Jews* (London: Weidenfeld and Nicolson, 1987), pp. 91–92.

The Israelites did this because of their profound conviction that the God who had revealed himself in the past was actively present in their contemporary experience, and it was important for succeeding generations that the honest story of their encounter with God should be accurately preserved for people yet to come. The recording of the past testified to God's sufficiency for the future.

Therefore, as these remorseful Israelites pray, they have a keen sense of solidarity with their forefathers. God had met them throughout the centuries and, despite their appalling sinfulness, had not abandoned them. As they reflect on the past, they derive comfort even from the mistakes of their ancestors. The past is not dismissed as antiquated and irrelevant data, for through it they have discerned one of the greatest of all truths: that God has never dealt with his people as they deserved. Their story demonstrates how lovingly and generously God has guided, corrected, restored and equipped them. With such an alert sense of history, they cannot possibly feel forsaken. Believers of earlier centuries have things to say which are strikingly up to date. This earlier experience of God was not shaped in ideal circumstances and, if their forefathers could discern more of God's nature in the grim events of previous centuries, so could their successors in the fifth century.

So, as the Israelites meet for prayer, their history reminds them that God has raised up particular individuals for his service. They recall God's choice of Abraham, his change of name and the Lord's promise to him (7–8, 23),[27] the call of Moses and God's reassuring message at the burning bush (9).[28] These servants experienced tough times, but God was on their side. The story of Egypt's plagues (10)[29] and their deliverance at the Red Sea (10–11)[30] testifies to God's presence with them in adversity. They take heart as they recall the guiding and protecting pillars of cloud and fire (12, 19),[31] the giving of the Law, as God *came down* on Mount Sinai to speak to them (13),[32] and his provision of food and drink in the wilderness (15).[33]

History has its sombre warnings as well as its rich encouragements. They cannot forget the disobedient pilgrims who did not enter Canaan (15–16),[34] the unbelieving plan to return to Egypt under a different leader (17),[35] and the golden-calf idolatry (18).[36] But God never dealt with them as they might have feared. Despite their sins in the wilderness, they had received from his abundant resources. His people *lacked nothing* (21);[37] even their clothes and sandals did not wear out (21).[38]

---

[27] Gn. 11:31 – 12:5; 15:1–20; 17:5.   [28] Ex. 3:7.
[29] Dt. 4:34; 7:19; 26:8; 29:2–3; 34:11.   [30] Ex. 15:5, 10.
[31] Ex. 13:21–22; Nu. 14:14.   [32] Ex. 19:11, 20.   [33] Ex. 16:4; Nu. 20:8.
[34] Nu. 13:31–33; Dt. 1:26–27; 2 Ki. 17:14; Je. 17:23.   [35] Nu. 14:1–4.
[36] Ex. 32:4, 8; Dt. 9:16.   [37] Dt. 2:7.   [38] Dt. 8:4; 29:5.

They remember the divine allocation of Trans-Jordanian territory (22),[39] and their entry into and conquest of the land promised to them (24).[40] They benefited from Canaan's fertility and natural resources (25, 35)[41] but, sadly, the more they received, the more they ignored the generous Giver. They recall their forefathers' appalling disobedience and rebellion (26a)[42] and the silencing of courageously outspoken prophets (26b).[43] Nevertheless, in the period of the Judges, as earlier (27),[44] God repeatedly answered their cry of distress (27b).[45] Even though they were faithfully admonished by Spirit-inspired messengers (30),[46] the arrogant people persistently refused to listen (30).[47] Yet God does not totally forsake them (31).[48]

As they looked back, God provided his people with renewed encouragement and necessary perspective. Recalling what God has done for us in our personal lives, even setting it down in writing, can enrich our prayer lives and enlarge our vision of God. Many believers in our own time keep a spiritual journal,[49] deliberately noting down how the Lord has helped them over specific issues, and recording the manner in which their own experience of his greatness and grace has been enriched through these events.

3. Discerned in prayer

The Israelites, however, were far more than avid collectors of historical data and scribblers of interesting facts. They knew that the mere remembrance of what God had said in Scripture and done in history would not automatically enrich their experience of him. It was when, as an act of will, they entered God's presence to pray, with the challenge of these words and the recollection of these deeds fresh in their minds, that their appreciation of God's nature and character was heightened. What God had said in Scripture and demonstrated in history were channelled in believing prayer to enlarge their vision of God.

They were particularly helped by the recollection of prayers offered by their predecessors in times of immense need. Prayerful leaders in earlier days called on God and he had not disappointed them, and the prayer-experience of seven believers encouraged Nehemiah's contemporaries as they too came before God with their

[39] Nu. 21:21–35; Dt. 2 – 3; Pss. 135:10–12; 136:17–22.

[40] Dt. 4:1; 7:24; 8:1; 9:1–3; 10:11; 11:8; 31:7; Jos. 1:6; 5:6; 11:12, 17; 14:12; 21:43–44; Jdg. 1:4; 4:23.   [41] Nu. 13:20; Dt. 6:11; 8:7–9; 32:13–14.

[42] 1 Ki. 14:9; 2 Ki. 17:15.   [43] 1 Ki. 18:4; 19:10, 14; 2 Ch. 24:19.

[44] Jos. 24:7; Jdg. 2:15.   [45] Jdg. 4:3; 6:6; Ps. 107:6, 28.

[46] 2 Ki. 17:13; 2 Ch. 24:19–20; Zc. 7:12.   [47] Je. 11:7–8; 42:19–21; Zc. 1:4.

[48] Je. 4:27; 5:18; 30:11; 46:28.

[49] Edward England (ed.), *Keeping a Spiritual Journal* (Crowborough: Highland, 1988).

own prayer of sincere confession. Many of this prayer's striking phrases and sentences are drawn from the petitions and intercessions of believers like Hezekiah (6),[50] Jeremiah (6, 10),[51] Moses (6),[52] Daniel (10, 17),[53] Solomon (27)[54] and David (31),[55] as well as the contemporary priest, Ezra (8).[56]

Our experience of God will never be extended or enlarged if we are merely 'bookish'. The intellectual grasp of Christian truth is vital, and we are to worship the Lord with our minds, but a believer's knowledge of God can never be a purely cerebral experience. We come to know him not only by reading about him but by spending time with him. We will certainly understand more about God through our reading, but to grow in maturity we must come to know him personally through the experience of prayer. It is that dimension of deeply personal involvement which makes this prayer in Nehemiah 9 such a moving and helpful passage.

P. T. Forsyth used to insist that human speech can never be put to any higher use than prayer, but prayer requires time. It will be necessary to allocate a certain period in the day when we respond to the teaching of Jesus: 'go into your room, close the door and pray to your Father'.[57] The delight of prayer derives from the discipline of prayer. We long for easy ways of knowing God when we are guilty of devoting less time to him than we would to the development of a human relationship. How could we possibly expect to enjoy someone's friendship if we only read about what they are like and about how good they have been to others, but never spent time with them ourselves?

4. Focused in adoration

The Levites invite the people to pray with the exhortation, *Stand up and praise the LORD your God, who is from everlasting to everlasting* (5). Before they come to their necessary confession, they are to think first about the God who alone can hear, pardon and change them. Their prayer begins and continues with an affirmation of the uniqueness of God. He is faithful, eternal and unchanging. He is *their God* (3, 4), the God who has revealed himself uniquely to Israel in the covenant (32) and who has pledged himself to them in love. Such an unchanging God, *from everlasting to everlasting*, could never go back on his word.

---

[50] 2 Ki. 19:15, 19; Is. 37:16, 20.
[51] Je. 32:17, 20–21.
[52] Dt. 10:14.   [53] Dn. 9:9, 15.   [54] 1 Ki. 8:33–34; 2 Ch. 6:21, 24–25
[55] 2 Sa. 24:14; 1 Ch. 21:13.   [56] Ezr. 9:15.   [57] Mt. 6:6.

Throughout the prayer, the people constantly reflect on God's nature and character as well as his mighty works in history. Adoration is at the heart of true prayer. Sir Thomas Browne urged his seventeenth-century contemporaries to 'think magnificently about God'.[58] Many of our difficulties in contemporary Christian living can be traced either to a narrow, restricted doctrine of God or, more likely, to a concept of God which, though thoroughly biblical, is totally unrelated to life in our world. Analysing the weakness of modern evangelicalism, David Wells refers to 'the weightlessness of God', not 'that he is ethereal but rather that he has become unimportant' or marginalized. He believes that the problem in evangelical churches 'is not inadequate technique, insufficient organization, or antiquated music'. Our sense of inadequacy or experience of ineffectiveness can be traced to our understanding and experience of God. It is 'that God rests too inconsequentially upon the church. His truth is too distant, his grace is too ordinary, his judgment is too benign, his gospel is too easy, and his Christ is too common.'[59]

These worshipping people in fifth-century Jerusalem gloried in the incomparable magnificence of their glorious God. It was not an item in a theological compendium, but a dynamic truth which captivated their minds, enriched their emotions, stirred their consciences and motivated their wills. When they prayed, the greatness of God became a dominant theme as they reminded one another that God is *great, mighty and awesome* (32). Their forefathers had *revelled* in his *great goodness* (25), yet even while they were *enjoying* such *great goodness* they had stubbornly refused to *turn from their evil ways* (35). It was because of his *great compassion* (19) that they were not abandoned during the wilderness wanderings for, however rebellious they were, in his *great mercy* he refused to *put an end to them* (31). They were in *great distress* (37), but their prayer brought clearly to their remembrance the uniqueness, reliability and sufficiency of their God, and in that assurance lay their confidence, peace and security.

5. Deepened through failure

The Israelites' prayer is an eloquent confession of faith in a great God, but it is also a genuine confession of sin on the part of a guilty people. When these worshippers reflected on the nature of God, they became acutely aware of the seriousness of their sins and those of their rebellious ancestors. As Job, Isaiah and Peter also discovered,

[58] Quoted in A. J. Gossip, *In the Secret Place of the Most High* (London: Independent Press, 1950), p. 120.
[59] David F. Wells, *God in the Wasteland* (Leicester: IVP, 1994), pp. 88, 30.

a personal encounter with God creates a more alert sensitivity to sin.[60] God's holiness exposes our impurity, his generosity censures our greed, his faithfulness challenges our disloyalty, his love unmasks our self-centredness. We note that their confession of sin was sincere, specific and realistic.

The people's confession was sincere; that was evident from their sorrow. They came before God *fasting and wearing sackcloth and having dust on their heads* (1). It was not an affected acknowledgment of occasional mistakes. They behaved and dressed as grief-stricken mourners, agonizing over their transgressions. Nothing could minimize the enormity of their offences. Their forefathers had experienced abundant blessing in spite of their persistent rebellion (16–25), a testimony to the omnipotence of grace. They had been repeatedly disobedient in spite of continuing blessing (26–31), an illustration of human sinfulness. They did not deserve God's forgiveness, and nothing anyone might do or say could merit it. They could only cry for mercy.

Moreover, that confession was specific. The people did not hide behind vague phrases and specious language. They itemized their sins, spelling them out in ugly detail. Throughout their history they had been *arrogant* (16) towards God, in much the same way that the Egyptians had dealt *arrogantly* (10) with them. They belonged to a disobedient and forgetful people who failed to *remember the miracles* God had *performed among them*, and, ungratefully rebellious, had appointed their own *leader in order to return* to Egyptian slavery (17). Deliberately breaking the first two commandments, they practised idolatrous worship *when they cast for themselves an image of a calf*, and became guilty of appalling blasphemy as they worshipped this offensive idol saying, *This is your God, who brought you up out of Egypt* (18).

Over the centuries, the Israelites had disobeyed God's Law, putting it *behind their backs*, and had murdered those courageous messengers who urged them to obey it (26). Even when, in answer to their cry for help, God sent them deliverers (27), they quickly forgot such mighty acts of undeserved salvation, and once again *did what was evil* in the sight of God (28). God often warned them about the serious consequences of these repeated sins but they continued in their arrogance, disobedience (29), stubborn independence, pride and heedlessness (30).

As the Israelites prayed, they contrasted God's tenacious loyalty with their own persistent evil: *you have acted faithfully, while we did wrong* (33). Although the Lord had given them such a *spacious and fertile land*, they had not responded to such generosity with

---

[60] Jb. 42:5–6; Is. 6:1–5; Lk. 5:8.

grateful homage: *they did not serve you or turn from their evil ways* (35). What the Puritans used to call their 'darling sins' meant more to them than their devoted Lord. This disastrously wrong choice was entirely due to their repeated dismissal of God's Word. Even their national and religious leaders, who ought to have been models of spiritual loyalty, rejected the truth which had been entrusted to them: they *did not follow your law; they did not pay attention to your commands or the warnings you gave them* (34).

The specific nature of the people's confession is important. They did not merely describe themselves as sinners; they spelt out how they had sinned. When we ask for cleansing, we sometimes heap our iniquities together, labelling them as common faults and mistakes, even excusing ourselves that everyone fails in one way or another. But, in confession, the universality of sin should not obscure the particularity of our offences. If we are to appreciate the wonder of God's forgiveness, our sins need to be identified as the distinctly individual, personal and damaging transgressions they really are, and not mechanically lumped together in some ritualistic phrase at the beginning of a formal prayer. We must name them honestly before God as we ask that they might be washed away; only in this way will we admit their seriousness and acknowledge our shame.

The confession of the Israelites was also realistic. The prayer recognizes the solidarity as well as the individuality of their sins. It may seem strange to us that they had so much to say about the sins of their forefathers, and we may ask why they grieved so much about transgressions they had not personally committed. They had not personally rejected Moses' authority (17) or built that calf of gold in the desert (18); they were hardly responsible for the execution of prophets nor had they personally *committed awful blasphemies* (26). So why are they in sackcloth and ashes?

These people were the first to acknowledge that the awful thing about sin is its power to communicate itself. Nobody sins in secret. When we sin we grieve God, damage ourselves and eventually affect others because we become something less than the people we might otherwise be. These praying people knew that, although they had not been present at the wilderness rebellion, it was a stark example of their own propensity to idolatry and lawlessness. They had not been in the garden physically when Adam sinned, but he was not there simply as solitary man but as representative man. As Paul insisted, in one sense, all of us were present at Eden,[61] for Adam's disobedience to God's command is mirrored every day in human experience. A first-century Jewish writer rightly maintained that

[61] Rom. 5:12–19.

'each of us hath been the Adam of his own soul'.[62] The nation's sins were starkly portrayed on this vast historical canvas, but these believers were honestly admitting that examples from the past illustrated the sins of the present. The iniquities of their forefathers had not been left behind, rooted in distant history. They had been passed on to their children and grandchildren. Their moral failure had left a legacy of disobedience and disloyalty that had communicated itself to successive generations right down to their own century and beyond. At the beginning and close of the prayer they did not simply acknowledge the sins of their forefathers; they confessed their own. It was not simply the mistakes of a corrupt ancestry: *They stood in their places and confessed their sins and the wickedness of their fathers* (2). They talked about *our sins* (37), not 'their sins'. They knew that both the iniquities of yesterday and their present offences had brought them into *great distress*.

The itemizing of their transgressions heightened their indebtedness to the Lord. It was through these experiences of serious moral failure that they had discovered the compassionate and merciful nature of God. When we sin, all is not lost if the experience of personal repentance and assured cleansing heightens our understanding of God. It is forgiven people who are most sincere in worship, most devoted in service and most effective in witness.

6. Enriched in suffering

Although most of their troubles could be traced to their sins, the people of Israel had, as a nation, been through immense hardship which was not always the consequence of their rebellion. They were hardly to blame for the sufferings in Egypt (9) as they laboured under cruel taskmasters (10). Throughout their history, thousands of good people had sighed for deliverance. But it was through these troubles that God came to them, and it was in adversity that they proved his abundant sufficiency. Suffering is never a lonely visitor to the human life. The Christian soon becomes aware of immense resources which accompany every experience of hardship. Our worst afflictions become the expositors of grace.

The Israelites discovered their best things about God when life was hard and difficult. Once prosperity came, they were in danger of forgetting God, and imagined they could rely on their own slender and inadequate resources.[63] But trouble drove them to God, and it will do the same for us. In the cruel years of persecution for nonconformists in late seventeenth-century England, Stephen

---

[62] 2 Baruch 54:19; R. H. Charles (ed.), *The Apocalypse of Baruch* (London: SPCK, 1917), p. 73. [63] Dt. 6:10–12; 8:10–14.

Charnock told his London congregation that the goodness of God is evident in afflictions. Sometimes the Lord 'takes away the thing which we have some value for, but such as his infinite wisdom sees inconsistent with our true happiness'. Through trouble we discern our need of him, and by means of unwelcome experiences he 'sharpens our faith, and quickens our prayers'. We see God more clearly and ourselves more realistically; he uses adversity to bring us 'into the secret chamber of our own heart, which we had little mind before to visit by a self-examination'.[64]

By the close of this prayer, these Israelite worshippers had certainly seen themselves as they really were, and they were under no illusions about their spiritual superiority or moral worthiness. More importantly, through their grief they were given new insights into the generosity and reliability of their unchanging, compassionate and merciful God. If trouble does that for us, we are privileged people indeed.

[64] Stephen Charnock, *Discourse on the Existence and Attributes of God: The Goodness of God*, in *Works*, vol. 2 (Edinburgh, 1864), p. 361

Nehemiah 9:1–37
11. 'But in your great mercy'

We have been looking at the means by which Nehemiah's contemporaries had their vision of God enlarged in chapter 9. Still in the same chapter, we turn now to trace the specific features of their portraiture of God in order to see what these attributes meant in their everyday experience. Ten aspects of God's nature and character emerge in this prayer, and they are as important for us today as they were for these Judean believers in the fifth century BC. As they responded to the Levites' call to prayer (4) they were led into the presence of an active and responsive God.

1. God reveals his nature (9:5)

He is the eternal God. As these spiritual leaders urge the people to seek God, their vision of his greatness is first set within the limitless framework of eternity. Their Lord was not a merely national deity or narrowly restricted tribal god, confined, parochial and limited. 'From everlasting to everlasting thy glorious name is blessed' (5, NEB). The Levites' opening exhortation to praise recalls David's prayer at the reception of gifts for the building of the temple and the exultant words of the psalmists: 'Praise be to the LORD, the God of Israel, from everlasting to everlasting'.[1] When confined and oppressed by life's restrictions, the Israelites rejoiced in a God of infinity.

Within recent decades, these Judean people had experienced intense hardship and innumerable difficulties, several of which are vividly described by Nehemiah. In the previous century, their grandparents had made the long trek of about a thousand miles across the deserts and wastelands of the ancient world in order to return from prosperous Babylon to a broken and deprived Jerusalem. To one prophet of those years in exile, such depressed people seemed

[1] 1 Ch. 29:10; Pss. 41:13; 90:2; 103:17; 106:48.

like a deep valley full of shattered skeletons, and we hardly wonder at Ezekiel's haunting question: 'Can these bones live?'[2]

To return to such a bereft city and countryside was a venture of faith, and their confidence in God had been generously rewarded. But it had been difficult. The holy city had been ruthlessly devastated by the Babylonian armies. Houses, temple and walls had to be rebuilt. The builders could be proud of their walls, but over the years there had been much to discourage them. When the new temple was dedicated, it looked a mere 'nothing' when contrasted with the magnificent edifice raised by Solomon centuries before.[3] Although there had been periods of relative prosperity,[4] life since the return had also been characterized by droughts, famine, poverty, oppressive threats from alien neighbours, burdensome taxation by the Persian authorities, and during the wall-building even their lives had been in danger. The prayer's introduction on the lips of those Levites reminded them to raise their eyes to wider horizons. They were to adore the *everlasting* God. There was more to life than Jerusalem and its neighbouring towns, villages and fields. They are not locked in to the present. God has indescribably happy plans for the ultimate future of his people. Present trials and threatened hardships are the tiniest fragment of his total purposes for them. Their lives are to be viewed within the context of a vast eternity; everything is under his almighty control.

At times we may become discouraged by the painful circumstances of life, and its unexpected adversities seem to hem us in. Our thoughts become channelled within the narrow limits of our present existence, and we are in danger of imagining that this life is everything. But believers know that it is not the sum total of God's plan for his people. They remember the incomparably vast setting of eternity. In contrast, contemporary unbelievers avoid all mention of an ultimate future. A modern journalist suffering from a terminal illness concluded that the 'imperative to behave well' is 'just about the only tiny moral truth that the twentieth century has been able to extract from the wasteland left by scientific materialism'. He wrote that, in 'a universe without God or an after-life, which is what most of us are reluctantly obliged to accept', the best we can do is to 'make ethical creatures of ourselves'.[5]

Though totally committed to the highest moral ideals, the Lord Jesus and his servants in the early church preached about eternity as

---

[2] Ezk. 37:1–2.   [3] Hg. 2:2–3.   [4] Hg. 1:4–6.

[5] *The Daily Telegraph*, 17 August 1995, p. 13. After some months of reading (including a careful study of the gospels) this journalist, Martyn Harris, found himself giving 'reluctant assent' to 'the intellectual coherence of Christianity', the uniqueness of Christ and his saving death, and in doing so lost his acute fear of death; see Martyn Harris, *Odd Man Out* (London: Telegraph Books, 1996), pp. 299–307.

well as ethics, future security as well as present standards. They reminded their contemporaries of the reality of heaven. Knowing that his disciples would soon be denied his physical presence, Christ pointed them to a guaranteed future in a better life to come. When work was hazardous for the apostle Paul, he refused to 'lose heart'; temporary hardships were far outweighed by the prospect of the eternal glory. The letter to the Hebrews addressed a church threatened by renewed persecution but, like the patriarchs, its readers were to look for 'a better country – a heavenly one' which God had prepared for them. James urges his readers to be patient because of the Lord's promised coming. Peter reminds his friends that, one day, the Chief Shepherd will appear; then they will receive an unfading crown. John rejoices that when he appears 'we shall be like him, for we shall see him as he is'. Through periods of bitter persecution, the early Christians believed in the inevitable unfolding of the Lord's sovereign purposes; they too worshipped a God 'who lives for ever and ever'.[6] That eternal perspective saw them through some desperately dark days; it will not do less for us.

By contrast, our contemporaries studiously avoid any mention of an ultimate future. Death is taboo in the vocabulary of the West and the subject is guaranteed to embarrass a secular conversation. It is shrugged off, hastily dismissed or diverted by a flippant joke. Yet what unspeakable folly to ignore the one inescapable event to which every single individual is moving – the inevitable termination of life in this world.

The secularist avoidance of death, denial of eternal judgment, and cynicism about heaven has had its subtle repercussions in the modern church; the topics are not prominent in contemporary Christian proclamation. In many churches, the doctrine of the second coming of Christ and related themes has been relegated to the circumference of Christian thought and, in some places, dismissed altogether. Yet, as Gordon Rupp once put it, Christians believe in 'Last Things First'.[7] They deserve to be reminded frequently that the God who is *from everlasting to everlasting* has made generous provision for the secure eternal future of all who turn to him through Christ. It is a topic to shout from the housetops, not whisper at street-corners.

2. God proclaims his uniqueness (9:6a)

God has no rivals. Surrounded as they were geographically with competing religious allegiances, the prayer's opening sentences

---

[6] Jn. 14:1–3; 2 Cor. 4:17–18; Heb. 11:16; Jas. 5:7–8; 1 Pet. 5:4; 1 Jn. 3:2; Rev. 4:9–10.
[7] Gordon Rupp, *Last Things First* (London: SCM, 1964).

provided these worshippers with an opportunity for public commitment to the only true God. Other claimants to deity were non-existent figments of corrupt human imagination. As these covenant people made their uncompromising confession, *You alone are the LORD*, they affirmed their obedience to the first and second commandments. In time, their testimony to God's uniqueness became the prayer of devout Jews, expressed each day in Deuteronomy's *Shema*: 'Hear, O Israel: The LORD our God, the LORD is one.'[8]

Other gods were a fraudulent nonentity, yet the attraction of idolatry was a constant hazard throughout Hebrew history. The darker moments of the prayer's confession reminded them of the golden calf in the wilderness and the blasphemous audacity of those who claimed that this impotent idol had delivered them from their Egyptian oppressors (18). When they constructed that degrading image, they were publicly denying the opening words of the Decalogue where the Lord identified himself as the one who had brought them out of the land of Egypt. In contrast to such blatant disloyalty, this prayer affirmed that there are no other gods. The only true God has no rivals.

You alone are the LORD is a significant biblical affirmation for our time, especially in the face of two contemporary challenges – idolatry and pluralism. Modern people have idols other than grotesque statuettes; their idols reign in the heart. They worship prosperity, popularity, pleasure and power, and those who idolize these invisible icons persistently turn their backs on the only God. Further, the pluralistic nature of late twentieth-century Western society will not tolerate this uncompromising biblical exclusivism. It prefers a 'pick 'n' mix religion', a view which regards all religions, ancient and modern, as of equal worth. Many of our contemporaries prefer to select acceptable elements not only from the older world religions but also from the new, such as the bizarre ideas in New Age with its primary focus on the pre-eminent 'self' ('self-awareness' and 'self-fulfilment'), rather than on the reality of human sin and the crucial need for a divine Saviour.[9] But, in a memorable prayer at the close of his earthly ministry, the Son of God defined 'eternal life' as knowing 'you, the *only* true God, and Jesus Christ, whom you have sent'.[10] In faithful testimony to the uniqueness of Christ, the contemporary Christian must be prepared to bear what has been described as 'the scandal of particularity': 'Salvation is found in no-one else, for there is no other name under heaven given to men by which we must be saved.'[11]

[8] Dt. 6:4 (*Shema* = Hebrew 'Hear').
[9] D. A. Carson, *The Gagging of God: Christianity Confronts Pluralism* (Leicester: Apollos, 1996), pp. 412, 330–332.   [10] Jn. 17:3.   [11] Acts 4:12.

3. God displays his power (9:6b)

He is the Creator God. The prayer traces the history of God's people from the opening stories in Genesis to their contemporary scene. Its beginning in creation is a testimony both to God's uniqueness and his total sufficiency for all our needs.

The reference to creation is a further affirmation of faith, particularly relevant in the fifth century BC. Nehemiah had worked for years in a Persian palace. Persian religion was essentially a religion of the court, and Nehemiah must have been familiar with its teaching. The Persian people memorized the sayings of Zoroaster and passed them on to their children. They were fascinated by the world of nature and enquired wistfully how it all came into being.

> This do I ask thee, O Lord, tell me truly;
> Who is the Creator, the first father of Righteousness?
> Who laid down the path of the sun and stars?
> Who is it through whom the moon now waxes, now wanes?
> All this and more do I wish to know, O Wise One.
>
> This do I ask thee, O Lord, tell me truly;
> Who holds the earth below and the sky as well
>   from falling?
> Who (created) the waters and the plants?
> Who harnesses the (two) courses to wind and clouds?
> Who, O Wise One, is the creator of the Good Mind?[12]

Their rhetorical questions invited the response that creation was the work of the good god of Zoroastrianism, Ahura Mazda. But those who prayed this prayer in Nehemiah 9 were supremely confident that Israel's God alone *made the heavens, even the highest heavens, and all their starry host, the earth and all that is on it, the seas and all that is in them. You give life to everything, and the multitudes of heaven worship you.* The prayer did not only exalt God's power in making this world out of nothing; it was a witness to their neighbours in the surrounding nations, some of whom vainly worshipped the creature rather than the creator.[13] They bowed down to the stars, ignorant of the Lord who made them.

The prayer was not narrowly polemical, however. It testified to an inspiring truth which has sustained God's people through difficult times. A God who made everything out of nothing[14] can do anything. Nothing whatever is beyond the ability of such a mighty God. When John Bunyan encouraged his persecuted friends in the

---

[12] From the Gathas, the hymns of Zoroaster, *Yasna* 44:3–4, quoted in R. N. Frye, *The Heritage of Persia* (London: Weidenfeld and Nicolson, 1962), p. 34.
[13] Rom. 1:22–25.   [14] Gn. 1:1–2.

late seventeenth century, he reminded them of Peter's advice to suffering Christians in the early church: 'So then, those who suffer
according to God's will should commit themselves to their faithful
Creator and continue to do good.'[15] As Bunyan expounded that text,
he told his readers that 'nothing can die under a Creator's hands ...
The cause of God for which his people suffer, had been dead and
buried a thousand years ago, had it not been in the hands of a
Creator.' He continued:

> Who could have thought, that the three children could have lived
> in a fiery furnace, that Daniel could have been safe among the
> lions, that Jonah could have come home to his country, when he
> was in the whale's belly, or that our Lord should have risen again
> from the dead: but what is impossible to a Creator?

The Bedford pastor then wrote with impassioned conviction: 'A
Creator can make such provision for a suffering people in all respects,
as shall answer all their wants.'[16]

Creation work is not confined to the stories in Genesis for, as
Jesus made clear, God continues to be wisely, skilfully and powerfully at work in the world, 'to this very day'.[17] The God who can
give life to everything will not leave his people without strength,
peace and hope. Furthermore, he not only has the desire and power
to help them but, as the prayer reminds us, the agents as well. The
multitudes of heaven are the angelic host, the supernatural messengers of his purposes. 'The heavenly bodies, often themselves
objects of worship,[18] here are worshippers of Yahweh'.[19] New
Testament Christians believed that angels were not only engaged in
the worship of heaven but employed in service on earth. A first-
century suffering church was assured that they are constantly on the
errands of their Creator, 'ministering spirits sent to serve those who
will inherit salvation'.[20] Secularistic cynicism must not be allowed
to rob us of these certainties; the angels are still with us.

4. God keeps his promise (9:7–8)

The prayer abounds with references to the initiative and activity of
God. The people gloried not only in what he did at creation but in
what he has continued to do in the world he made: *You made the
heavens ... You give life ... You ... chose Abram ... You found his
heart faithful ... you made a covenant with him to give ... You*

[15] 1 Pet. 4:19.
[16] John Bunyan, *Seasonable Counsel, or Advice to Sufferers* (1684), in *Miscellaneous Works*, vol. 10, ed. Owen C. Watkins (Oxford: Clarendon, 1988), pp. 76–77.
[17] Jn. 5:17.   [18] Dt. 4:19, *cf.* Ps. 148:2.   [19] Clines, p. 193.   [20] Heb. 1:14.

have kept your promise (6–8). The prayer focuses on several aspects of divine sovereign actions in the life of Abraham.

God *chose* Abraham. From this frail human source, a man on the threshold of the grave with a wife well beyond child-bearing years,[21] this unique nation was born. God selects unlikely people from undistinguished places (*Ur of the Chaldeans*) to fulfil his plans so that men and women cannot boast about their own achievements.[22]

God *changed* him. His name, *Abram*, 'high father', probably denoted someone with a modest claim to public recognition, a person of significance among his neighbours, but such a title meant little beyond the confines of the local community. God transformed his frail life, changing his name to *Abraham*. The herdsman who was 'as good as dead' became 'father of a multitude'.

God *knew* him. The Lord knew that Abraham's motives were pure and his allegiance true. The omniscient God *found his heart faithful*. Before these people confess the iniquities of their fathers and their own, they acknowledge that he is aware of everything. There are no secrets. He has seen into the deepest recesses of their corrupt hearts and minds. Even when he looked into Abraham's life, he did not see a man of flawless morality. Abraham was a sinner like everybody else, but he was a man determined to trust God, and his tenacious loyalty was recognized in heaven.

God *used* him. *He made a covenant with him to give to his descendants the land.* This man of faith received the covenant promise that God's chosen people would inherit a land of their own. Although it was inhabited by Canaanite nations, all the earth belonged to God, so God made Abraham a pledge that he would become the father of the promised race and his progeny occupants of the promised land.

In trusting and obeying God's word, Abraham had left a noble example to his descendants.[23] The people confess that it was one they did not follow, but their recollection of Abraham's life was a testimony not to the patriarch's worthiness but to God's faithfulness. He always does what he says: *You have kept your promise.* The reliability of his word is guaranteed by the integrity of his character: *because you are righteous.* A God of truth is incapable of deception; his people are secure when, like Abraham, they accept what he says as infallible fact.

[21] Heb. 11:11–12. [22] 1 Cor. 1:26–28.
[23] Gn. 12:1–7; 13:14–17; 15:1–6; 17:1–22; 18:1–15; 22:1–18; Heb. 11:8–19

5. God manifests his love (9:9–12)

As the prayer continues, its story leaps from Abraham to Moses. It moves from the creation of the nation to its salvation, from God's grace in establishing a community to his power in redeeming them. Once again, God chooses the most unlikely personality to achieve his plans, a refugee who had fled from Egypt forty years earlier, guilty of manslaughter.[24] But God uses the weakest of people, especially those who are haunted by earlier failures. Who could have imagined that that quick-tempered courtier in mid-life would be called to new work when he was a shepherd in his eighties. All things are possible with God.

In recalling the Exodus story, the prayer focuses on God's love and power, a perfect combination. Love *saw the suffering* of the oppressed Israelite slaves, and his power did something about it. Many people have love but no power to help, whilst others have forceful power but minimal love. Love without power is helpless; power without love is dangerous. God is both loving and powerful.[25] He determined their destiny, saw their suffering, heard their prayers and changed their lives.

He acted for them in love and power but not solely for Israel's sake. In the Exodus event his declared uniqueness and promised reliability were at stake: *You made a name for yourself which remains to this day* (10). In announcing his name to Moses at Horeb he was declaring his character; the 'I am who I am' is the eternal, unchanging God.[26] He is ever-present (for he has always been and will always be the same), never-failing ('the God of your fathers'),[27] and all-powerful ('I have promised to bring you up out of your misery').[28] The redemption of his people was undeniable historical proof that he would do what he said. He has his name to think about.

When the redeemed people idolized their golden calf, Moses was summoned to the mountain top. The covenant must be renewed even among sinners. There, God 'proclaimed his name ... "The Lord, the Lord, the compassionate and gracious God, slow to anger, abounding in love and faithfulness"' (covenant loyalty).[29] When they left Egypt, the great 'I am' demonstrated the invincibility of his power; now he declares the immutability of his love. He is true to his name and loves them still.

In the century before Nehemiah, Daniel sought God in words similar to these in chapter 9. In the dark days of the exile he was glad to recall that, in delivering a captive people from Egypt, God had

---

[24] Ex. 2:11–15; Acts 7:22–29. [25] Ps. 62:11–12. [26] Ex. 3:13–14.
[27] Ex. 3:15–16. [28] Ex. 3:17. [29] Ex. 34:5–6.

'made ... a name' for himself 'that endures to this day'.[30] Daniel pleaded with the Lord to do it again, and not for the exiles' sake only: 'For your sake, O Lord ... see the desolation of the city that bears your Name.' They did not deserve a new exodus but cast themselves on his 'great mercy'. The man of prayer pleaded because he knew that God was true to his name and his people were its witnesses in a pagan environment. He asked God to do it for them again 'because your city and your people bear your Name'.[31]

At the exodus he had answered their prayers (9), vanquished their enemies (10), overcome their fears (11) and guided their steps, *to give them light on the way they were to take* (12). As Nehemiah's contemporaries prayed, they knew that God had certainly done it yet again in delivering them from Babylon. He had not changed, and they could certainly rely on his good name.

Throughout history, the exodus story has spoken with renewed appeal in vastly different contexts. Helpless slaves in the New World voiced their dreams in plaintive song: 'Let my people go'. Many thousands of innocent people who suffered in the holocaust cried for a similar deliverance and dreamt of a promised land. Contemporary liberation and black theologians interpret these narratives afresh and plead for better things. Over the centuries, captive people have turned to this story as a sign of hope. The days of oppression are not over, and in this cruelly divided world, thousands long for change. In addition to political oppression, ethnic conflicts and appalling racial injustice, there are closer and more subtle tyrannies. Millions throughout our world are enslaved to destructive lifestyles, avarice, gluttony, drug abuse, alcoholism, sexual promiscuity, gambling, pornography, and in their own strength they cannot break free. The story of what God did for thousands of broken Hebrew slaves is a model of what he continues to do in changing human lives. It is little wonder that when the early Christian people expressed the wonder of their salvation, it was in categories which reminded them of the exodus. Through his redemptive work, Christ had become their deliverer. The Passover Lamb had been slain in their place. The judgment was past. As released pilgrims they were destined for a new land.[32]

6. God unfolds his will (9:13–15)

The pagan gods were dead and silent but the living God *came down* and *spoke* with his people at Sinai. He told them he would be with them,[33] and how could they have God at their side and be destitute?

[30] Dn. 9:15.   [31] Dn. 9:17–19.   [32] 1 Cor. 5:7; 1 Pet. 1:18–19; Mk. 14:12.
[33] Ex. 33:14.

He was true to his word and lavished choice gifts upon them, meeting all their needs: moral (13, *just and right* laws and *decrees and commands* which were *good*), physical (14, a *holy Sabbath*) and material (15, *bread from heaven* and *water from the rock*), as well as spiritual needs. Everything he had said and done was for their blessing. He had taken a solemn vow *with uplifted hand to give them* (15) the land, and would not go back on his word.

When God spoke to them they could trust his promises (8) because they reflected his character. They knew he was righteous (13, evident in his *just and right* laws), good (13, demonstrated in his *good* decrees), thoughtful (14, making provision for a day of rest), generous (15, *in their hunger you gave them bread . . . and in their thirst you brought them water*) and dependable (15, *sworn . . . to give*).

7. God demonstrates his mercy (9:16–18)

Yet, in spite of all the Lord had said and done, *they, our forefathers . . . did not obey* God's Word (16). In the light of such abundant generosity, the Israelites' contrasting disloyalty comes as an immense shock – until we examine our own hearts. Had we been numbered among the wilderness pilgrims, we are not likely to have behaved much better. Their sin is serious, but what makes it tragic is its persistent repetition throughout history. It is the story of wayward humanity, not just of rebellious Israel. We too have been guilty of stubborn pride (16, *arrogant and stiff-necked*), wilful disloyalty (16, *did not obey*), studied heedlessness (17, *refused to listen*), appalling ingratitude (15, 17 *you gave . . . they failed to remember*), blatant rebellion (17, *appointed a leader in order to return to their slavery*), pathetic idolatry (18, *cast for themselves an image of a calf*), and unashamed profanity (17, *committed awful blasphemies*). We too are doomed, unless a merciful God comes to rescue us.

8. God shows his generosity (9:19–25)

The praying people rejoiced not only in what God had done but also about what he had not done. Because he was *slow to anger and abounding in love* he *did not desert them* (17) when they sinned against him. There was so much that they did not do towards him. They did not appreciate his protection. Even on the day they worshipped the golden calf, the pillar of cloud still towered high above the camp, sheltering the idolaters from unseen dangers. As they went to bed that night, the protecting wall of fire still shone brightly. They did not remember his mighty deeds on their behalf

(17). They did not obey his law (26a) nor value his message but, in arrogant rebellion, silenced his messengers (26b).

In his wrath, the Lord might have done all manner of things, totally deserved, but they were his treasured people. The Israelite offenders deserved God's punishment or abandonment but because of his *great compassion* (19) he refused to let them go.

He did not withdraw his presence (19). Although they were sickeningly idolatrous, he could *not abandon them in the desert.* Those massive symbols of his unfailing presence, the daytime *pillar of cloud did not cease to guide them on their path, nor the pillar of fire by night to shine on the way they were to take.*

He did not refuse his help (20a). In their idolatry, they had openly rejected his teaching but, lovingly and persistently, he continued to speak and gave his *good Spirit to instruct them.*

The Lord did not withhold his provision (20b). Despite their disobedience to his Word, indifference to his mercies, and rejection of his authority (17–18), he continued to meet their daily needs: *You did not withhold your manna from their mouths, and you gave them water for their thirst* (20). *For forty years*, the consequence of their wilful disobedience, he *sustained them in the desert* (21).

Rebels though they were, *they lacked nothing.* In totally unmerited generosity, God did seven things for them. He gave them geographical direction (19), spiritual insight (20a), material provision (20b), adequate clothing (21a), physical stamina (21b), military success (22, giving them *kingdoms and nations*) and numerical strength (23), making *their sons as numerous as the stars in the sky.*

God insisted on being true to his promise (23, to Abraham) even though they had broken theirs. The disobedient and rebellious fathers died in the wilderness as God had predicted, but *their sons went in and took possession of the land* (24). Those children proved the continuing favour of God. He secured their land, provided their homes and guaranteed their food. They had more than enough. What an astonishing contrast after the wilderness years. Now they were in *fertile land* (25), the undeserving recipients of *all kinds of good things.* What privileged people they were. Water was life's most precious commodity and the necessary wells were *already dug* for them. God gave them *vineyards, olive groves and fruit trees in abundance. They ate to the full and were well-nourished: they revelled in your great goodness* (25). One imagines they might respond to such rich mercy with unceasing gratitude, but they did not.

Before we condemn them, we need to ask whether we count God's blessings and recall his goodness in our lives. Every opportunity for prayer ought to begin in adoration, acknowledging who God is, then continue in thanksgiving, recognizing what he has done for us. All too often, we crave for more, forgetting what we already have.

9. God exercises his patience (9:26–31)

The next section of the prayer covers those decades which followed the settlement in Canaan, particularly the events described in the historical books of the Old Testament. It is a sad story of loveless-ness towards God and indifference to his Word: *But they were disobedient and rebelled against you; they put your law behind their backs.* They did not merely ignore what God had said but took steps to ensure that they would not have to listen to it again; they ridiculed and killed those who proclaimed it.[34] The repeated cyclic pattern of prosperity, arrogance, apostasy, judgment, penitence and restoration – typical of the stories in the book of Judges – is recited in this honest prayer: *they committed awful blasphemies.* They did not only use offensive speech about the Lord (18, 26); they held him 'in great contempt'.[35] *So you handed them over to their enemies . . . but when they were oppressed they cried out to you . . . you heard them . . . you gave them deliverers . . . But . . . they again did what was evil* (27–28).

God patiently absorbed their repeated disloyalty. He knew that the only way to bring them back to their covenant relationship was to give them over *to the hand of their enemies.* Only by intense hardship of that extreme kind would they become aware of their dependence on the Lord. When things went well for them, they did not merely forget God; they turned to other gods. It was exactly like an unfaithful partner in a marriage who was generously forgiven after having an illicit affair with someone else. Then, a short while later, the same thing happened again, and not once but repeatedly. It is an impossible strain on life's most special relationship. A human being could hardly bear it but the Lord, grieved by their monotonously repetitive infidelity, fully forgave them and *delivered them time after time* (29).

The Israelites' abandonment of the covenant relationship was evident from their determined rejection of God's Word. They were repeatedly urged to *return* to the law but they *disobeyed* God's *commands* and *sinned* against his *ordinances* (29). In doing so, they were deliberately choosing the path of death, for the man who treasures God's ordinances *will live if he obeys them.* But the people *turned their backs* on God as they chased after material things, destructive pleasures and useless idols. They put God's law *behind their backs* (26) and, just as they would treat a contemptuous thing, they hurled it away. But *for many years* the Lord was *patient with them* (30). God raised up and the *Spirit* inspired faithful and courageous

---

[34] 2 Ch. 24:20–22; 36:15–16; Mt. 23:34–37; Acts 7:51–52.   [35] Blenkinsopp, p. 298.

prophets,[36] but the people *paid no attention* so, God *handed them over to the neighbouring peoples* knowing that, under the pressure of adversity, they would remember the Lord who loved them. In his *great mercy* he *did not put an end to them or abandon them*, for he is *a gracious and merciful God*.

Trouble still drives self-sufficient people into the arms of a loving God. When all goes well for them in life, they can do without him. He patiently waits, knowing that everything may not always be well for those who are arrogantly *stiff-necked*. The prodigal forgot his father when he was feasting at sumptuously laden tables surrounded by approving friends, but when his money ran out and his stomach was empty, he thought about home.[37] There are times when, sadly, only sorrow can bring people to their senses.

10. God proves his faithfulness (9:32-37)

As this comprehensive prayer draws to its close, the scene changes from the story of a degrading past to the distressing present – with the treasured hope of a better future. They turn from the heartaches of the years gone by to the *hardship* of their own times. How they approach God is significant and relevant.

The praying people adore his greatness. As they gradually move from confession to petition, they turn from their evident failures to his immense compassion. Their *great, mighty and awesome* God has persistently kept *his covenant of love* (32), despite the repeated flirtations and blatant disloyalty of his adulterous people.[38] He will surely rescue their contemporaries as well.

They magnify his constancy. Their past disloyalty and present distress has affected every strata in society: *kings . . . leaders . . . priests . . . prophets . . . fathers . . . people*. That is the agonizing thing about sin; it spreads rampantly and, like a ghastly disease, infects one generation after another. But the Lord did not treat them as they had repeatedly dealt with him. They persistently broke their side of the agreement but he resolutely refused to break his: *In all that has happened . . . you have acted faithfully, while we did wrong* (33).

The people acknowledge his justice: *you have been just*. If they were to be forgiven, their sins could not be overlooked. They would not admit sin's ugliness until they suffered its consequences. So, from the times of *the kings of Assyria*, when the Northern Kingdom was chastised for its idolatrous disobedience, *until today*, the people could trace the chastising hand of God.

They recognize his sovereignty. The Lord allowed them to go

---

[36] Possibly recalling the prophetic indictment voiced by Zechariah a few decades earlier (Zc. 7:11-12).   [37] Lk. 15:11-20.   [38] Ho. 2:2-13.

through those experiences of intense pain so that they would come back to him. These severe judgments were an expression of his universal sovereignty and tokens of his persistent love. The armies of the Assyrians, Babylonians and Persians, like the Egyptians, Canaanites and Philistines before them, were only victorious in conquering God's people because the Lord had willed it so. He *handed them over* (27), *abandoned them to . . . their enemies* (28) and *handed them over to the neighbouring peoples* (30) just as, earlier, he *handed the Canaanites over to them* (24). Their history was not a series of disconnected political accidents and military failures; he was at work in it all. Those prophets, whose ministry they had despised (26, 30), proclaimed God's sovereign rule. Isaiah identified the ruthless Assyrians as the rod of God's anger.[39] Later, Jeremiah urged his contemporaries to accept that Babylon's threatening king was nothing other than God's servant,[40] fulfilling the divine purposes for Judah's chastisement. It was the Lord who 'handed them over' to Nebuchadnezzar.[41] The Babylonians were themselves defeated later, because the same sovereign God raised up a Persian prince to be his people's deliverer.[42]

The Israelites remember God's Word. Their greatest sin has been disobedience to what he has said. The *law* was abandoned, the *commands* unheeded, the *warnings* ignored (34). Because they refused to serve God (35), they are slaves to others (36). They are still under the dominion of another ruler. The Persians were not cruel overlords but God's people were not entirely free, and heavy taxation frequently brought them into dire poverty. A severe produce-tax meant that their hard work on the land was primarily for the benefit of others. Only a great God (19, 32) who does great things (25, 27, 31, 35) could relieve such *great distress* (37).

Israelite history testified to the Lord's goodness, however, and not only to their wickedness. Though weighed down by guilt and tormented by their sinful record across the centuries, they can still revel in that great goodness. The prayer exalts the God who across the centuries has done so much for them. Twenty blessings are itemized in their recital of his generous mercies. He has given himself to the work of creating (6), choosing (7), encouraging (8), hearing (9), delivering (10–11), guiding (12), meeting (13a), teaching (13b), protecting (14), feeding (15), forgiving (17), loving (17), accompanying (19), clothing (21), empowering (22), sustaining (21), multiplying (23), prospering (25), correcting (26–27) and rescuing them (27). Looking back they could trace not only their own appalling unworthiness but his abundant faithfulness.

---

[39] Is. 10:5.   [40] Je. 25:9; 27:6; 43:10.   [41] Je. 32:24.   [42] Is. 41:2–4, 25; 45:1–6.

What mattered most, though, was that they emerged from this experience of prayer with an enlarged vision of God. We too need the same expansiveness of thought as we consider all that the Lord has said to us and done for us. We are sometimes content with narrow and restricted concepts of God. A bigger vision of the Lord's great ness and sufficiency will affect us in three main ways.

First, it challenges our irreverence. In their periods of prosperity, the Israelite people began to take God for granted and foolishly imagined that they could live as they liked. They had adopted morally selfish and spiritually careless lifestyles, casually dismissing the covenant obligations they had accepted as his believing children and submissive servants. We too can become flippant about spiritual issues and indifferent or apathetic about the things that matter most of all. If that happens, it is because we have become content with a severely limited doctrine and experience of God. As these people prayed, they became increasingly convinced of God's holiness and righteousness. Many of their neighbours in surrounding nations had gods they could buy off or placate with the odd sacrifice here and there, but no such offers were open to the Israelites. If God is holy, then they must be holy too. They must never return to the outrageous idea that they could sin as much as they liked without it affecting their relationship with him. Similarly, we too must be holy.

A bigger vision of him also banishes our despondency. These Israelite worshippers became increasingly aware of their sins and those of their forefathers. Their sense of failure was crippling and demoralizing. They had lost endless opportunities to demonstrate their love, holiness and commitment. Could they ever trust themselves with the idea of a new beginning? The portrait of God which emerges from this chapter is that of a merciful and forgiving God. He will certainly accept them if they come in genuine penitence and cast themselves upon him for the strength to conquer sin in the future. He will accept us too.

Thirdly, a bigger vision of God overcomes our inadequacy. What if new temptations arise, as they most certainly will? Can the Israelites be sure they will be given the moral strength to conquer insidious allurements or vicious onslaughts, and rise to new heights of love and loyalty? The vision of God in this prayer reminds them that God can change and transform the most impossible situations. He delights in taking weak and vulnerable people and providing them with all the necessary resources for living. Abraham and Moses are the only two Israelites who are singled out by name in the prayer, but their experience was not unique in the lives of isolated individuals. They witness to a God of invincible power and unlimited resources, who can take unlikely people and make them into strong and effective instruments of his sovereign purposes. What he did for them he would do not only for their Israelite successors but for all who belong to Christ. All Christian believers are 'Abraham's seed' and inheritors of these unfailing promises[43] of total sufficiency and unlimited grace.

These believers in Nehemiah's time sought that kind of confidence as they entered the future. Because they and their forefathers had shamelessly and repeatedly broken their side of the covenant agreement with God, now was the time publicly to affirm their promises of love and loyalty. It was the moment not only for penitent prayer but for a renewed commitment.

[43] Gal. 3:29.

Nehemiah 9:38 – 10:39
12. 'Making a binding agreement'

At the conclusion of their prayer, the people made a renewed sur-render to the God of the covenant.[1] Those who belong to him must behave as he demands, and the time had come to affirm their loyalty in the presence of their families, friends and neighbours. Their com-mitment to God took the form of a series of written promises: *In view of all this, we are making a binding agreement, putting it in writing, and our leaders, our Levites and our priests are affixing their seals to it* (9:38).

This passage invites us to consider four aspects of Nehemiah's covenant.

1. The importance of the covenant

Covenants are important from a biblical, historical and con-temporary perspective.

First, written agreements of this kind have figured prominently in biblical history. God made different covenants with Noah and Abraham, and later initiated an agreement with his people through Moses, committing himself to them as their unique God.[2] They in turn were to demonstrate their response to him by obeying his law. We have already seen that, although the Lord was utterly faithful to his people, the Israelites frequently broke their part of the agree-ment. At specific times in their history they realized with sorrow how serious that disloyalty had been, and leaders such as Joshua and kings like Hezekiah and Josiah framed their people's renewed com-mitment in written covenants.[3] The narratives describing these covenant renewal ceremonies in Judah were recorded by the gifted

---

[1] Some scholars, *e.g.* Williamson, believe that historically this covenant follows Nehemiah's reformation in chapter 13.

[2] Gn. 6:18; 9:8–17; 15:18; 17:1–22; Ex. 19:5; 24:1–8.

[3] Jos. 24:25–27; 2 Ch. 29:10; 34:29–32.

author of the books of Chronicles, probably during the exile or soon after, and such stories must have been well known by believers like Nehemiah who treasured the history of their people. When they added their names to this covenant, they were doing something which was in line with the best traditions of their forefathers.

Secondly, covenants have also been important in Christian history. Following the precedent of biblical covenants, a number of sixteenth-century congregations prepared written accounts of their corporate commitment to the Lord and to one another. Some of the English Puritans recorded their personal promises of love and loyalty to the Lord. Joseph Alleine's covenant, publicized by his brother, Richard, became a model for other Christians to copy. Later, men like Jonathan Edwards, David Brainerd and John Wesley framed their personal commitment to the Lord in the form of written promises as they surrendered their lives wholly to him. Some seventeenth- and eighteenth-century Nonconformist commitments took the form of corporate covenants as local church members pledged themselves to honour God in specific ways and appended their names to such promises. Wesley compiled a New Year Covenant Service for the Methodist people, which continues to be an important feature in the spiritual life of their churches.

Thirdly, many of our contemporaries have also found it helpful to draw up covenants in order to give expression to their commitment to Christ concerning precise issues. The Lausanne Covenant is a recent example of corporate commitment to evangelism and social action on the part of evangelical leaders from all over the world. The value of a covenant is that it saves our laudable desires from hovering in a pious void. Instead, we make firm decisions in God's presence to do his will over particular contemporary issues.

Many present-day Christians have also found it personally helpful to draw up a covenant with the Lord, identifying certain areas in their lives where it is helpful to make a definite commitment to Christ about such matters as their daily communion with him, their lifestyle, priorities, relationships, possessions, witness and church work. Sometimes when we hear a challenging sermon we want to be better Christians, but fail to make a definite response to God's Word through the preacher. We ought to take time to channel our desires into practical decisions, putting them in writing and, like the 'man with a very stout countenance' in part one of *Pilgrim's Progress*, say, 'Set down my name, Sir'.

2. The structure of the covenant

A study of covenants in the ancient near-east has shown that these agreements followed a common literary structure and, with a history which predated Moses, such treaties are likely to have influenced the compilation of covenants in Israel. Political covenants of this kind were frequently drawn up between a stronger (suzerain) power and a weaker (vassal) nation. They usually began by outlining the historical relationship between the two parties in the agreement, paying special attention to the generosity of the suzerain. Then followed the covenant's basic stipulations, before a description of the specific and practical ways in which this more general commitment is to be applied. It often went on to require that a copy of the written agreement be deposited in the temple of the god and that the covenant's terms be declared publicly on given occasions. Those who signed went on to agree to blessings and cursings which would follow the keeping or breaking of the covenant, and the covenant concluded with a brief recapitulation of its terms.

It is clear that, whether influenced by this treaty pattern or not, this literary structure is found in Nehemiah 9 – 10. The extensive prayer in chapter 9 eloquently describes the relationship between the Lord and his people and appropriately emphasizes the generosity of God. The basic stipulation of this Nehemiah covenant is that his people promise to obey God's Word. They publicly agree to *follow the Law of God given through Moses the servant of God and to obey carefully all the commands, regulations and decrees of the LORD our Lord* (10:29). This general statement is followed by a series of specific ways in which this commitment to God's law is to be applied[4] in various aspects of their lives: domestic (mixed marriages), commercial (Sabbath trading), agricultural (seventh-year laws), social (cancellation of debts), religious (support of God's house) and economic (regular contributions). Finally, Nehemiah's covenant concluded with an appropriate recapitulation: *We will not neglect the house of our God* (10:39).

3. The relevance of the covenant

However, the terms of this covenant in Nehemiah 10 may seem largely irrelevant to life in our world today. It pertains to a small country in the middle east under Persian domination and its determined separation from the religious ideas and practices of its neighbours. It concerns the life of mainly rural communities, their farms and fields, land laws, the observance of holy days, financial support for their temple, the maintenance of its staff and how such

---

[4] For a stimulating discussion of how the Mosaic law was interpreted and applied in this covenant, see D. J. Clines, 'Nehemiah 10 as an Example of Early Jewish Biblical Exegesis', in *Journal for the Study of the Old Testament* 21 (1981), pp. 111–117.

171

contributions were to be made. It appears alien to life in an increasingly mobile, highly technological, largely urban society as it enters a new millennium. Yet, when we look more carefully at the distinctive features of this covenant, we begin to realize that its topics do not belong exclusively to the fifth century BC. Its themes are prominent in our world: they relate to crucial contemporary issues such as the authority of Scripture, Christian witness in a pluralistic society, the sanctity and stability of marriage, employment conditions, human and animal rights, conservation, 'green' issues and money management. Here is teaching for our century as much as for theirs.

This does not mean that as Christians we are mechanically to adopt every aspect of this teaching. If we do that, we shall find it necessary to arrange for public worship on Saturdays and, if we are farmers, ensure that our fields are left fallow every seven years. Plainly, some of the items in this covenant cannot directly relate to us. There is no temple to be supported in Jerusalem, and the sacrificial system is no longer in operation. How then can these stipulations apply to us in the modern world? We have been given a whole Bible – Old and New Testaments – and these passages must have something to say to us. We readily appreciate that we have things to learn from Nehemiah's character and personal example as a man of God, but how can we rightly interpret Nehemiah's covenant and related passages?

Christopher J. H. Wright suggests that Old Testament ethical teaching of this kind provides the Christian reader with a helpful paradigm, 'a model or example for other cases where a basic principle remains unchanged, though details may differ'. All of us who have had to learn other languages are familiar with paradigms, perhaps a verb-pattern which demonstrates how the endings or suffixes will appear for similar verbs. Wright illustrates this use of a paradigm model by relating it to the life, teaching and ministry of Jesus. When we are called to 'follow' Christ that is not meant to be interpreted literally, otherwise we would all have to become carpenters, wear first-century clothing, enlist a dozen helpers, attend synagogue worship and travel throughout modern Israel. The example of Jesus is important but, when he used the concept of 'following', Christ was not encouraging slavish repetition, even for his contemporaries. Most of them would not become homeless itinerants but they would be his devoted followers. What it means surely is that we 'move from what we know Jesus *did* do to what we might reasonably presume he *would* do in our changed situation. The overall shape and character of his life ... becomes our pattern or paradigm, by which we test the "Christ-likeness" of the same components of our own lives.'[5]

With this as our model, the account of Nehemiah's covenant has important things to say to us as we look beneath the Israelite legislation to *why* these people were committed to act in these particular ways. The principles behind this teaching are as vital for us as for them. How we apply the teaching will be different in our lives from what it was in theirs, but our application will be as meaningful, practical and relevant as theirs was intended to be.

Moreover, as an exercise in commitment, Nehemiah's covenant has much to say to us in contemporary society. Many of our contemporaries find commitment exceptionally difficult. They prefer not to be tied to firm allegiances. The main political parties lament that even people who agree with their policies are reluctant to join, for fear that 'belonging' may mean that more may be expected of them than they are prepared to give. Cohabitation has increased annually in British society over the past thirty years.[6] Couples are unwilling to commit themselves to a marriage relationship; they want to be free to experiment and to break it off if they become disillusioned with the other partner. Churches discover that although Christians are pleased to attend worship, even on a regular basis, they are not so willing to join the membership of a particular congregation, preferring to drift from one church to another as the mood takes them. Whilst missionary societies are glad that candidates are offering for service, they note that it is often for periods of short-term work, rather than to the lifelong commitment characteristic of an earlier generation. Unreserved commitment, both costly and sacrificial, is decidedly unpopular in our day.

4. The nature of the covenant

The covenant made by Nehemiah and his contemporaries opened with a vow of total allegiance to what the Lord had said to them *through Moses the servant of God* (29). The initial promise to obey God's Word was of a general and introductory nature: they promised to *follow the Law of God ... and to obey carefully all the commands, regulations, and decrees of the LORD our Lord*.

This was, first of all, a personal commitment. The names of Nehemiah and fifty-seven other leaders (10:1–27) were appended to a written document. Some are clearly patronymic, ancestral or family

---

[5] Christopher J. H. Wright, *Living as the People of God* (Leicester: IVP, 1983), pp. 40–45.

[6] John Haskey, 'Trends in Marriage and Cohabitation: the decline in marriage and the changing patterns of living in partnerships', in *Population Trends* 80 (HMSO), pp. 5–15.

names, rather than personal names: for example, 10:1–8 lists several priests who returned much earlier with Zerubbabel (12:1–7). To this agreement they fixed their seals in token of their promise to abide by its conditions; they signed not only on their own behalf but as priests, Levites and leaders who were representatives of the people. It was not a vague statement, formally assented to by a vast and nameless crowd, but one which was signed by responsible people who, before they added their names and personal seals, had ensured that those they represented shared their determination to please God by honouring and obeying his Word. Moreover, every individual Israelite was personally involved, not just the signatories to the covenant. The *rest of the people* (28) were fully identified with their leaders, and their number appears to have included some who had come to faith from a pagan background. Citing a similar commitment by 'proselytes' at Ezra's passover,[7] Clines maintains that those *who separated themselves from the neighbouring peoples for the sake of the Law of God* is 'not a way of describing the people as a whole', but refers to those who, accepting 'the full obligation of the law', had 'joined themselves to Israel'.[8] All these, established believers and recent converts, *together with their wives and all their sons and daughters who are able to understand – all these now join their brothers the nobles, and bind themselves with a curse and an oath to follow the Law of God* (10:28–29).

Secondly, this was a public commitment. It was affirmed and recorded in the presence of many witnesses; the people who had prayed publicly now made their promises public as well. Though personal it was not individualistic, as if it were a matter which merely concerned the solitary believer. The issues affected society in general, and everyone was testifying openly to their neighbours that they had presented themselves afresh to God. Commitment of that kind is an important part of effective Christian testimony. Baptism provided the early Christians with a form of witness which publicly declared to their neighbours their resolute loyalty to Christ.[9]

Thirdly, it was practical. The people did not merely assent to a series of generalized statements in carefully chosen words. They committed themselves to specific actions which would characterize their lives and authenticate their witness. The agreement would radically change their lifestyle and affect every aspect of their daily conduct. Being a Christian is something more than giving our intellectual assent to a series of doctrinal propositions. It means committing ourselves to the way of life which Christ has determined and exemplified for us. In biblical teaching, doctrine and deeds are inseparable; belief affects behaviour.

[7] Ezr. 6:21.   [8] Clines, p. 205.   [9] Acts 2:41; 8:36–38; 9:18; 10:47–48; 16:15, 33.

In Christian life and witness so much is lost because we are indefinite. The devil is not worried by our pious aspirations. He is troubled when, in obedience to God, for the glory of Christ and in the power of the Spirit, we make firm practical decisions to *do specific things for the Lord.*

The Israelites' initial promise in Nehemiah's covenant to obey God's Word was the general stipulation. It was followed by five promises of how that obedience was to be worked out in precise issues of personal, family and community life. We shall turn to these in our next chapter.

Nehemiah 10:30–39
13. Being specific

After their pledge of loyalty to God's Word, Nehemiah and his contemporaries make a public commitment about five precise issues in their daily life. The implications of their promise to the Lord were costly.

1. Pursue his will (10:30)

God's will for his people was that they might maintain an uncompromised testimony across the centuries and share his unique message with other nations. That would only be possible if they steered clear of syncretistic worship. The form in which that danger was most likely to mar their message was through life's most intimate relationship, marriage. Those who agreed to this covenant *separated themselves from the neighbouring peoples for the sake of the Law of God* (28). When they began to spell out the covenant's practical implications, they started by making this vow: *We promise not to give our daughters in marriage to the peoples around us or take their daughters for our sons* (30). It is important to bear several things in mind when we read this pledge, lest we are tempted to regard it as distasteful ethnic superiority which modern Christians strenuously resist.

Israel's problem was that by wrong relationships their distinctive witness would be nullified. God's destiny for them was that they might be a missionary people,[1] so it was vital that their message was not corrupted. In a culture where they were ceaselessly exposed to neighbouring religions, other gods came to have a fascinating attraction for them. The notorious golden-calf incident was neither the first nor the last time that they had bowed down to

---

[1] Is. 42:4, 6; 45:20–24; 49:6; 55:4; 56:6; Lk. 2:32; Acts 13:47; see H. H. Rowley, *Biblical Doctrine of Election* (Guildford: Lutterworth, 1950).

idols.[2] It is against this background that we must understand the prohibition about mixed marriages. At this point in the history of God's people, it was crucial that their witness to God's truth should remain pure and unadulterated. There were scriptural, historical, moral and contemporary reasons why marriages with pagan people were disastrous.

First, there were clear biblical warnings about the danger of corrupting their faith through an unsuitable marriage. When two people in the ancient world made a marriage agreement, they normally confirmed their commitment in the presence of their gods and gave each other's idols a prominent place in their new home. For Israel's neighbours such syncretism was perfectly permissible; the more gods the better. But the Lord's people had entered into a covenant which began by affirming God's uniqueness. They had vowed not to recognize, let alone worship, other gods.[3] Joshua warned his contemporaries that if they intermarried with people from idolatrous nations, their partners would become 'snares and traps' to them, whips on their backs and thorns in their eyes.[4] The fact that some of Nehemiah's contemporaries had married people from other religions was further evidence of their studied indifference to God's Word. If they were to commit themselves unreservedly to obey his Law, the first thing was to acknowledge their sin in disregarding God's warnings about marriage.

Secondly, there was abundant historical evidence that forbidden marriage alliances of that kind had been disastrous in Israel's spiritual and moral life. Surely they could learn from the past. In another context (13:26), Nehemiah refers to the notorious instance of Solomon's apostasy, his marriage to women from other nations who set up shrines to their gods in Jerusalem, and its disastrous effect on the spiritual and political life of God's people. Their idolatry through Solomon's wives led directly to the division of the kingdom into north and south, Israel and Judah. Later in Israel's history, Ahab's marriage to the Sidonian queen Jezebel led to the widespread promotion of Baal worship in the northern kingdom, with disastrous moral consequences as well as the murder of the Lord's servants, the prophets.[5]

Thirdly, there were moral reasons why the Israelite people were forbidden to marry partners from other nations. It had been made clear to them that the Lord regarded these gods as 'detestable'. The

[2] Gn. 35:1–4; Jos. 23:7, 16; 24:14–15, 23; Jdg. 2:1–3, 11, 17, 19; 3:5–7; 5:8; 6:10, 25–34; 8:33; 10:6, 10, 13–16; 18:14–24; 1 Sa. 7:3–4; 8:8; 19:13; 12:10; 26:19; 1 Ki. 9:6, 9; 11:4–6, 10; 12:25–33; 14:9; 16:25–33; 2 Ki. 17:7–41; 22:17; 23:24; Je. 7:18; 9:14; 14:14; 44:15–25; Ho. 2:13, 17; 11:2.   [3] Ex. 20:1–5.
[4] Jos. 23:12–13, cf. Gn. 28:1; Ex. 34:16; Dt. 7:3.
[5] 1 Ki. 11:1–13; 16:29–33; 18:4, 13, 22; 19:10.

worship of these 'foreign gods' involved their worshippers in rituals and ceremonies which the Lord regarded as 'detestable' practices.[6] These often included cult prostitution and other sexual obscenities. God's revelation to his people made it clear that they were to be like him. He is holy, so they must be holy. He is compassionate, so they must be also. He is righteous, so they must live in a way which reflects his righteousness.[7] A God of truth cannot tolerate worshippers who tell lies.[8] Those who honour a just and merciful God will not behave dishonestly and unkindly in the world.[9] It was unthinkable that people who had committed themselves to God should be involved in immoral religious practices.

Fourthly, Nehemiah and his colleagues were aware from the contemporary scene that it was disastrous for an Israelite believer to marry someone committed to the worship of other gods. In literature outside the Old Testament, we have a clear illustration of the continuing corruption of Israel's faith through the gradual infiltration of ideas and practices from other religions. The danger was not confined to the period before the exile. It was prevalent in Nehemiah's time also. In Egypt, close to Aswan, there is an island in the Nile where a military colony with Jewish residents lived in the 5th century BC. Aramaic papyri discovered on this island (once known by its Greek name, Elephantine) demonstrate that the worship of these colonists had been corrupted by the adoption of pagan religious ideas alongside their Israelite faith. The papyri mention Sanballat of Samaria, so there are clear historical affinities with Nehemiah's lifetime.[10] In other words, the corruption of Israel's faith was not simply an antiquated danger but a present reality. If it continued in Judah, the message entrusted to God's people would become corrupt and eventually indistinguishable from the wide variety of syncretistic religions of the period.

But Nehemiah did not have to go as far as Egypt to prove that Israel's distinctive message could be compromised. Nehemiah's older contemporary, Ezra, discovered that even priests in Judah had broken God's law by marrying women with other religious allegiances, so leading the way in 'unfaithfulness' to the covenant.[11] A later passage in Nehemiah (13:23–24) vividly portrays many homes in Judah where married partners had introduced religious ideas and practices from other countries and had taught their children the

---

[6] 1 Ki. 11:5, 7; 14:24; Ezr. 9:1. The Ammonite religious ritual included child sacrifice (Lv. 18:21; 2 Ki. 23:10, 13), as did that of the Moabites to their god Chemosh (2 Ki. 3:27).   [7] Lv. 11:45; 19:1; Dt. 24:17–22; Ezr. 9:15; Is. 45:25; Je. 12:1.
[8] Ex. 20:16; Lv. 19:12.   [9] Lv. 19:13–18.
[10] For the Elephantine texts, see A. Cowley, *Aramaic Papyri of the Fifth Century*, document 30, and B. Porten, *Archives from Elephantine: The Life of an Ancient Jewish Military Colony*.   [11] Ezra 9:1–2.

languages of Ashdod, Ammon and Moab rather than the Hebrew of their fathers. These children were growing up in an environment where they could not understand God's Word, because the language in which it was written and spoken was not known to them, even though they lived in Judah.

In declaring this prohibition, the Lord was concerned about both the purity of their faith and the holiness of their lives. It was not ethnic differences which were at issue but spiritual loyalty, ethical purity and doctrinal integrity. The law about mixed marriages was essential to Israel's missionary vocation. It was not about crude nationalism or ethnic exclusivism. After all, members of other races were free to embrace Israel's faith if they abandoned their own and gave themselves wholly to the Lord. People of other religions were free to join the Israelites when they left Egypt as God's redeemed people, provided they fully embraced Israel's faith. Ruth the Moabite is a later example of someone from another faith who turned to the Lord and was fully welcomed into the life of God's people. But once she said 'Your God shall be my God', she did not continue to worship 'Chemosh, the detestable god of Moab'. Jeremiah's Ethiopian friend Ebed-Melech obviously came from a pagan background with a name like that. Molech was 'the detestable god of the Ammonites', and to be named 'servant of Molech' indicates that he did not have Israelite ancestry, but he had put his trust in the only true God.[12]

Israel had been entrusted with the most wonderful message in the world and nothing was to be allowed to corrupt it. The truth had to be faithfully preserved and not contaminated by alien and contradictory religious ideas. It was to be handed on from generation to generation, until a few hundred years after Nehemiah its great truths were passed on to a devout Israelite couple who lived in Nazareth. They too would teach it to the unique child who was born, miraculously, into their home, Jesus the Son of God. He was to love, share, fulfil and expand that message so that, without adulteration, it might be taken to the ends of the earth and to the end of time. That is why these seemingly rigorous laws did not allow committed members of the covenant to mar their message and invalidate their witness by marrying outside their faith.

In daily life we are more influenced by other people than most of us care to admit. The early church's leaders knew that. The Corinthians lived in a grossly immoral environment, and Paul reminded them of an old saying of their poet Menander, 'Bad company corrupts good character.' That would mean that certain relationships, known to damage their faith, were best abandoned, and as soon as possible. He recalls words from Isaiah, 'Therefore

[12] Ex. 12:38, 48–49; Ru. 1:16; 2:12; 1 Ki. 11:7; Je. 38:7–13; 39:15–18.

come out from them and be separate.' John urged his Christian friends not to love the world or anything in it which might destroy their distinctive witness. James put the issue more starkly than any when he insisted that 'friendship with the world is hatred towards God.' Peter told his churches that believers need to live in this world as 'aliens and strangers' destined for eternity, God's servants, not the world's slaves.[13]

We are not to cut ourselves off from our contemporaries in order to preserve our faith. We live among people because God has made us as social beings; we need each other. A person who craves for total isolation is psychologically unwell. But, more significantly for Christians, we are glad to be among people in everyday life because we want to know, love, serve and win them. We must live in the world but the world must not live in us. It is a delicate balance. With his fine sense of humour, Luther put it beautifully: 'Temptations of course cannot be avoided, but because we cannot prevent the birds from flying over our heads, there is no need that we should let them nest in our hair'.[14]

Before we leave this covenant's prohibition about mixed marriages, it is important to relate its message to two crucial modern issues: Christian marriage and contemporary religious pluralism.

In Western society, the institution of marriage is seriously under threat. Cohabitation is on the increase and, as divorce figures escalate with every passing decade, large numbers of our contemporaries seriously question the need for marriage. Christians are now presented with an unprecedented opportunity to witness to the uniqueness, enrichment, security and permanence of heterosexual marriage as instituted by God and confirmed by Christ. Israel's sensitivity to the religious dangers inherent in marriage to a person who did not share the Israelite faith is echoed in the New Testament. Scripture places a similar obligation on Christians not to 'be yoked together with unbelievers'. Paul taught the Corinthians that, if a committed Christian 'unites himself with the Lord', then marriage to an unbeliever is an act of disloyalty to Christ as well as disobedience to God's Word.[15] If Christians marry partners who do not share their personal commitment to Christ, the road ahead is likely to be fraught with tension, frustration and unhappiness. However tolerant the unbelieving partner may be, occasions are bound to arise when love and loyalty are certain to be tested. If love for Christ is not a shared experience in marriage, no believer can be as happy as God desires.

In a pluralistic environment this teaching about the danger of mixed marriages in Israel recalls the biblical teaching about the

[13] 1 Cor. 15:33; 2 Cor 6:14, 17; 1 Jn. 2:16; Jas. 4:4–5; 1 Pet. 1:17; 2:11, 16.
[14] Quoted in Roland Bainton, *Here I Stand* (New York: Mentor, 1950), p. 176.
[15] Gn. 2:24; Mt. 19:4–6; 2 Cor. 6:14; 1 Cor. 6:17.

uniqueness of the Christian gospel. God's Son entered this world as its only Saviour, knowing that there was no other way by which men and women could receive eternal life. We have an obligation to understand the message of other religions and not caricature what their adherents are saying about their own faith. In a society properly concerned about human rights, we must value people's freedom to believe, and befriend and love them as people for whom Christ died. There may be helpful social and community projects which Christians can usefully share with people of other faiths or no faith, but the distinctive message of the Christian faith must not be compromised by allegiances or events (like Inter-Faith services) which suggest that all religions are equally valuable and basically heading in the same direction. The claim of Jesus that no-one comes to the Father but by him[16] is a crucial testimony in a culture which is offended by the distinctive message of the Christian gospel. In such a compromising context, the unique claims of Christ must be lovingly and unequivocally affirmed.

2. Honour his day (10:31a)

The covenant was further renewed with another promise: *When the neighbouring peoples bring merchandise or grain to sell on the Sabbath, we will not buy from them on the Sabbath or on any holy day.* In Nehemiah's time, it was necessary for Israel's law about the Sabbath to be clearly understood, publicly affirmed and frequently applied.

The Sabbath law must be *clearly understood.* The people had to appreciate afresh why keeping that day 'holy' was such an important component in their personal and corporate life. The weekly Sabbath had been given so that they might honour God, enjoy rest, help others and declare truth.

It was instituted, first, as a day to honour God: 'the seventh day is a Sabbath to the LORD your God'. It was set apart from other days and given to God so that they might offer their worship to him, undisturbed by the inevitable distractions of everyday life. Secondly, it was a day to enjoy rest. Leisure and relaxation is a vital ingredient in effective living, and God set a pattern for them by resting after his unique work in creation: 'he rested on the seventh day'.[17] The Lord knew that during their Egyptian slavery they worked day after day without a break, and such cruel and prolonged experience must never be repeated in Israelite life. Thirdly, it was a day to help others. It was not only the Israelite householder and his family who were to

[16] Jn. 14:6.   [17] Ex. 20:8–11.

181

enjoy this rest but also their servants, animals, neighbours and visitors, 'the alien within your gates'. Servants were not to be degraded by ceaseless work, and their Sabbath law ensured that, however mean their employers might be, Israelite employees had a compulsory rest day automatically written into their employment contracts.

God was also concerned about animal welfare as well as human rights. Their donkeys, horses and cattle enjoyed the Sabbath as well. Moreover, every stranger or refugee visiting their locality must also be physically refreshed by the Sabbath rest. The detailed Sabbath legislation ensured that the Israelites did not enjoy the Sabbath at other people's expense. When the commandments were repeated by Moses before God's people entered the promised land, the Sabbath law reminded them of Egypt's tyranny. Such heartless cruelty must be a thing of the past: 'Remember that you were slaves in Egypt and that the LORD your God brought you out of there with a mighty hand and an outstretched arm'.[18]

Fourthly, the Sabbath was a day to declare truth. The day was a silent witness to God's supremacy. Sabbath was a magnificent witnessing opportunity. Once God's people found themselves in their own land they would naturally have business contacts with people from other nations, cultures, customs and religions. However well an Israelite's business was prospering, on one day of the week he was required to close his shop or cease work on his farm. The Lord gave them that one day when all their neighbours could know without any doubt that they had an allegiance to God which far transcended their business interests, domestic concerns or social obligations. To their unbelieving neighbours it proclaimed, in intensely practical terms, the truth that God comes first. He had told them to make that day special and what he said must be done.

The Sabbath law must be *publicly affirmed*. However familiar God's people were with this law, once they settled in the land they would always be confronted with the temptation to neglect the Sabbath. In Babylon, when they were living in an alien culture, it may have required considerable moral resolve to withdraw from business and social life on the seventh day. When they kept the day special, Sabbath marked them out as people different from others and on occasions even made them the butt of local ridicule. Each succeeding generation had to be reminded of this fourfold purpose of the Sabbath, and Nehemiah's covenant renewal provided them with a public opportunity to declare to others their obedience to God in this personal, practical and public regulation.

The Sabbath law must be *frequently applied*. Several centuries had

[18] Dt. 5:12–15.

passed since the original promulgation of the law at Sinai. The wilderness pilgrims were a nomadic people, and their commercial transactions of a simple and basic kind were conducted largely within their own community. In those days there would have been no question of buying from a fellow Israelite on the Sabbath, as most were eager to maintain the holiness of the day. But, once they had settled in Canaan, life was different, and throughout their history it was necessary to apply the Sabbath law afresh to each generation, bearing in mind new cultural situations in which they found themselves. The prophets sometimes had occasion to act as exponents and interpreters of the fourth commandment, bringing a ministry of outspoken correction, necessary encouragement and serious warning, as well as a reminder of what it was intended to be.

In the eight century BC, Amos's teaching about the Sabbath was a sharp rebuke. He exposed the materialistic and unjust traders of the northern kingdom, who exploited the poor and were irritated that their corrupt business practices could not take place every day of the week: 'When will ... the Sabbath be ended that we may sell wheat?'[19] Such greedy people had no regard for God's Word and no compassion for his deprived children.

Isaiah's Sabbath teaching was a rich encouragement. He insisted that, far from being inhibiting, the keeping of Sabbath was a 'blessed', God-pleasing and joyous experience, a sheer 'delight' for people intent on honouring God.[20] In the next century Jeremiah's teaching was a serious warning. He condemned those merchants who were carrying their goods into Jerusalem on the day appointed for worship and rest, and warned such disobedient citizens that their desecration of God's day would lead to the destruction of the city.[21]

During the exile, Ezekiel's teaching was a necessary challenge. He reminded his contemporaries in Babylon of Moses' teaching that the Lord had instituted the Sabbath 'as a sign between us, so they would know that I the LORD made them holy'. Ezekiel said that for centuries, even during the wilderness wanderings, God's people had disregarded his teaching about the priority, value and witness of their special day.[22] There in Babylon they had an opportunity in a pagan environment to demonstrate on that one day in each week that God came first in their lives.

Now that God's people were back in Jerusalem and on the other side of the exile experience, they had to be reminded afresh of the importance of the Sabbath in their personal and community life. It was still a unique 'sign' or badge to their neighbours of their obedience to God, care for themselves and compassion for others, their servants, animals and neighbours.

---

[19] Am. 8:5.   [20] Is. 56:2, 4, 6; 58:13–14.   [21] Je. 17:21–27.   [22] Ezk. 20:11–24.

Nehemiah's contemporaries were in a new situation and this naturally gave rise to fresh questions about the Sabbath. Though selling was not permissible on that day, some asked whether it was in order for them to purchase goods on the Sabbath from Gentile merchants in the city. Others wanted to know whether the rules about Sabbath trading were confined to the seventh day or to be applied to other holy days as well. With uncomplicated definiteness, this Nehemiah covenant applied the fourth commandment to life in contemporary Israel: goods were not to be bought on the Sabbath nor *on any holy day* in the year.

God's provision of this special day in each week is an important 'paradigm' or model for believers. From the days of the early church, Christians made the Lord's Day, the celebration of Christ's resurrection on the first day of the week, their appointed day for worship, service and rest. It is important for Christian believers to heed the obvious warnings in the New Testament about legalism and not to fall into that subtle trap in their commendable desire to keep the Lord's Day special. Christ's legalistic contemporaries complained that he 'worked' by performing healing miracles on the Sabbath. Jesus made it clear that such restrictive legalism was not God's will for his people. Such 'work' glorified God, testified to Christ's uniqueness as 'Lord even of the Sabbath' and brought incalculable joy to others.[23] Both Israel's Sabbath and the Christian Lord's Day were instituted for the believer's spiritual and physical benefit and not as a cumbersome and restrictive burden.

Sunday presents Christians with an ideal opportunity to honour God in public worship and witness. Additionally, it ought to provide opportunity for rest, relaxation, reading and prayer, as well as service for Christ. That might include doing things together as a family, or helping a broken family to have some experience of 'family' love, calling on some lonely person, visiting sick people at home or in hospital, offering hospitality in our homes, writing letters to missionaries and others. Setting the day apart for God ought to mean that its special character is maintained so that, on this day, the Lord is honoured, we are enriched and other people are helped. Although we cannot insist that our unbelieving contemporaries respect Sunday as God's special day we ought certainly to encourage our contemporaries to 'keep Sunday special'.

Those who emphasize the Sabbath as a creation ordinance are right in reminding us that 'all work and no rest' is a recipe for physical and family breakdown. G. A. F. Knight makes the point that neither the great world empires nor Israel's immediate neighbours 'ever thought of "stopping" work (as the word means literally) one day in

[23] Mk. 2:23 – 3:6.

seven so as to give ordinary people, the masses of humanity, a complete day of rest.' It was God's unique provision not only for his covenant people but, through them, for everyone, so that 'those same commonfolk might be taught to possess a God-centred theology'.[24]

3. Value his world (10:31b)

The people went on to promise: *Every seventh year we will forgo working the land.* Now that they were enjoying their new-found security in Jerusalem and Judah, it was a time to return to the covenant's decrees regarding property, especially their farms and fields. This provision was another aspect of *the Law of God given through Moses the servant of God* (29). It went back to the expansion of the fourth commandment's Sabbath law in Exodus 23:10–11 and Leviticus 25:1–7, 18–23. In complying with this regulation that their fields must not be sown in the seventh year, the Israelites were asserting four important things.

First, the Israelites were declaring God's ownership. Had the land been the personal possession of the farmer, he was free to do whatever he liked with it, but in unequivocal terms the law stated that every farmer was nothing other than a trusted tenant. The land belonged to the Lord: 'the land is mine and you are but aliens and my tenants'.[25] This Sabbath-year rule was a regular, visible reminder to Israel's so-called land-owners that the fields they tilled were not their own personal property. God had entrusted the land to them, and they were his accountable stewards. If he said his fields were to be left fallow, then they must be left fallow. It is a graphic reminder to us that everything we have and are comes from God. Paul told the Corinthian believers that their physical bodies were God's possession. He had given them life and it was to be used for his glory: 'You are not your own; you were bought at a price. Therefore honour God with your body.'[26] The apostle told his readers in Rome that those bodies must be surrendered entirely to God so that he might use them as vehicles of worship and service.[27]

Secondly, the Israelites were illustrating truth. God had devised this provision, and other similar ones, to impress upon his people the truth that proper care of the land is vital. As Jonathan Sacks points out, the three great commandments of periodic rest – Sabbath, the seventh year and Jubilee – were 'powerful forms of environmental education', impressing upon us that we are not to

---

[24] G. A. F. Knight, *Isaiah 56–66*, International Theological Commentary (Grand Rapids: Eerdmans, 1985), pp. 4–5.   [25] Lv. 25:23.   [26] 1 Cor. 6:19–20.
[27] Rom. 12:1–2.

pursue 'short-term gain at the cost of long-term desolation'.[28] The soil needs time to recover after six years' hard work. It was not only people and animals who were to have a regular period for rest; the land must also have a time to be restored, recover its natural nutriments and replenish its resources.

In our day, thousands of people all over the world are rightly concerned about questions of ecology and conservation. We need this timely reminder about 'green' issues in the Bible. The earth belongs to the Lord, and we are not to pollute the air, plunder forests, contaminate rivers, and act as though this world's resources can be ruthlessly exploited for our own private use.

Thirdly, the people's act of obedience expressed love. When the fields were left fallow for a year, a certain amount of produce would automatically re-seed, and in time the fields could yield a modest natural harvest. God's word demanded that in that year such produce belonged not to the tenant farmer but to deprived people in the local community: 'Then the poor among your people may get food from it, and the wild animals may eat what they leave. Do the same with your vineyard and your olive grove.'[29] There is nothing to suggest that, initially, this seventh-year land law was applied simultaneously throughout Israel. That possibly developed later, but at least in the earlier centuries the country's farmers would reach their seventh year at different times, so in any locality there was a likelihood that somewhere or other there would be fallow fields, olive groves and vineyards for the poor to collect a modest food supply.

Here again, a compassionate God is telling his children that they must be like him. He is God of the poor as well as the prosperous, and he cares passionately for the widow, fatherless, orphan and alien in Israel.[30] In our day, no Christian can be indifferent to the serious deprivation, hunger and homelessness in many Third World countries. We must offer something more than sympathy and prayer if we wish to honour the God who loves the needy.[31]

Fourthly, the Israelites were confessing their faith. When the farmer was confronted with the practical implications of this law, it was natural for him to question how he could live in any year when he was denied the normal cycle of seedtime and harvest: 'What will we eat in the seventh year if we do not plant or harvest our crops?' The seventh-year rule was a graphic teaching aid: obeying God means trusting him. God promised that he would send 'such a blessing in the sixth year that the land will yield enough for three years'.[32] There are times in all our lives when obedience to God involves us in a venture of faith. We cannot always see the way ahead

[28] Jonathan Sacks, *Faith in the Future* (London: Darton, Longman and Todd, 1995), p. 209.   [29] Ex. 23:10–11.   [30] Dt. 10:17–18; 24:17–22; 26:12–13; 27:19.   [31] Mt. 25:31–46; Jas. 1:27; 2:14–17; Jn. 3:17–18.   [32] Lv. 25:18–22.

with the clarity we would like but, if we are doing what he says, he will never disappoint us. Adequate resources will never be lacking.

4 Reflect his love (10:31c)

Israel's citizens also promised that, when that seventh year came round, they would *cancel all debts*. Here was another indication of the Lord's compassion. In his scale of values people matter more than things: the welfare of the debtor took precedence over the prosperity of the creditor. Nehemiah had already encountered economic and social problems due to serious poverty in the community, and he had taken active steps to put them right (5:1–19), but the plight of the poor continued. Debt in Israel was rarely due to careless mismanagement; it could normally be traced to unexpected family deprivation, such as the death or serious illness of the wage-earner, the collapse of a family business, or adverse physical conditions such as famine. In such dire circumstances, deprived people had to borrow money and, although lending with interest was not permitted among Israelites,[33] the burden of repayment was often crippling.

The cancellation of debts probably means the postponement during the sabbath year of any obligation to repay the debt, thus giving the debtor more time to earn money. It is possible, of course, that *cancel* here means the total removal of all obligation to repay at any time. Deuteronomy's warnings to the 'tight-fisted' lender,[34] reluctant to part with money as the seventh year was approaching, can certainly be read in that way. It may, on the other hand, simply be exposing the 'hard-hearted' lender, who did not want his money to be put on loan for a long period during which the debtor could take advantage of the seventh year's freedom from repayment.

What made debt such an agonizing burden in Israel was the incidence of economic slavery; people in desperate circumstances might be compelled to sell themselves or their children as slaves as a way of meeting their financial obligations.[35] This naturally had the most damaging effects on Israel's family life, always regarded as one of their nation's great strengths.

Debt is a crippling burden, whatever the generation, and millions of our contemporaries suffer because of it. Money-management is an important topic in our time, and Christians need to set a good example by ensuring that they do not adopt lifestyles which are beyond their predictable income level. Churches may take advantage of special courses available to help people who find it difficult to

---

[33] Ex. 22:25; Lv. 25:35–36; Dt. 23:19–20.   [34] Dt. 15:1–11.   [35] 2 Ki. 4:1.

manage on limited financial resources. Local or combined congregations often have within their membership gifted and experienced people who can hold seminars, give talks or offer personal advice to people who are finding it difficult to make ends meet. It would be a practical and compassionate expression of our interdependence as limbs in the body of Christ.

5. Support his work (10:32–39)

The closing pledge in the covenant-renewal is its longest. It concerns *the house of our God* – a phrase which appears in every verse throughout this concluding vow, apart from *the house of the LORD* in verse 35. The earlier promises have dealt with home and family, shops and markets, farms and fields, plenty and poverty, and the theme now turns from life in the city or countryside to the work of the temple, built about eighty years earlier under the inspiration of their leaders Jeshua and Zerubbabel, and the prophets Haggai and Zechariah. It was one thing to build it, but quite another to maintain it. When the Israelites rebuilt their temple in 516 BC they were, in accordance with Persian custom, given generous help for its construction and maintenance by King Darius,[36] but it is possible that in changed circumstances, Persian support for Judah's religious life was either curtailed or withdrawn. Jerusalem's temple stood at the heart of the country's religious, moral and political life. In symbolic terms it proclaimed the presence and power of God among his people and the centrality of spiritual things. In this covenant promise, the people were committing themselves to the worship and service of God and, in doing so, wished to declare openly their determination to honour him in every aspect of their lives.

The passage covers an impressive series of promises to support God's work in a variety of different ways, and suggests a number of insights into the importance of Christian giving.

1. The Israelites recognized the necessity of *responsible giving* (32, 35). In making the promise, they declare that they will *assume the responsibility for carrying out the commands to give . . . for the service* of God's house. It was a solemn obligation before God to do all that was required to support the temple's worship and maintain the priority of spiritual and moral values in the life of the nation.

2. The people responded to God's Word by *obedient giving*. It was not an impulse of sudden generosity, a passing emotional gesture out of profound relief that their city wall had been rebuilt. Their giving was an expression of practical obedience. Those who love him will do what he says. They were *carrying out the commands to*

---

[36] Ezr. 6:6–15.

give (32), *as it is written in the Law* (34, 36). It was yet another practical outworking of the covenant's initial promise to *obey carefully all the commands, regulations and decrees of the LORD our Lord* (29). God has been good to his people, and generosity was expected from them. Their public commitment to follow the Law of God given *through Moses* (29) would affect the amount of money in their purses. If they made the required annual payment towards the upkeep of the temple for the provision of its offerings, the arrangement of its festivals and *for all the duties of the house of our God* (33), it meant they would have that much money less for themselves. It was a further practical affirmation that God came first in their lives.

Their public agreement to give *a third of a shekel each year* (32) is an interesting adaptation of the law given to Moses concerning the upkeep of the tabernacle in the wilderness. When the Israelites left Egypt, every person over twenty years of age was to bring a larger sum, half a shekel of silver, as 'an offering to the LORD'. This 'atonement money', a one-off payment at the time of a census, was regarded as 'a ransom' for each life at the time the people were counted.[37]

3. The promise recognized the necessity of *obligatory giving*. There was nothing remotely optional about the support of God's work. Everyone was required to give in one form or another. Everybody would benefit from the ministry of the temple and everyone must support it. A work for all must not rely on the charity of a few. A great deal of magnificent Christian service, evangelistic, educational, medical and social, at home and overseas, depends on the generosity of a minority who are willing to make immense sacrifices that the work be maintained and continued. That was not God's plan for the support of his servants. The promise focuses on two vital aspects of the temple's ministry to God's people, to offer praise and to secure pardon.

All the people had cause to praise God for his generous gifts. He had been good to them and money was needed *for the regular grain offerings and burnt offerings; for the offerings on the Sabbaths, New Moon festivals and appointed feasts; for the holy offerings* (33). Sacrifices presented them with an opportunity to express in symbolic terms how much they loved God. They were also a means of supporting the priesthood, who regularly shared in the meals provided by the offerings. Moreover, such occasions were specific opportunities for bringing families and communities together; many of the offerings were times when the offerer as well as the priest shared the food in a communal meal. They were, additionally, times when deprived people from the community could be generously fed.

[37] Ex. 30:11-16.

189

Thanksgiving is a vital element in our spiritual life; there is always a gift to acknowledge.

Every person also had reason to seek God for his promised cleansing. Support was always necessary for the upkeep of the temple and its priesthood so that guilty people could present *sin offerings to make atonement for Israel* (33). They might rejoice in a wide variety of different gifts from God, but the greatest was his promise to forgive them when they sinned. The Levites would be supported by these gifts for God's house. They were the teachers and pastors in Israel, and from their rich store of scriptural knowledge they could reassure the people that God would wash their sins away, blot them out, sweep them away like a cloud, hurl them into the depths of the sea, put them behind his back, separate them from the offender as far as east is from west, and remember them against them no more.[38] But they stood in need of something more than a reassuring word. The sin offering convinced them visually that their transgressions were forgiven.[39] Christian believers have the assurance not only of God's unfailing promises to cleanse us, but also of the assurance that, in Christ's unique death on the cross, he offered himself in our place as a substitutionary sacrifice. If we acknowledge our iniquities, repent and seek his pardon, our cleansing is assured on the basis of what Christ has uniquely done and what God has clearly promised. Because every believer in Israel needed the ministry of the temple and its staff, everyone was required to support it.

4. The people also recognized the need for *systematic giving*. There was nothing remotely haphazard about it. Everything was carefully planned. *Each year* they were to bring their third of a silver shekel (32) for the upkeep of the temple and its worship. In addition, lots were cast to determine when each of their families was to bring to the temple, *at set times each year*, their *contribution of wood* to burn on the altar (34). *Each year* they would make an offering of *the firstfruits* of their crops and fruit trees (35). There was an orderliness about these offerings. People knew precisely what was expected of them and exactly how and when they were to make their offerings to the Lord.

5. The reference to the wood offering suggests that *proportionate giving* played some part in the people's contributions to the temple. In Israel's sacrificial system there was a clear recognition that not everybody could afford the same kind of offering; provision was always made for poor citizens to offer less than the wealthy. The cost of a young bull, male goat or lamb for a sin offering was totally beyond the ability of many, so they were able instead to offer two

[38] Ps. 51:2; Is. 43:25; 44:22; Mi. 7:19; Is. 38:17; Ps. 103:12; Je. 31:34.
[39] Lv. 4:1 – 5:13.

doves or young pigeons, and if they could not even afford that they were to bring 'an ephah of fine flour for a sin offering'.[40]

The wood offering may have given many poor people in Israel an opportunity to make a gift to the Lord which would demand time rather than money. Wood was a relatively scarce commodity in Israel. When the original temple was built, wood was imported from Lebanon. Before Nehemiah travelled to Jerusalem, he first asked King Artaxerxes for timber for the building of the city's gates, walls and his own house (2:8). A regular supply of wood was also necessary if the sacrifices were to be offered *on the altar of the LORD our God, as it is written in the Law* (34). The Mosaic law made no provision for a wood offering, so it is clear that the phrase *as it is written in the Law* refers to the command in Leviticus 6:12–13: 'The fire on the altar must be kept burning; it must not go out.'

Many of the poorer people in Israel who could not make expensive offerings were certainly able to collect wood and were pleased to do so, even though it would take them many hours to gather just a modest amount. We are not always in a position to give substantial amounts of money for the Lord's work, but one of the most precious commodities we can offer is our time. Time to pray, to meditate on God's Word, to listen to what he is saying to us, to think about what we might do for him, to distribute some Christian leaflets to people's homes, to listen sympathetically to other people's problems and difficulties, to visit or write to a lonely person, to do some practical act of kindness for a neighbour – all in the name of Christ. It is not the amount we give which is important; it is the spirit in which we make our offering and the element of costliness it entails – that is what counts. And for many people, time is their most costly commodity.

6. These citizens also knew that they were called to *sacrificial giving*. They were to bring to God's house *each year the firstfruits* of their crops *and of every fruit tree* (35). The firstfruits were the choicest by far. To offer the first was a vivid way of declaring three important things. First, that the Lord is the giver of all good things. Secondly, that everything belongs to him and, thirdly, that he is worthy of the best they can offer. The Mosaic law of the firstfruits said that God's people were to 'bring the best'[41] and that these choice offerings would be given to the priests.[42] Deuteronomy's account of the firstfruits is set within a formal presentation when a public confession of faith was recited at the altar by the giver.[43]

What is new about this covenant promise in Nehemiah is that the firstfruits *of every fruit tree* were also to be brought as offerings, as well as their crops and vegetables. Once again, we have another

---

[40] Lv. 5:11–13.   [41] Ex. 23:19; 34:26.   [42] Nu. 18:8–13.   [43] Dt. 26:1–11.

example of the way the law of Moses had to be re-interpreted and applied afresh to new circumstances within the life of God's people. The people are also to *bring the firstborn* of their *sons . . . cattle . . . herds and . . . flocks . . . to the priests ministering there* (36). The custom in Israel was that a 'redemption price' was paid to the priest on the birth of the first son and in respect of the firstborn of certain animals.[44] What is clear is that when the Lord had given so generously to them, it was hardly appropriate to withhold their gifts to him.

7. *Prescribed giving* is another feature in this account of the offerings presented by God's people. They are to bring not only *the first* of their *ground meal, new wine and oil* but also *a tithe* of their crops to the Lord. Giving a tenth of their produce or income to the Lord has a long and dignified history in the life of God's people,[45] and many Christians throughout the world regard it as an appropriate guide and a useful 'paradigm' for Christian giving.

8. Additionally, we have here an account of *comprehensive giving*. The *tithe* of the people's *crops* (37) was for the maintenance of the Levites, but those who were supported must themselves give a tenth of what they receive. The Lord's servants were not exempt from the Lord's command about giving: *The Levites are to bring a tenth of the tithes up to the house of our God, to the storerooms of the treasury* (38). There was not one set of rules for the people and another for the pastors and teachers. The Levites would benefit from the generous and regular giving of God's people, and they in turn were to help to maintain the priesthood. The Levites were to be a continuing example of total obedience to God's Word. The message was the same for the leaders as it was for the people.

9. Finally, here is an example of *organized giving*. The people were told not only how much was to be given but also who was responsible for the collection of the gifts. It was to be in the hands of the main beneficiaries, the Levites, but they were always to be accompanied by another responsible person, well honoured within the spiritual life of Israel: *A priest descended from Aaron is to accompany the Levites when they receive the tithes* (38). Financial matters ought always to be conducted in a manner which removes any possibility of suspicion or accusation regarding the misappropriation of funds. From this passage it is abundantly clear that such provisions are not peripheral or marginal, nor do they convey the hint that the person who handles the money cannot be trusted. Rather, they are important safeguards to protect an innocent person

---

[44] Nu. 18:12–19.
[45] Gn. 14:17–20; Lv. 27:30; Dt. 14:22–29; 26:12–15; Mal. 3:8–12; Mt. 23:23, note 'without neglecting the former'.

who might well be unjustly accused of improper use of the Lord's money.

To look back over the five promises made by these citizens is to be reminded of truths which are as vital for Christians as for these Israelite believers in the fifth century BC. These people were confessing God's sovereign control over every aspect of their lives, at home and at worship, on their farms, in trading and commerce, in their social contacts and spiritual obligations. Learning from this paradigm, Christian believers wholeheartedly confess that Jesus is Lord of their relationships (30), time (31a) and possessions (31b–39).

Nehemiah 11:1 – 12:26
14. Vocal archives

We have already noticed how Nehemiah's personal memoirs are supplemented at different points with written records from the archives of God's people. The book has five lists in all. At an appropriate point in the early narrative (3:1–32), the reader is provided with a description of the various sections of Jerusalem's wall and the names of those involved in the rebuilding operation. Later (7:1–73), Nehemiah shares his natural concern that the newly fortified city might have sufficient people living within it to guarantee its future development and protection. In the course of initiating a registration of families, he discovered a 'genealogical record', which he inserts into his narrative, a list of almost 50,000 exiles, the first to return to Judah in the previous century under the leadership of Zerubbabel and Jeshua. There is a third list (10:1–27) which names those people who committed themselves afresh to God's Word in the covenant-renewal event which followed the completion of the rebuilding project.

We have now reached a section in the book where we are given two further lists. Nehemiah returns to his plan to populate Jerusalem with sufficient citizens to ensure its developing economy and safety, and inserts a list of those people who went to live in the city (11:3–24) and of those whose homes were elsewhere in Judah (11:25–36). The fifth and last list (12:1–26) provides us with details of those priests and Levites who returned with the first exiles under Zerubbabel and Jeshua in 538 BC and their successors, including details of Jerusalem's hereditary high priests (10–11), updated by a later editor, to the time of Alexander the Great.

History was immensely important to God's people, but they were not fusty antiquarians, eager to collect information about their forebears simply for the sake of compiling family trees. These are reliable records and they certainly trace roots but they are something more. From these lists it is possible to discern some important spiritual principles in the mind of Nehemiah, his devout predecessors and contemporaries who collected, treasured and edited this material. We are not reading a dusty and irrelevant catalogue of names and families; these archives convey a series of far-reaching biblical truths.

1. The necessity of partnership

Jerusalem had to be repopulated if it was to develop a vigorous economic, social and spiritual life. With its broken fortifications and missing gates, the city had been neither an attractive nor a safe place to live, and most of the returned exiles felt happier and more secure in the smaller towns and villages. People from those more rural communities had gladly made themselves available for the rebuilding of the walls, but now the work was completed they soon returned to their own homes and families. Only a minority of Judah's total population lived within the city's walls, and Nehemiah knew that their weak numbers must be dramatically increased if the city was to enjoy a healthy commercial life. In order to repopulate the city he adopted the principle of the tithe, so that one person in ten was expected to move from their country homes to establish a new life within Jerusalem (1). These Israelites recognized that the city's community life could only be developed at great personal cost to themselves.

Most of the families living outside the city depended entirely on the land for their daily existence, and there was considerably greater opportunity for simple farming in the surrounding countryside. Over the years they had developed a normally adequate, if precarious, pattern of life, tilling, sowing and reaping in their fields, gathering their crops of wheat, barley, grapes and olives, growing vegetables for their own consumption and for market, and caring for a few sheep or cattle. Few of these people would choose to leave familiar communities where all of them had grown up since the first return of exiles a hundred years earlier. For most of them, the change of location would be a highly traumatic experience, moving from a largely rural to an urban community. It was a costly transition from the spacious, expansive countryside to a more confined and restricted pattern of life. It meant leaving their homes, wider family, neighbours, work, friends and familiar locations and setting up a new life in a radically different environment.

Many of our contemporaries can sympathize with them. Ours is a highly mobile society. In the UK alone, 27% of people plan to move within the next twelve months. A change of location for employment is an increasingly common aspect of modern life. Redundancy has compelled many people to seek work in other parts of the country, with the loss of the familiar and all the consequent disruption to homes, families, the education of children, loss of Christian support and fellowship from a church they may have known and loved since childhood or youth. When such unexpected or unsought changes occur, it is good to reflect on the neglected story of these newly settled citizens in Jerusalem, reminding ourselves of some of the things which may have been in their minds as they packed their simple belongings and made that trek towards the city with their children.

The first thing which strikes us about Nehemiah's unadorned account of this repopulation is the people's total subservience to God's will. In order to determine who was to make the sacrifice, the people *cast lots* to discern whether they were among the *one out of every ten* destined *to live in Jerusalem* (1). In their culture, the casting of lots was one means of discovering the divine will.[1] For centuries they had treasured the conviction of Israel's wise men that 'the lot is cast into the lap, but its every decision is from the LORD'.[2] About five thousand of these contemporaries of Nehemiah were prepared to subject themselves and their whole future to the unfolding of God's sovereign will for their lives. What they preferred was secondary to what God desired. Discovering God's mind about their future took priority over every other consideration. It is not always easy for us to discern the will of God, though he is more eager to reveal it than we are to discover it. Any one of us is capable of making wrong decisions in life, but Christian believers who genuinely seek God's will and have a single eye to his glory are less likely to make serious misjudgments about the big issues in life.

In our different culture we would not choose to discern his purpose by means of lots. We are enriched with greater spiritual privileges and resources than those which were at their disposal. Now, the Holy Spirit is the indwelling friend and guide of every Christian, and he will direct us if we are eager for his guidance as surely as he led Paul and his colleagues.[3] Sadly, there are times when we may want to pursue our own way, and we can be wilfully indifferent to what God's mind may be about our decision-making. However primitive the casting of lots may appear to be to us in our more sophisticated culture, one can hardly fail to admire the faith, love, sacrifice and heroism of people who were prepared to uproot themselves from familiar surroundings in Judah and sever established friendships because, by this means, they were persuaded that it was the will of God for them to do so. Their exemplary surrender and

---

[1] Lv. 16:8; Jos. 18:6–10; 1 Ch. 24:5, 31; 25:8; 26:13; Ne. 10:34; Jon. 1:7; Acts 1:26.
[2] Pr. 16:33.   [3] Acts 16:6–7; Rom. 8:14.

uncomplaining sacrificial response to God's will is one of the neglected dimensions of Nehemiah's story.

2. The primacy of holiness

Almost as if to complement this aspect of undoubted denial, another perspective is introduced into the narrative. We are told that these people who responded to Jerusalem's practical need went to live in *the holy city* (1). As a devout believer, Nehemiah was fascinated by the holy, that which has been 'set apart' for the Lord's use. He knew that the priests were holy people in that they worked exclusively for God.[4] He reminds us that the Sabbath is a holy day (9:14; 10:31; 13:22) and that other occasions in Israel's year have also been designated as 'holy' (10:31). The sacrifices offered in the temple are also holy (10:33), and his contemporary, Ezra the priest, rightly emphasizes that all God's people need to be holy.[5] Here we are twice told that the city itself has been set apart for the Lord's special use (1, 18). To live in Jerusalem and be given the opportunity to serve God in such a holy place would be regarded by these newly enlisted citizens as an immense privilege. That would serve to outweigh their natural sense of disappointment about leaving the familiar and stepping out into the unknown. To be associated with the holy was to be involved in a project specifically designed to glorify God; sharing in such an enterprise was an honour not to be missed.

But there is something more here. To live in *the holy city* might well be regarded as a high privilege but it was also a challenging responsibility. It is one thing to have a home in a holy city; it is quite another to make the home holy. Living in a holy context did not automatically transmit holiness to the individual citizen. Richard Baxter reminded his minister friends that 'a holy calling will not save an unholy man'.[6] Each life had to be made holy by giving everything over to God. William Law made this point when he encouraged his eighteenth-century contemporaries to live holy lives: 'As a good Christian should consider every place as holy, because God is there, so he should look upon every part of his life as a matter of holiness, because it is to be offered unto God.' Law maintained that

> ... all things are to be used and regarded as the things of God ... Things may and must differ in their use, but yet they are all to be used according to the will of God. Men may and must differ in

---

[4] Lv. 21:5–8.   [5] Ezr. 9:2.
[6] Richard Baxter, *The Reformed Pastor* (1656), ed. J. T. Wilkinson (London: Epworth, 1939), VI.vii, p. 163.

their employments, but they must all act for the same ends, as dutiful servants of God.

He rightly insisted that 'there is no other true devotion, but this of living devoted to God in the common business of our lives'.[7]

Seventy years before Nehemiah and his partners repaired the walls, two different men exercised a crucial prophetic ministry in Jerusalem. They urged their contemporaries to demonstrate their commitment to spiritual priorities by rebuilding the temple, but they also made it clear that holiness could not be achieved merely by external things. The temple was an excellent reminder of great spiritual realities, but they must not make the mistake of Jeremiah's contemporaries by imagining that a religious building guaranteed divine favour. Haggai stressed the point that holiness could not be conveyed by physical contact and, in the same period, Zechariah urged Jerusalem's citizens to anticipate the time when everything in Jerusalem would be holy, not just the temple. On that day, 'Holiness to the Lord' would be inscribed on the bells of the horses carrying tradesmen's wares and on every cooking pot in their houses, not just on the sacred vessels of God's house.[8] A *holy city* would be a contradiction in terms if inhabited by unholy people.

3. The privilege of service

The narrative contains an intriguing and enigmatic comment about the way people were recruited for the repopulation programme. We have already seen that lots were used to obtain many of those 'one in ten' people who were required, but it is also clear that, alongside those whose names were discerned through lots, there were others who freely offered themselves for this new work: *The people commended all the men who volunteered to live in Jerusalem* (2).

It is possible that, once the need was known, some people enlisted immediately as prospective citizens and that lots were cast to bring that list of volunteers to the required number, but, alternatively, the volunteers may have supplemented the people whose names had been revealed by lots. Perhaps some of the volunteers were men and women who offered to go in the place of their neighbours and friends, people whose circumstances were such that they were in a better position than others to respond to this fresh need. Whatever the nature of the volunteers, they are a reminder of that vast army of people who, with no compulsion other than the pressure of love, have willingly offered themselves to the work of the Lord.[9]

[7] William Law, *A Serious Call to a Devout and Holy Life* (London: Methuen, 1950), part IV, pp. 46–47, 59.   [8] Hg. 1:2–15; 2:10–14; Zc. 14:20–21.
[9] Jdg. 5:2, 9; 2 Cor. 8:5.

This description of the methods used to obtain Jerusalem's new citizens reminds us that, across the centuries, God's work has been undertaken by both conscripts and volunteers. There have been those who, deeply aware of their own limitations, never considered themselves remotely worthy of the Lord's service; they only accepted responsibility because of a deep sense of compulsion. They knew that they had been called by God and could not possibly refuse. Others became overwhelmed, not so much by their own human limitations as by the exciting challenge of the task. Evident opportunity dwarfed personal inadequacy. They realized that men and women were urgently needed for the work and offered themselves freely to be used as and where the Lord cared to call them.

Writing about ministry in the late sixth century, Gregory the Great made use of two great Old Testament accounts of a prophetic call as he sensitively contrasted Jeremiah the conscript with Isaiah the volunteer.[10] There is room for both in the Lord's work. Gregory makes the point that both men were motivated by love. Jeremiah's response is 'based on the love of God' and Isaiah's 'on love for the neighbour'. Isaiah 'desired the active life in the office of preaching, moved thereto by the wish to benefit his neighbours', but Jeremiah preferred to express his love for God in a life of quiet devotion, so naturally he 'remonstrated against being sent'. Jeremiah feared that by preaching 'he should forfeit the benefit of quiet contemplation', while Isaiah feared 'that by not preaching he might suffer harm for the lack of arduous work'.[11] Those who serve God, whether with the eagerness of Isaiah or the caution of Jeremiah, must do exactly what those two prophets did. Gladly or reluctantly there has to be a total surrender to God's sovereign purposes so that we are ready to do whatever he has in mind for us.

4. The variety of ministry

When we examine these two lists of Jerusalem and Judah's residents (11:4–36) and of Israel's priests and Levites (12:1–26), we find ourselves confronted with a wide range of gifts and abilities which these people brought to God's work.

There were people with fine leadership qualities. In addition to Jerusalem's *leaders* (1), Judah's *provincial leaders* (3) came to live alongside them in the city, setting a noble example to those of their contemporaries who would also be required to uproot themselves by leaving their homes to populate Jerusalem. Many qualities are

[10] Je. 1:4–8; Is. 6:8.
[11] Gregory the Great, *Pastoral Care* I.7, in *Ancient Christian Writers*, vol. 11, ed. Henry Davis (Westminster, Maryland: Newman Press, 1950), pp. 32–33.

required for effective leadership, but few can be more important than exemplary conduct.

It is not enough to tell people what they must do; the leader must become a visible model of obedience, holiness and love. For that reason leaders need to cultivate their own spiritual lives so that they do not contradict their message. Both Paul and Peter urged their first-century colleagues in ministry to take care of themselves so that they did not become a bad advertisement for the gospel.[12] Richard Baxter emphasized the importance of example: 'He that means as he speaks will surely do as he speaks.' Preachers are specially vulnerable; congregations have every right to an embodied sermon and not merely an eloquent one. Baxter warns his colleagues that their mission can easily be ruined. 'One proud, surly, lordly word, one needless contention, one covetous action may cut the throat of many a sermon and blast the fruit of all that you have been doing.'[13]

Furthermore, there are people in these lists with administrative skills. The newly populated city had its *chief officer* and an additional colleague who kept a watchful eye over *the Second District of the city* (9). These local government officers had to ensure that the city's streets and markets were kept clean, that proper sanitary arrangements were maintained and wise building regulations honoured – such important matters were not overlooked by the Mosaic law.[14] There was little point in having new walls to the city if old sins destroyed its life from within.

Other people were equipped with maintenance experience. Two of the heads of the Levites *had charge of the outside work of the house of God* (16). The temple had to be kept in good repair and these men were entrusted with overall responsibility for the care of the fabric. Churches and Christian organizations all over the world are grateful for the dedicated practical skills of men and women who care for their buildings, many of them in an entirely voluntary capacity. Their unobtrusive work is done for their Lord rather than their church. The service of such devoted people is hardly likely to reach the pages of church history books, but their loving service is not forgotten in the place where the best records are kept.

5. The priority of worship

Others had responsibility for the temple's worship. *Seraiah*, the *supervisor in the house of God*, was probably the high priest of the

---

[12] Acts 20:28; 1 Pet. 5:1–3.   [13] Baxter, *Reformed Pastor* VI.vi, p. 162.
[14] Dt. 23:12–14; 22:8.

time, and he was supported by a team of priests *who carried on work for the temple* (11).

Their spiritual ministry was supplemented by people with evident musical gifts. Mattaniah was the Levite assigned to the work of *the director who led in thanksgiving and prayer* (17). Clines suggests a slight textual emendation[15] which would describe the director as the 'psalm-reader (who) praises (*i.e.* leads the songs of praise) at prayer (time)', just as David had commissioned his predecessor Asaph to do. Centuries earlier, Israel's greatest king had encouraged the people to do those two things: 'Give thanks to the LORD' (praise), 'call on his name' (prayer).[16] Praise and prayer are central to the spiritual life of God's people.

In thanksgiving we acknowledge God's generosity. The praise element ought always to come first. All too easily we crave for more without recalling what we have already received. To neglect thanksgiving is to ignore one of the Christian's distinctive characteristics; the godless do not do it.[17]

In prayer we seek God's help. Whenever we pray we are making the confession that we cannot live without God. We are openly testifying to our reliance on him. We are no longer depending on our own frail resources. As Forsyth says, prayer 'relaxes the tension of our self-inflation'.[18] Biblical narratives and Christian history testify alike to the primacy of prayer in the life of the believer. All the great characters of Scripture prayed and across the succeeding centuries men and women have made it a daily priority to spend time with God. The Indian Christian, Sadhu Sundar Singh, prayed earnestly after his costly conversion and testified, 'I used to ask for specific things. Now I ask for God . . . How our life is transformed when we are in the company of a noble friend. Then how much more will communion with the One who is good beyond all measure transform us.'[19]

The temple's services were occasions when thanksgiving and prayer were best expressed in song. *Uzzi was one of Asaph's descendants, who were the singers responsible for the service of the house of God* (22). Mattaniah, *the director who led in thanksgiving and prayer* (17), is also described in the list of returning priests and Levites as 'in charge of the songs of thankgiving' (12:8). There were two choirs, and these shared in responsive worship as they offered *praise and thanksgiving, one section responding to the other, as prescribed by David the man of God* (12:24).

Music has played an immense part in the worship of the Lord's

---

[15] Clines, p. 217. [16] 1 Ch. 16:7–8. [17] Rom. 1:21.
[18] P. T. Forsyth, *The Soul of Prayer* (1916), p. 24.
[19] B. H. Streeter and A. J. Appasamy, *The Sadhu* (London, 1921), p. 93–94.

people, and throughout history the church has been indebted to soloists, choirs, instrumentalists and musical groups who have offered their gifts to the Lord and enriched our praise and prayer in churches throughout the world.

These lists of names testify to the spiritual commitment of many hundreds of Jerusalem's citizens. Besides the leaders and prominent people such as *priests, Levites, temple servants and descendants of Solomon's servants* (11:3), there were innumerable others, whose different qualities, skills, abilities and expertise had been willingly and gratefully offered to God. The builder's hammer was no less expressive of sincere devotion than the chorister's voice.

6. The grace of humility

Everybody recognizes the necessity, responsibility and privilege of gifted leadership, but not everybody can lead. It is not because, in Gilbertian terms, 'when everyone is somebody then no one's anybody';[20] it is simply that innumerable tasks are devotedly performed by men and women who are happy to accept less prominent roles in God's work. In addition to respected leaders and chief officers, this list also contains the names of people who were content to serve as deputies, assistants, colleagues and partners of those in more eminent positions. We read about *associates, who carried on work for the temple* (12). Even Mattaniah *who led in thanksgiving and prayer* was *second among his associates* (17). *The temple servants lived on the hill of Ophel, and Ziha and Gishpa were in charge of them* (21). Somebody had to be responsible for their welfare, but not everybody could have the job. There will be *servants* as well as leaders. The list of priests and Levites who returned with Zerubbabel and Jeshua gives the names of the personnel concerned but it also refers to the important ministry of *their associates* (12:7–9). Their names are not listed but their service is remembered.

The story of Christian work and witness over the years is something far more enriching than a record of great names and remarkable events. It is about millions of unremembered but committed believers, ordinary church members, forgotten ministers, evangelists, tract-distributors, Bible Class leaders, Sunday School teachers, sick visitors, caterers, cleaners, door stewards and, most important of all, undaunted intercessors. When A. R. Vidler wrote his history of the nineteenth-century church, he said he wished he had been able to say more

[20] From Gilbert and Sullivan's light opera *The Gondoliers*.

... about the ordinary life of Christian people in parishes and congregations which has gone on steadily from generation to generation and without which there would be no church history worth mentioning. It does not hit the headlines and it slips easily through the net in which historians try to catch what is unsteady and non-recurring and more readily open to public inspection.[21]

These are the kind of people who are content to be *associates*, believers who realize that whatever is done, whether in leadership from the front or in supportive partnership, must be done not for the praise of the individual but for the glory of God. Peter reminded the first-century churches that all our service, applauded or unsung, is an opportunity from God, for others and to his glory alone.[22]

There will always be a need for men and women who are committed to work as loyal supporters and reliable partners. Great Christian enterprises across the centuries would never have been possible had it not been for the unacclaimed sacrificial ministry of people who were ready to play a subservient role in the work of Christ. William Wilberforce could never have achieved what he did for the freedom of slaves had it not been for years of arduous back-room work by Thomas Clarkson. The researcher in Wisbech was as vital as the parliamentarian in Westminster. Without a reliable person behind him, constantly obtaining vital information, the reformer's work would have been impossible.[23] D. L. Moody's vigorous evangelistic preaching was used to bring thousands to personal faith in Christ, but few people knew how it all began on that Saturday morning in 1855, when Edward Kimball invited the young Moody 'to come to Christ who loved him, and who wanted his love and should have it'. Moody remembered that there were tears in Kimball's eyes.[24] Edward Kimball was a reticent witness with no gift for preaching but those tears were as eloquent as Moody's finest sermons. The forgotten Sunday School teacher made an incalculable contribution to the story of nineteenth-century evangelism. The church's best story is that of self-effacing service and interdependent partnership. The apostles knew the strategic importance of supportive colleagues, and their letters frequently testify to their invaluable contribution and encouraging practical help.[25]

---

[21] Alec R. Vidler, *The Church in an Age of Revolution* (Harmondsworth: Pelican, 1961), pp. 9–10.   [22] 1 Pet. 4:10–11.

[23] Ellen Gibson Wilson, *Thomas Clarkson* (London: Macmillan, 1989).

[24] John Pollock, *Moody without Sankey* (London: Hodder and Stoughton, 1963), p. 24.

[25] Rom. 16:1–16, 21–23; 2 Cor. 8:16–24; Phil. 2:19–30; 2 Tim. 4:11–12, 19–21; 1 Pet. 5:12–13.

7. The importance of the family

From the descendants of Judah: Athaiah son of Uzziah . . . son of . . .
(4). As we look back over these lists, we realize that there is
something more here than a catalogue of dedicated individuals. They
refer throughout to the families into which these workers were born
and where their faith in God was encouraged and nourished. Their
parentage is traced through six or seven generations with its clear
acknowledgment of the crucial role of the family. As loving and
secure units of personal care and spiritual education, families were
intended to play an enormous part in the life of God's people. These
lists and similar genealogies in Scripture testify to the reality of
Israel's commitment to share God's Word with children and working
members of the 'household': 'One generation will commend your
works to another; they will tell of your mighty acts.'[26]

In contemporary society, families are highly vulnerable and
exposed to increasing danger. It is estimated that at least 40% of new
marriages in the UK are likely to end in divorce, and recent studies
suggest that 'the likelihood of divorce is higher among those whose
childhood home was disrupted by marital breakdown'.[27] If divorce
rates persist at their present level, more than one in four children
living in married-couple families will experience divorce in their
family before reaching the age of sixteen.[28]

These lists in Nehemiah reflect a family structure which provided
children with emotional security, material necessities, physical care,
intellectual encouragement, moral values and spiritual teaching. The
Israelites' commitment to the priority of family care is a rebuke to
contemporary casualness about marriage. It reminds modern believers that they have a responsibility to encourage, nurture and protect family values, and that, in tragic situations of family breakdown,
local churches have a vital role to play in offering love, understanding, support, practical care and security.

One of the church's most strategic opportunities in the contemporary world may be to provide, sensitively and unobtrusively,
that measure of compassionate understanding: 'I was a stranger and
you invited me in'.[29] People will hardly see Christ in us if we cannot
help them in crisis.

[26] Ps. 145:4.
[27] John Haskey, 'The proportion of married couples who divorce: past patterns and
current prospects', in *Population Trends 83*, HMSO (Spring 1996), pp. 25–36.
[28] John Haskey, 'Children who experience divorce in their family', in *Population
Trends 87*, HMSO (Spring 1997), pp. 5–10; see also *Journal of Marriage and the Family*
53 (1991), pp. 43–58. [29] Mt. 25:35.

Nehemiah 12:27–47
15. Our 'chief end'

The Israelite leaders reflected on God's goodness in enabling them to complete the rebuilding of the walls in such a short space of time. They wanted to offer praise to God publicly for his guidance, help and protection, and to dedicate not only the restored walls but their reformed community to his glory. Nehemiah's vivid narrative of this service of thanksgiving presents us with important biblical guidelines regarding the nature, centrality and purpose of worship.

Worship is 'worth-ship'. The word describes those acts of the mind, heart and will whereby we gratefully acknowledge the worth of our God. There can be no other human activity which is so lofty and spiritually determinative as that of adoring God. Christians in the Reformed tradition have described it as the main purpose of human existence; our 'chief end is to glorify God and to enjoy him for ever'.[1] Worship is more than vocal and aural participation in a public service as we offer prayers, sing hymns and songs, hear readings, make offerings and listen to Christian preaching. It is the total submission of all that we have and are to everything we know of God. William Temple described adoration as 'the most selfless emotion of which our nature is capable, and therefore the chief remedy for that self-centredness which is our original sin and the source of all actual sin.'[2]

Yet, although Christians formally recognize the priority of worship, they do not have a common mind regarding its character and form. The topic has a prominent place on the contemporary church's agenda as believers discuss, often vehemently, themes as varied as participatory worship (the congregation's greater involvement rather than 'the ministerial monologue'), charismatic worship (the active use of the gifts described in 1 Corinthians 14), ecumenical worship (to what extent believers need to be in total doctrinal

[1] Westminster Shorter Catechism.
[2] William Temple, *Readings in St John's Gospel* (London: Macmillan, 1950), p. 68.

harmony to worship together), inter-faith worship (whether adherents of different world religions can meet together for meaningful worship), contemporary worship (the differences between more traditional as opposed to modern worship patterns, or the combination of both), 'balanced' worship (the relationship between Word and Spirit in worship), 'excellence in worship', 'user-friendly' services and the impact of our worship-patterns on non-believers, and so on. The topics are not mutually exclusive; in several cases, discussion about one merges naturally into another. The controversy is likely to continue.

Believers have talked about the subject a great deal; few would argue that the debate has necessarily inspired better worship. One of the most pressing issues which needs to be at the heart of contemporary discussion is not what pleases us in worship but what most honours God. All too often the subject is discussed from highly subjective perspectives, and that is not particularly helpful. We have different, even divergent, preferences, and without help from Scripture cannot confidently assert what pleases God most about worship. The purpose of worship is not to provide us with an exultant feeling inside. Euphoric worship may vary little from the inspiration and delight which a person experiences on hearing a Brahms or an Elgar symphony. In other words, the value of worship patterns cannot be determined on merely subjective grounds, that is, whether *we* find it helpful. What is 'helpful' to us, may not even be acceptable to God.

People throughout the world are tireless in their pursuit of different religious exercises – adoring idols, kneeling on hard floors, abstaining from food, beating their bodies, mechanically turning prayer-wheels, lighting candles, reciting repetitive mantras, embarking on sacrificial pilgrimages – all because they passionately believe these acts are 'helpful' for relieving their guilt, shedding their anxieties, obtaining their pardon, registering their allegiance and guaranteeing their security. But, even though they may have a highly subjective notion that these deeds are 'helpful', it does not mean for a moment that they honour the only true God. Some of them are actually condemned in God's Word, so it is to that book we need to turn if we want clear guidance on this spiritually crucial topic.

We are on firmer ground when we deliberately minimize our personal preferences in worship styles and endeavour to examine the subject with as much objectivity as is humanly possible. Clear biblical teaching about the nature and content of worship is likely to prove a better guide. If we genuinely believe in the unique authority, reliability and relevance of Scripture, then we are right in expecting that the Bible will have important things to say to us, not only about how biblical characters worshipped (descriptive passages, such as the one before us), but also about how we might best follow their example (where the descriptive becomes, with the support of other biblical passages, prescriptive); not just something to read with interest but to copy with enthusiasm.

This account of a biblical celebration of adoration, thanksgiving and dedication has not been preserved by Nehemiah as a pattern for us to follow exactly, otherwise we will need two choirs walking in opposite directions around our communities, accompanied by gifted musicians playing stringed instruments, trumpets and cymbals before entering a worship-building. What is here, however, is another model or paradigm. It invites study, not with a view to reproducing it item by item, but to discover what was intended by its different elements and how, supported by other passages of Scripture, we might identify appropriate patterns of worship in the contemporary church.

A careful reading of the narrative in Nehemiah 12 directs us to ten aspects of this important theme of acceptable worship.

1. Its purpose

The purpose of this act of worship in the fifth century BC was to celebrate what God had done, thank him for such astonishing generosity, and dedicate the people and their work to his glory. The Levites were *brought to Jerusalem to celebrate joyfully the dedication with songs of thanksgiving* (27). Grateful celebration, thanksgiving and dedication are the three main themes, and they take us to the heart of what worship is really about.

First, the Israelites magnify his name. *Celebration* is a primary aspect of worship. It does not begin with what we are doing when we pray or sing or speak or ponder in adoring silence. It begins with who God is, what God has said and done. We glory in those unique acts which took place before ever we had the desire to think or say anything to him. In worship we extol with all our powers the initiative of God as we recall all that he has done, said and is to his people.

Secondly, the people acknowledge God's gifts. *Thanksgiving* was another main aspect of their worship. They marvelled at God's astonishing and totally undeserved generosity to them and, with a sense of adoring wonder, give public expression to their immense gratitude. This congregation's commitment to thanksgiving is deliberately repeated throughout the passage. In addition to this introductory explanation (27) of what happened that day, we are told that the choirs were appointed *to give thanks* (31), and then, after processing around the newly built walls, both the choirs *that gave thanks* (40) entered the temple.

Our thanksgiving needs to be specific. It is not enough to express our gratitude formally in well-worn phrases. Thanksgiving must be itemized, so that we appreciate all the ways in which we are indebted to such a generous God. Nehemiah and his partners had many reasons to offer their thanks to the Lord.

They were thanking him that day for divine guidance, that Hanani had met his brother in the citadel of Susa and shared the burden of his people's needs, and that Nehemiah had made such an immediate response; for sovereign direction, that Persia's king had allowed his cupbearer to go to Judah; for those material resources that Artaxerxes had given them; and for safe travel throughout a hazardous journey across a vast desert.

Nehemiah was thanking God for willing colleagues who had shared his burden for the city and were willing to give themselves to such arduous and dangerous work. They were all thanking God for constant protection from their enemies, and for the strength to continue when the going was tough; for unselfish dedication on the part of a huge team of workers and for that steadfast continuance which enabled them to bring the work to a successful conclusion; for spiritual confidence that, even though dogged by discouragements and ridiculed by their enemies, they had continued to trust him. Most of all, they were thanking him for their completed building enterprise, which they now wished to dedicate to his glory.

Moreover, the thanksgiving was not a one-off devotional act which took a few hours. It continued long after the day of dedication was over. A concluding note to the passage (45–46) makes it clear that *songs of praise and thanksgiving to God* were offered not only that day but also on subsequent occasions in the people's worship.

Thirdly, the Israelites offer themselves in *dedication*. To dedicate means to put over 'the work of human hands to God's ownership'.[3] It is not enough just to celebrate God's achievements in history and experience, and to thank him for such merciful intervention. Worship demands the surrender of ourselves, and the surrender to him of all that he has given to us.

These three elements of celebration, thanksgiving and dedication are given expression by our total being, the intellectual, emotional and volitional aspects of our personality. In celebration, the mind recalls what God has said and done, the revelatory and redemptive initiatives of God; in thanksgiving, the heart is moved with gratitude; in dedication, the will is surrendered to him.

Moreover, we discover that these three elements have a prominent place in the New Testament concept of worship. The note of celebration is captured in the word frequently used by the crowds as they acknowledge the worth of the victor in the games stadium. They

[3] Clines, p. 228.

cried out, '*Axios! Axios!*' ('You are worthy of our praise!'). Celebration is central in the book of Revelation's portraiture of the adoring multitude in heaven, and reflects the pattern of early Christian worship. The multitude celebrate who God is: 'You are worthy [*axios*] our Lord and God . . . for you created all things, and by your will they . . . have their being'. They magnify Christ for what he has done for us: 'You are worthy [*axios*] . . . because you were slain, and with your blood you purchased men for God'.[4]

The exultant throng in heaven typify ideal worship in that they not only gave honour to God but thanks as well.[5] Thanksgiving is given rich expression whenever God's redeemed people meet around the Lord's Table. Just as Jesus gave thanks at the Last Supper, so do believers as they remember with gratitude his sacrificial death for them on the cross.[6] One of the early names for this service, 'Eucharist', is derived from *eucharistos*, 'thankful'.[7] Thanksgiving is a missing element in the lives of some Christians, yet it is impossible to read Paul's letters without realizing that, even during imprisonment, he was thankful for so many good things in his life.[8]

The apostle Paul also emphasizes this third element, the offering of ourselves, with his vivid reminder that the surrender of our bodies as 'living sacrifices' is the Christian's 'spiritual act of worship'.[9]

2. Its nature

The secret of acceptable worship is not simply what we do but how we do it. The worship of these citizens was a radiantly joyous experience. The Levites came to Jerusalem *to celebrate joyfully the dedication* of their walls (27) and *on that day they offered great sacrifices, rejoicing because God had given them great joy*. It was not only the choirs who were elated: *The women and children also rejoiced. The sound of rejoicing in Jerusalem could be heard far away* (43).

This opportunity to magnify God was a supremely happy occasion. Whenever these people came together for worship, their hearts overflowed with true joy. It happened earlier when the temple's foundation was laid, when its building was completed and the Passover celebrated.[10] In Nehemiah's time, that congregation which had met in the square to hear the reading of Scripture celebrated 'with great joy, because they now understood the words that had been made known to them' (8:12). As they participated in the Feast of Booths, 'their joy was very great' (8:17), which was exactly how the Lord had told them to celebrate it.[11]

[4] Rev. 4:11; 5:9. [5] Rev. 4:9; 7:12; 11:17. [6] 1 Cor. 11:23–24. [7] Col. 3:15.
[8] Rom. 1:8; 1 Cor. 1:4; 15:57; 2 Cor. 2:14; Eph. 1:16; 5:4, 20; Phil. 1:3; 4:6; Col. 1:3, 12; 2:7; 3:15, 17; 4:2; 1 Thes. 1:2; 2:13; 3:9; 5:18; 2 Thes. 1:3; 2:13; 1 Tim. 1:12; 2 Tim. 1:3; Phm. 4. [9] Rom. 12:1–2. [10] Ezr. 3:12–13; 6:16, 22. [11] Dt. 16:14–15.

Worship was never meant to be a doleful and drab experience. God's people are to come before him with joyful songs.[12] They have more to delight their hearts than anyone else in life. Yet, at times, Christian worship can be painfully dreary and monotonous, even depressing. That is not what God intended. Worship is meant to be the natural overflow of jubilant spirits. Christianity is the happiest religion in the world. Other worshippers rarely hurry to their shrines and temples with happy spirits.

That cheerfulness and delight ought to find its richest expression in corporate worship, when our incomparable joys are recalled, confirmed and shared. It is a desperately poor witness if unbelievers come into church services and find them dull and boring, as they look at sombre faces and hear people singing at a tediously slow pace in a funereal atmosphere. Such criticism has all the dimensions of caricature, of course, but many of us have had some experience of such a service, and it ought not to be. Those who lead worship have the responsibility of striking the clear notes of celebration, thanksgiving and joy right at the beginning, so that Christians are reminded why we are present and how we should worship.

3. Its variety

There was nothing stereotyped and monochrome about this worship occasion in Jerusalem. Those responsible for leading it used a wide range of musical gifts to express their adoration and praise. Worship is meant to be a shared experience to which a variety of participants bring their particular gifts. That day many people travelled specially to the city, in order to sing God's praise and use their gifted voices to enrich the worship: *The singers also were brought together from the region around Jerusalem . . . for the singers had built villages for themselves around Jerusalem* (28–29).

Instrumentalists shared in the procession with *the music of cymbals, harps and lyres* (27), and *priests with trumpets* (35, 41) also took their part, along with those who played *with musical instruments prescribed by David the man of God* (36). Those *harps* were portable stringed instruments carried by the musicians, and the various instruments expressed the different moods reflected in the great psalms. The blowing of trumpets and the crashing of loud cymbals was perfectly appropriate to exalt the greatness of God, but the quieter tones of stringed instruments would more fittingly convey their expressions of gratitude for God's mercy to sinners like themselves.

Choral music was given the most prominent place, as many singers

[12] Ps. 33:1; 100:2; 145:7.

joined the *two large choirs* which encompassed the walls *to give thanks* on behalf of all the people (31, 38, 40, 42).

One naturally wonders which of the psalms might have been used to give adequate expression to their gratitude to God that those walls had been rebuilt at last. It is tempting to think of Psalm 48 as a possibility, with its reference to the secure defences of 'the city of our God':

> Walk about Zion, go round her,
>   count her towers,
> consider well her ramparts,
>   view her citadels,
>   that you may tell of them to the next generation.
> For this God is our God for ever and ever;
>   he will be our guide even to the end.[13]

4. Its priority

However skilled the instrumentalists and choristers, Scripture emphasizes a quality which takes priority over musical ability and the eager participation of gifted people in worship. The hearts of the worshippers are of greater importance than their voices. The Lord is not moved by lofty words and captivating tunes if he discerns unworthy and unacceptable things in our lives. Before the procession moved off, the priests and Levites *purified themselves ceremonially* and went on to purify *the people, the gates and the wall* (30).

Although leaders and people participated in a ritual act of cleansing, it was far from being mere cultic formality. Such acts were important in Old Testament times, and symbolized inward purification. They were designed to direct the people's attention to the necessity of a clean heart. If believers want to stand in the 'holy place' of worship, they must first have 'clean hands and a pure heart'. The psalmist knew that the external ritual would achieve nothing if the worshipper treasured unconfessed sin. He prayed, 'Create in me a clean heart, O God ... You do not delight in sacrifice, or I would bring it ... The sacrifices of God are a broken spirit; a broken and contrite heart, O God, you will not despise.'[14] Isaiah exposed the sin of those worshippers who trampled the courts of God's house with their expensive sacrifices, but whose offerings had become a wearisome burden to the Lord. Such people lifted their arms in prayer, but stained hands and chattering lips made their sacrifices obnoxious to a God who looked for clean hearts and upright lives. The prophet needed that cleansing himself. Before he could offer acceptable worship to God, he had to acknowledge the sin of

---

[13] Ps. 48:1, 2, 8, 12–14.   [14] Ps. 24:3–4; 51:10, 16–17.

'unclean lips'. Only when that sin was purged away was he ready to hear the call of God to service.[15]

In New Testament times, Jesus looked for something more than ceremonial purity. During his ministry he frequently encountered religious zealots who were far more concerned about external cleansing than inward holiness. He exposed the Pharisees for fastidiously washing 'the outside of the cup and dish' whilst inwardly they were 'full of greed and self-indulgence'.[16] God looks within, to the deepest recesses of our hearts and minds. He knows whether the words on our lips are matched by the quality of our lives.

5. Its traditions

With an appreciative sense of history, this congregation acknowledged their indebtedness to the great traditions of worship in the past. They enjoyed a sense of continuity with those who had worshipped before them. The list of returned exiles which precedes this account of the dedication of the walls recalls that, since David's reign, the psalms had enriched responsive worship. They gave their celebrations an awareness of the corporate nature of their worship and provided a measure of congregational involvement. The Levites gave 'praise and thanksgiving, one section responding to the other, as prescribed by David the man of God' (24). Responsive participation helped to prevent the congregation from being mere observers of something conducted by the leaders but from which they felt strangely detached.

Similarly, those who played instruments were encouraged that their offerings of praise in music had been *prescribed by David the man of God* (36). Likewise, their *singers* united their voices in praise *according to the commands of David and his son Solomon* (45).

This company of worshippers was pleased to continue the tradition of temple worship which had enriched the nation's spiritual life for centuries: *For long ago, in the days of David and Asaph, there had been directors for the singers and for the songs of praise and thanksgiving to God* (46).

As these choirs processed around the rebuilt walls, the event was novel but their words and music expressed their indebtedness to the past. They were sensitive to the fact that, long before they were born, their forefathers had adored God, recalled his mercies and surrendered themselves to his work. The psalms they sang contributed an enriching dimension to their worship.

Sadly, the debate about worship in the contemporary scene is marred by a reluctance on the part of both traditionalists and

[15] Is. 1:11–15; 6:5–8.   [16] Mt. 23:23–28.

'moderns' to acknowledge that they have an enormous amount to give and receive from each other. Newly composed worship-songs convey a freshness, immediacy and vitality to worship. Their words are not as familiar as some of the older hymns, though many of them have the great merit of keeping close to the text of Scripture. However, they can be sung as repetitively and unthinkingly as the older material; freshness is not guaranteed by recent composition.

On the other hand, many of the great hymns of our faith, rich in teaching, devotion and language, have sustained millions of believers through difficult and bewildering times. Such a legacy is not a matter of indifference to sensitive worshippers. Contemporary Christians need to combine the older material and the new. Singing the great psalms of their spiritual history helped these Jerusalem worshippers to give expression to three things about their faith.

First, these psalms confirmed the reality of their faith. There are experiences in life when our own faith may be severely tested and we are buffeted and bewildered, even bereft. In such times the lamp of our personal faith may flicker, but these great songs from the past speak powerfully about a faith which is bigger and stronger than our own immediate experience of God. They renew our confidence, reminding us in our frailty that our faith is shared by a vast multitude who have sung these great songs before us and have been sustained by them. We are upheld by them just as they were fortified by the heroism and devotion of their forefathers. As we sing these magnificent psalms, we lose our sense of solitariness in suffering, and realize we are part of a vast worshipping company of people throughout history who have proved the reliability and sufficiency of God.

Secondly, these psalms expressed the continuity of their faith. They rejoiced that the Lord had guided and guarded them across the centuries, and they testified to his unswerving faithfulness. He had not done so because they had deserved it. More often than not, they had disappointed him and failed to live up to those high and noble standards he had set for them, and the resolutions they had made of love and loyalty. But, although a huge majority had let him down, there had always been a remnant of faithful, believing people. He had called, equipped and used his sincere worshippers and willing servants in every generation, and as these choirs processed they witnessed to that miraculous continuity. When we look back over Christian history, we are aware that, time without number, God's people have failed and been less than they ought to have been, but we are debtors to that past, whatever its failings. The torch was passed on from generation to generation, never by perfect people, but by men and women so indebted to the grace of Christ that they could not possibly keep the message to themselves.

Thirdly, these psalms declared the solidarity of the Israelites' faith. As they used these great psalms, they gave expression not simply to the faith of the past but to the great truths which unite God's people in every generation. In his day, Luther contrasted the spirituality expressed in the psalms ('little Bibles', as he called them) with that found in the popular miniature biographies of the saints, sold at fairs and markets throughout late medieval Europe. In the psalter 'we find, not what this or that saint did, but what the chief of all saints did, and what all saints still do. In it is shown their attitude to God . . . and their manner of life and behaviour in face of manifold dangers and sufferings.' Our faith is not a solitary experience, and these great words from the past unite us with the redeemed people of God throughout the centuries. As Luther says, when we hear, read or sing these words, we receive the assurance that we are 'in the company of the saints . . . because all of them join in singing' these great songs with us. We 'can use their words to talk with God as they did'. Here is 'a valid passport with which we can follow all the saints without danger', this 'beautiful, bright, polished mirror, which will show you what Christianity is'. It is one of God's vast and 'immeasurable benefits'[17] to be used for our good.

We are debtors to the past. The great psalms, hymns and spiritual songs recall the experience of God's people across the centuries and remind us of all they have contributed to our spiritual lives. Believers do not lightly dismiss such a rich heritage. The early believers were no more perfect than we are. There may be times when we are aware of great biblical doctrines which our forefathers neglected, but there are also immense truths which we have ignored. We have so much to receive from them. Those who will be our partners in heaven have left us with superb material to enrich our worship.

6. Its witness

The procession of both choirs around the walls was a public act of witness, which culminated in a service of thanksgiving in the temple. It was never intended to be an exclusive conclave restricted to religious officials. Everybody in the nation was meant to know that the people were honouring God's name and exalting his goodness to them. The worshippers were clearly seen and heard as they made this joyous declaration of their indebtedness to God. As the two choirs processed and sang, accompanied by their instrumentalists, they walked in opposite directions *on the top of the wall* (31, 38). Everyone in the city could see what was happening, and for miles

---

[17] Martin Luther, 'Preface to the Psalms', in John Dillenberger (ed.), *Martin Luther: Selections from his Writings* (New York: Doubleday, 1961), pp. 40–41.

around people heard these songs of praise, because the *sound of rejoicing in Jerusalem could be heard far away* (43).

Every service of worship is an act of corporate testimony to God's nature, word and acts. A person without a clear faith who comes into a service of Christian worship ought to be in no doubt about what and why we believe. The centrality of the Lord needs to be the distinctive element in our worship, yet it can be subtly marginalized in the contemporary world. With an understandable ambition to make worship attractive, 'user-friendly' and relevant, there is a danger that modern worship patterns can be unconsciously modelled on media presentations, more reminiscent of a bouncy TV chat-show than an inspiring occasion for adoration and praise.

All occasions for worship (as distinct from evangelistic opportuni-ties) need to incorporate the essential elements of adoration, thanksgiving, petition, the assurance of forgiveness, the exposition of and submission to God's Word, the offering of our gifts as well as ourselves, intercession for our world and specific individuals in need, and commitment to future service. People who participate will ensure that, in sharing their distinctive gifts, they always direct atten-tion to their Lord and not to themselves. Whenever any of us share in the public aspects of worship, either singly or in groups, we do well to recall not only the ambition but the determination of John the Baptist when he said of Christ, 'He must become greater; I must become less'.[18] Everything we do is totally ineffective if it does not turn people's gaze to the Lord of glory.

7. Its vitality

This passage is memorable in its abundant use of superlatives. It describes the vitality of something that was really well done, with every participant determined to offer their best and make the occa-sion one which would always be recalled with joy. The Israelites were passionate and enthusiastic as they worshipped the Lord. They *celebrate joyfully* (27). These are not just choirs but *large choirs* (31). The priests offer *great sacrifices*, and they rejoice *because God had given them great joy* (43). There is nothing half-hearted about their worship. It is the overflow of supremely grateful hearts from people who have personally experienced the lavish generosity of God and the incalculable and undeserved blessings which have been showered upon them. They have revelled in his 'great goodness' (9:25), enjoyed his gracious gifts (9:35), cast themselves upon his 'great mercy' (9:31) and experienced his 'great compassion' (9:19). It is little wonder that they wish to offer *great sacrifices* (43).

[18] Jn. 3:30.

215

8. Its unity

This act of worship was an occasion which united not only the citizens of Jerusalem but people from the surrounding countryside. The urban and rural population rubbed shoulders as they rejoiced in the infinite mercy of God. Levites who lived some miles from the city *were sought out from where they lived and were brought to Jerusalem to celebrate* (27). *The singers also were brought together from the region around Jerusalem – from the villages* (28).

When it is conducted with sincerity, sensitivity and dignity, Christian worship can be a markedly unifying experience. People from all walks of life stand in equal need of the Lord's mercy, and all are debtors to his astonishing grace. Many of the things which might otherwise divide them become less than important in their united aim and privilege of adoring praise, thanksgiving and commitment.

It is sad that this great unifying opportunity has in some contexts become the source of painful division, largely because of extreme and intransigent positions, an unwillingness to acknowledge each other's insights, the serious lack of a tolerant and forgiving spirit, and the failure to appreciate that varied personalities may need different things in worship. Some people genuinely need quietness, time for reflection and a creative silence in worship, whilst others long for a more vivacious and exuberant expression of praise. If those who carried the cymbals had always clashed them loudly, people who played stringed instruments would be wasting their time. Both loud and soft instruments could be equally accommodated when everyone treasured no ambition other than the glory of God.

9. Its quality

This narrative gives us a distinct impression of the quality of the Israelites' worship. Everything was done well. There was nothing haphazard that day, and things were not hurriedly thrown together at the last moment. It had all been well thought out: the recruitment of the singers, the composition of the choirs, the combination of the instrumentalists, the route of the procession, even the training of the chorus: *The choirs sang under the direction of Jezrahiah* (42).

The Lord is worthy of our best, and it is sad that he does not always receive it. Life is full for many of us and there are so many pressures. Innumerable things clamour for attention, and worship often receives neither our best preparation nor our total commitment.

10. Its cost

The concluding verses (44–47) present us with another aspect of authentic worship: the offering of our money as well as our time and service for the Lord's work. For all its attractiveness, splendour and excitement, the great service of dedication would inevitably draw to its close, and provision must be made for the continuing worship of God's people. The priests and Levites, those living in Jerusalem and beyond, must be supported by the generous gifts which the Lord had described and commanded. The people had promised that such offerings would not be withheld (10:35–39), so the concluding paragraph of this narrative describes the appointment of those who would *be in charge of the storerooms for the contributions, firstfruits and tithes* (44). So it was that, *in the days of Zerubbabel and of Nehemiah, all Israel contributed the daily portions for the singers and gatekeepers. They also set aside the portion for the other Levites, and the Levites set aside the portion for the descendants of Aaron* (47).

In recording this narrative, our author is at pains to mention six characteristics of the people's giving to the Lord's work. It was organized (*men were appointed*, 44), specific (*contributions, firstfruits and tithes*, 44), grateful (because the ministry of God's servants had brought them such delight: *for Judah was pleased with the ministering priests and Levites*, 44), obligatory (*all Israel contributed*, 47), regular (*daily portions*, 47) and universal (everyone, including *the Levites* who were also to *set aside the portion* for the priests' support, *the descendants of Aaron*, 47).

The apostle Paul rightly insisted that God's servants and needy people must be lovingly and regularly supported, and early Christian worship provided an opportunity for the offering of money for the Lord's work.[19] No worship can be honouring to God if those who serve the Lord are deprived of life's basic necessities.

Sadly, in the light of Israel's later experience, this vivid description of Israel's generosity following the dedication service reads like a forgotten dream. When Nehemiah left Jerusalem and returned to his work at the Persian palace, things gradually began to deteriorate. One of the first things to suffer was the generous support of the Levites. That widespread and sustained neglect is one theme in the book's closing chapter.

[19] Rom. 12:8; 1 Cor. 16:1; 2 Cor. 8–9; Phil. 4:10–19; 1 Tim. 5:17–18; 6:17–18.

Nehemiah 13:1–3
16. 'There it was found written'

There is an absorbing realism about Scripture. It refuses to present us with a romantic portrait of life; things do not always develop as we hope. 'Good beginnings are no guarantee of happy endings'.[1] People with immense gifts do not always achieve their potential. The biblical narratives often present us with frustrated ambitions, disappointing failure, neglected opportunities and broken vows. Sin often spoils the story. Abraham attempts to deceive, Jacob cheats, Moses loses his temper, David commits adultery and Peter lies. The stark honesty of the Bible makes it such compelling and relevant reading.

Following the rebuilding of the walls, Nehemiah's story appears rich in promise. He vividly describes the people's eager attentiveness to Scripture (8:1–12), their gratitude for God's mercies (8:13–18), genuine repentance expressed in prayer (9:1–37), commitment to the covenant (9:38 – 10:39), earnest resolve to make Jerusalem a 'holy city' (11:1–2), joyous dedication of the newly repaired walls (12:27–43), delight in (12:44) and support for (12:45–47) their spiritual leaders, and practical determination to maintain pure worship (13:1–3). We feel it safe to imagine that, with such a background of love and loyalty, all will be well. But Nehemiah's closing chapter brings the book to a starkly realistic conclusion. It shows how easily the most spiritual community can find its standards subtly eroded as it gradually accommodates to the pressures of contemporary worldliness. At the dedication, the builders celebrated their moral victory in a battle against secularism and materialism, but they had not won the war.

This final chapter of Nehemiah demonstrates the disastrous consequences of poor leadership (4, 28), the damage caused by disobedience to God's Word (4–9), the insidious temptations of a materialistic society (15–18), and the danger of ignoring family values

[1] Southwell, p. 28.

218

(23–27). Nehemiah may have been tempted to bring his book to a more cheering and inspiring conclusion with his account of vibrant worship (12:27–43), diligent service (44–46), generous giving (47) and obedient listening (13:1–3) but, although true, it would have given a misleading impression of Judah's spiritual life in the mid fifth century BC.

The people's first offence was one from which all the others derived: they ignored God's commands (1–3). Each of the sins exposed in this concluding chapter stems from a common source: disobedience to God's Word. In the events here described, Nehemiah tackles the same issues which figured prominently in the public covenant renewal described in 10:28–39. Those themes to which they then gave their attention, and the vows they made in God's presence, emerge again in Nehemiah's final reformation story in chapter 13: obedience to God's Word (10:28–29), purity in marriage (10:30), the sanctity of God's day (10:31), necessary generosity for the upkeep of God's servants, the planned, practical support of priests and Levites, and care of the temple (10:32–39).

The passages in 10:28–39 and 13:1–31 are meant to be seen alongside one other, and there are clear literary links which encourage us to read each in the light of the other. The determined conviction which concluded the renewed covenant, 'We will not neglect the house of our God' (10:39), is followed by Nehemiah's later condemnation, 'Why is the house of God neglected?' (13:11).

The covenant of chapter 10 began with an affirmation of loyalty to God's Word (10:28–29). Nehemiah's concluding chapter begins with a description of Israel's carelessness about what God had said in *the Book of Moses* (1) concerning the purity of their worship. 'At that time' (1; *On that day* is the same phrase as in 12:44) during Nehemiah's governorship and possibly following the dedication, Scripture was read publicly. Those present realized how careless they had been about the wholehearted commitment of the worshipping congregation and its exclusive loyalty to God. They listened to Moses' words recalling the period when the Israelites were on the threshold of the promised land. The law made it clear that 'no Ammonite or Moabite or any of his descendants may enter the assembly of the Lord'.[2] The sin of these nations was exposed by God's Word. The Ammonite sin was one of heartless omission: *they had not met the Israelites with food and water*; while the Moabite transgression was that of ruthless commission: they *had hired Balaam to call a curse down* on the Israelite pilgrims (2). The narrative invites us to consider the sin of the Ammonite and the Moabite,

[2] Dt. 23:3–5.

and also the Lord's determination to bless and the Israelite resolution to obey.

1. The Ammonites' failure to help

All too often, our estimate of sin is limited to things we *do* which offend God, harm others and spoil ourselves. But Scripture does not encourage such a partial view of human failure. We can grieve God by what we fail to do, as much as by what we do. The Ammonites were given a 'one-off' opportunity to show kindness to the Israelite travellers, but they resolutely refused to do so. The exhausted pilgrims were in desperate need of food and water and asked that they might buy them in Ammon's market-places, but they were not allowed to purchase life's essential commodities. The Israelites had made a firm promise not to make their encampments in Ammonite fields. They were merely passing through the country and would keep to the main highways. Their treatment by this nation, and by the Amorites who occupied adjacent territory,[3] was cruel in the extreme, for the travellers had undertaken not to touch local vineyards and wells.[4] These unco-operative nations refused to sell food and water in the way that other nations had willingly done.[5]

Sins of omission are seriously regarded in Scripture. In the gospels, both narratives and parables expose the danger. The indignant Pharisee did not welcome Jesus with the customary eastern courtesies,[6] and nine of the cleansed lepers did nothing to express their gratitude.[7]

In Jesus' parables, failure to act is a recurrent theme. The rich man was unconcerned about the poor man at his gate and, preoccupied with his prosperous lifestyle, had not listened to God's Word.[8] The priest and Levite in the parable of the good Samaritan failed to help the dying victim on the road to Jericho.[9] The rich farmer did not think about eternity and failed to store up riches in heaven.[10] The foolish virgins failed to put oil in their lamps, and the timid servant did not use his talent profitably.[11] Those who stand before the eternal throne[12] are reminded of times when they neglected people who were deprived of life's greatest blessings and natural amenities, food and water (like the Israelite travellers), shelter, health and freedom. The contemporary plight of the hungry, thirsty, homeless, sick and persecuted is a stark reminder of Christ's parable. The tragedy flashes across our television screens and fills the columns of our newspapers

[3] Clines (p. 236) suggests that they were probably a closely related people and, for this reason, the text in Dt. 23 and Ne. 13 does not make specific mention of the Amorites, as does the narrative in Nu. 21:21; Dt. 2:26–30.   [4] Nu. 21:22; Dt. 2:28.
[5] Dt. 2:29.   [6] Lk. 7:44.   [7] Lk. 17:17.   [8] Lk. 16:19–31.   [9] Lk. 10:30–37.
[10] Lk. 12:13–21.   [11] Mt. 25:1–30.   [12] Mt. 25:31–46.

with such frightening regularity that we are in danger of becoming compassion-weary, and the impact shocks us no longer.

Christians of all people must not emulate the callous non-involvement policy of the Ammonites and Amorites who refused to help the needy. We need to discover imaginative ways in which we can offer our 'cup of water' in Christ's name,[13] and do something practical to help the world's hungry and deprived millions.

2. The Moabites' plan to hinder

The Moabite sin was of ruthless commission. Intent on thwarting Israel's purpose in entering Canaan, they hired the prophet Balaam *to call a curse down* on the Hebrew travellers. The reference to a hired prophet is an interesting feature in this setting and would hardly have escaped the notice of Nehemiah's contemporaries. At a strategic time during the building operations, those who opposed the project also 'hired' Shemaiah 'to intimidate' Nehemiah and prophesy against him. The same Hebrew word translated 'hired' (6:12-13; 13:2) is used in both instances, reminding the reader that there will always be those who deliberately set themselves against the Lord's work and servants. It also alerts us to the fact that the worst opposition frequently comes from unpredictable sources and by unexpected means. Jesus certainly proved that, and Paul often wrote about it.[14] But, although Balaam made repeated attempts to call down a damaging curse on God's people, all his efforts were totally frustrated. Both pagan king and compliant prophet had forgotten about God.

3. The Lord's determination to bless

Our God, however, turned the curse into a blessing (2). The worst designs of Israel's enemies were doomed to failure when God was on their side. Balaam may have been specifically chosen because of his high success rating. Those who had Balaam speaking against them were naturally fearful; people in that locality believed that his curses always worked: 'I know that . . . those you curse are cursed'.[15]

But this is to reckon without God. God addressed the pagan prophet, ordering him not to curse the Israelite travellers and, though the Moabite king was willing to increase the payment, every effort to secure Israel's downfall was brought to nothing. On four separate occasions[16] the hired prophet could only say encouraging things;

[13] Mk. 9:41.
[14] Lk. 22:2-3; 2 Cor. 11:13-15; 12:20-21; Phil. 1:15-17; 1 Tim. 1:18-19; 6:3-5; 2 Tim. 4:14; Tit. 1:10-11.   [15] Nu. 22:6.   [16] Nu. 23:7-12; 13-26; 23:27 – 24:14; 24:15-25.

destructive words died on his lips. Balaam had received his fee[17] as Shemaiah had his, but in both cases the money was wasted. God can take ugly situations and use them for his ultimate glory, our blessing and the enrichment of other people.

Little could have been more shattering for China's western missionaries than to be expelled from the country where God had sent them. After decades of devoted ministry, all their best work seemed to be in jeopardy. Communism was ousting Christianity. By 1951 all foreign missionaries had been forced to leave the country and, within a few years, their pastors, leaders and evangelists were sent to prisons and labour camps. Houses were searched for Bibles and, when found, immediately burnt. Church buildings were closed down. During the cultural revolution of 1966–76 not only the leaders but members of the churches were ruthlessly persecuted. Yet the most conservative estimate is that there are about 50 million Christians in China today. For over forty years the Christian church in that country was denied any direct, practical input from their fellow-believers in other parts of the world; their colleagues in other countries could do little but pray, but those prayers were abundantly answered as God *turned the curse into a blessing* (2). David Wang is persuaded that the 'phenomenal growth of the church in China is nothing short of a sovereign move of God'.[18]

Nehemiah's contemporaries needed this reminder of God's sovereignty from the Balaam story. They had been enabled to build Jerusalem's broken walls because God had been on their side. Despite intense and increasing opposition, all their enemies' attempts to destroy them had come to nothing. Verbal assaults, belittling ridicule, insidious threats, ingratiating invitations and deliberate attacks had all failed simply because 'the gracious hand of my God' was upon Israel's people and their leader (2:8, 18). The Lord can turn life's cruel experiences into something beautiful and enriching. His sovereign and compassionate purposes for his people can never be overthrown. That is why, writing about first-century deprivation and persecution, famine and sword, the apostle can affirm, 'If God is for us, who can be against us?'[19] The God who gave his Son for us will not deny us anything which he regards as vital for our daily life and work.

[17] Nu. 22:7.
[18] 'Lessons from the Prayer Habits of the Church in China', in D. A. Carson (ed.), *Teach us to Pray: Prayer in the Bible and the World*, World Evangelical Fellowship (Exeter: Paternoster, 1990), p. 247.
[19] Rom. 8:31.

4. The Israelites' resolution to obey

When they heard God's Word that the Ammonites and Moabites could not be *admitted into the assembly of God*, Nehemiah's contemporaries excluded from their worship not only people from those two nations but *all who were of foreign descent* (3). This does not mean, of course, that such people had no opportunity to believe in Israel's God. Other passages in the Old Testament make it clear that Gentiles could 'turn to God', but their conversion must be resolute, genuine and definite. Those Moabites who insisted on holding on to their Moabite beliefs were prohibited from attending Israelite worship, but the book of Ruth tells the story of a Moabitess who was not only *admitted into the assembly of God* but was one of King David's ancestors. Ruth made her public confession: 'Your people will be my people and your God my God.' Naomi recognized the genuineness of her daughter-in-law's faith and rejoiced that the young widow loved the God of Israel, 'under whose wings' she had come to take refuge.[20] As if to underline the radical transformation which the Lord can effect in human life, the phrase 'Ruth the Moabitess' is repeated throughout the book.[21] Moreover, as we have seen (10:28), such conversions were not restricted to Israel's past.

Syncretism was always a serious threat to the spiritual life of God's people. Whether captives in Egypt, residents in Canaan, exiles in Babylon or Persia, they were surrounded by pagan influences. If Israel was to hand on a unique faith from one generation to another, her vibrant message must not be compromised or adulterated by assimilating insidious elements from surrounding religions. The purity of Israel's faith had been crucially important during the exile. Babylon's idolatry and Persia's idol-free religion were an equal threat to God's people. In an alien materialistic culture, it cannot have been easy to maintain an uncompromising witness to the truth of God's Word. Unashamed commitment was a vital priority. The book of Daniel preserves stories which illustrate both the incipient dangers and exemplary heroism of God's servants who were steadfastly loyal to their unique faith.[22]

It was no less easy in the early church. Paul warned his readers in Rome about the danger of worldliness: 'Don't let the world around you squeeze you into its own mould'.[23] It is a continuing danger in the modern world, where to be a Christian one must swim against the fast-flowing stream of contemporary culture. We must live in the world but not let the world live in us.

Jerusalem's citizens were alerted to the importance of purity in

[20] Ru. 1:16; 2:12. [21] Ru. 2:2, 6, 21: 4:5, 10.
[22] Dn. 1:3–21; 3:1–30 (esp. 17–18); 6:1–28.
[23] Rom. 12:2, in J. B. Phillips' paraphrase, *The New Testament in Modern English.*

223

worship as *the Book of Moses was read aloud in the hearing of the people* (1). The daily reading of Scripture and its faithful exposition in relevant preaching is essential to Christian growth and maturity. When we study the Bible ourselves or listen to its interpretation in Christian teaching, God corrects, encourages and instructs. He corrects us as he identifies sins of omission and commission which need to be put right. He encourages us by reminding us that he can turn life's curses into blessings, and, as with these Israelites, he urges us to rectify those things which damage our lives, hinder others and disappoint him.

Nehemiah 13:4–31
17. Temple, market-place and home

Nehemiah had given twelve years to his work in Jerusalem (1:1; 2.1, 13:6), and once his main task was over he made his way back to Susa to report to the king. After an undefined period back in Persia, he obtained permission to make a return visit to Judah. He may well have been away for a few years, long enough for some of the men to have married foreign wives and raise families with children who did not know the Hebrew language (23–24).

In Jerusalem, things were not as their former governor had remembered them. He had exercised an exemplary influence on the everyday life of the people but, once he left the city, standards began to fall. Despite the fact that large numbers of its citizens and people from the surrounding countryside had put their seals to the covenant, things drifted badly. It probably did not happen suddenly, or dramatically. Gradually, people started to do things without asking whether God's Word had anything to say on the subject. They began to live for themselves rather than the Lord. They stopped giving generously for the support of the Levites as they had promised to do. Without their regular teaching ministry, men and women were no longer reminded of spiritual values. Israelites all over the country neglected Scripture's provisions for the Sabbath. Marriage and family concerns were no longer subject to divine direction. Soon, Judah's faith was adversely affected. Its religious (7–11), commercial (15–22) and domestic (23–27) life became less than God intended it to be.

Temple, market-place and home were no longer places where God's name was revered and his values honoured. The preceding chapter, with its arresting account of devoted choristers, reliable gatekeepers, gifted instrumentalists, greatly valued (12:44) priests and committed Levites is replaced by the story of despondent Levites (10), silenced singers (10), disobedient tradesmen (15), ungodly merchants (16), materialistic nobles (17) and spiritually negligent husbands (23). The exemplary leadership of Ezra and Nehemiah

(12:26) had given way to the damaging leadership of Eliashib (4, 7) and the unnamed son of Joiada (28).

This concluding chapter of Nehemiah is a warning against spiritual carelessness. It reminds us how easily and imperceptibly things can slip. A healthy spiritual life in one year hardly guarantees that it will always be so. At one time the name of Demas could be mentioned appreciatively in the same sentence with Luke. Then, both were reliable men, and Paul could write warmly from prison: 'Our dear friend Luke, the doctor, and Demas send greetings.' Towards the end of the apostle's life, the two names again appear in a letter's concluding paragraph, but this time Paul's final epistle tells a different story. The greatly loved physician is still at the apostle's side, using his skills to help God's servant in his closing days: 'Only Luke is with me.' But 'Demas, because he loved this world, has deserted me'.[1]

Individuals change, and so can churches. When John writes Christ's letters to the churches of Asia Minor, the believers at Ephesus possessed fine qualities – hard work, endurance, loyalty to the truth, discernment, courage and patience. But over the years they had lost the best: 'You have forsaken your first love ... Repent and do the things you did at first.'[2] These Ephesian Christians were warned that if they did not recapture their former love for Christ, their witness would first be diminished, then would disappear altogether. Despite their privileged beginnings,[3] immense resources (described in Paul's letter to the Ephesians) and later commendable experience,[4] the glowing lampstand was removed and the light extinguished in one of the greatest cities of the ancient world.

When Nehemiah returned to Jerusalem, the flame of Israel's distinctive testimony was flickering badly. If their lowering standards were allowed to continue in decline, the nation's unique spiritual influence would be diminished. God's people were meant to be 'a light for the Gentiles' and destined to take his 'salvation to the end of the earth'.[5] But traders and merchants from other countries noticed that they were no longer zealous for the Sabbath. The market-places of their towns and villages were as crowded on that day as on any other. When Nehemiah had returned to Persia, family life was sacrosanct, but now Israelite children were more influenced by their pagan mothers than their Hebrew fathers. Even the leading priests, God's role models of spirituality and commitment, were as guilty as anyone else (4, 7, 28).

---

[1] Col. 4:14; Phm. 24; 2 Tim. 4:10–11.   [2] Rev. 2:1–7.

[3] Acts 19:1–41; 20:16–38.

[4] Ignatius, *Letter to the Ephesians* (c. 117 AD?), I.1: 'Taking God as your pattern and example, you have indeed fulfilled to perfection the duties of brotherliness' (*Early Christian Writings: The Apostolic Fathers* [Penguin Classics: Harmondsworth, 1948], p. 75).   [5] Is. 49:6; Lk. 2:30–32; Acts 13:47.

Nehemiah did not restrict his concern to the capital city. Visiting the towns and villages of Judah (15), he saw that the deteriorating standards in Jerusalem were reflected elsewhere in the country. The city was holy in name alone (11:1, 18), no longer in reality.

The concluding paragraphs of Nehemiah's memoirs describe the reformation which took place under his vigorous leadership. Glaring sins had to be exposed and expunged, and damaging social problems publicly acknowledged and rectified. The final chapter of the story describes how various offences were put right. The people had grieved God during Nehemiah's absence in several ways.

1. God's house defiled (13:4–9)

The chapter's opening note about the exclusion of Ammonites and Moabites from the worshipping life of God's people introduces us to one of the serious sins which Nehemiah discovered on his return to Jerusalem. A prominent Ammonite, who had earlier done everything possible to frustrate the rebuilding of Jerusalem's walls, had been given spacious living accommodation in the temple. Tobiah had been a sinister and outspoken enemy of the work, yet *Eliashib the priest* had given this Ammonite select rooms which were *formerly used to store the grain offerings and incense and temple articles, and also the tithes of grain, new wine and oil prescribed for the Levites, singers and gatekeepers, as well as the contributions for the priests* (5). These rooms were not only used for storage purposes. Certain accommodation in the temple was set aside for those 'ministering priests, gatekeepers and singers' (10:39) who lived elsewhere in Judah but regularly visited the city and temple for work assigned to them at different times during the year. In order to provide room for Tobiah, these essential services were no longer available to those who were officiating in the house of God.

Although this Eliashib is unlikely to be the high priest of the same name (3:1; 12:10), Jerusalem's high priest can scarcely have been unaware of what was happening in the temple, and he cannot be free from blame. Those who assume positions of leadership must ensure that people to whom they have delegated responsibility are serving in a manner which glorifies God and meets the needs of the people.

The story of Tobiah's residence within the temple precincts is a cameo of serious warning. Eliashib had been entrusted with a privileged responsibility but, by cultivating the wrong relationships, he misused his office and frustrated God's work.

Eliashib was entrusted with a privileged responsibility. This priest *had been put in charge of the storerooms of the house of our God* (4). When the covenant was renewed, it was to these same rooms that the Levites brought their tithes (10:38), and it was there that the

Israelite people, along with the Levites, were 'to bring their contributions of grain, new wine and oil', commodities used for the daily sacrifices. This special accommodation was also used for keeping 'the articles of the sanctuary' as well as for housing the temple's visiting personnel.

Specific duties were often delegated to individual priests, and Eliashib had been assigned to this privileged task of ensuring that the storerooms were available for the purposes for which they were intended, so that Jerusalem's worship was maintained in a regular, orderly and dignified manner. These were places to receive the offerings, house the temple's sacred articles and accommodate the Lord's servants. Eliashib had the unique opportunity to do a necessary job in a manner which would honour God, but it all went wrong.

First, Eliashib cultivated the wrong relationships; he was *closely associated* with Tobiah. The term may indicate that he was linked to Tobiah's family by marriage.[6] In that case the chapter both begins and ends with the story of two priestly families (4, 28) who compromised their loyalty to God's Word. The Ammonite troublemaker had certainly established strong family ties with some leading Judeans. He had married into an Israelite family and his own son had done the same (6:18). It is possible that, in one way or another, Eliashib the priest had established a family link, however distant, with Tobiah. Whether this is so or not, close ties had developed between Eliashib and Tobiah, and the association was certainly not to the priest's advantage. Our lives can be ruined by damaging relationships. The apostles were eager that the early Christians should live in the world as consistent and attractive witnesses to the love and power of Christ, but these leaders knew only too well that, whilst involvement is a crucial necessity, absorption is a recurrent danger.[7]

Secondly, Eliashib seriously misused his office. He used a holy privilege for an unholy purpose. That *large room* (5) had not been intended as a convenient city *pied-à-terre* for a dangerous opponent of God's people. It was meant for higher things but, in his desire to please Tobiah, Eliashib had marginalized the spiritual priorities to which the room had been dedicated. Tragically, the priest's moral indifference and spiritual carelessness is not an act of isolated disloyalty. Throughout history there have been those who were given fine opportunities to further the Lord's work but who instead, by their inconsistent lifestyles, have brought dishonour on the name

[6] The same term is used in Ru. 2:20 to describe the relationship of Boaz to Naomi and Ruth.

[7] Rom. 12:2; 1 Cor. 5:9–11; 10:27 – 11:1; 15:33; 2 Cor. 6:14 – 7:1; Eph. 5:3–16; Col. 3:5–10; 2 Tim. 2:3–4; Tit. 2:1–10; 3:14; Jas 4:4; 1 Pet. 2:11–12, 15; 3:1–2; 4:1–4; 2 Pet 3:11–14; 1 Jn. 2:15–17.

of God and damage to their witness. Paul had Christian contemporaries who let the side down,[8] and his painful disappointments were not the last. Those of us who are entrusted with responsibility in Christian work must ensure that our lives do not contradict our message.

Thirdly, Eliashib frustrated God's work. The later verses (10–13) explain that, during Nehemiah's absence, the people withheld their gifts to the temple for the support of its personnel. Levites and singers had been compelled to give up their spiritual ministry to work in the fields so as to maintain their families. It is impossible to know which came first – the people's disobedience about giving (thus providing vacant rooms in the temple which Tobiah could occupy), or the priest's transgression (in using a room for improper purposes) so that there was nowhere for their gifts to be stored nor anywhere the neglected singers and gatekeepers might stay. During the period between Zerubbabel's arrival and Nehemiah's administration, such gifts for the support of the Levites, singers and gatekeepers had been faithfully provided on a regular basis (12:47), but the improper occupancy of these rooms by an enemy of God's people disrupted that generosity and sent the wrong messages to the Israelite people. It suggested that materialistic advantage takes precedence over spiritual opportunity.

Fourthly, the further warning of this painful saga is that sin is never an isolated phenomenon. One transgression leads inevitably to another. The sin of greed, which made the people neglect the practical support of the Levites, may have created empty rooms in Jerusalem's temple, rooms soon occupied by a totally unsuitable person. Neglecting to do good often spawns an opportunity for evil. A failure to love and show kindness to someone in need can give rise to emotional pain, a sense of neglect, the complaint of negligence, criticism by others – and so the iniquity begins to multiply. Sin always spreads. The careless or cruel word seldom dies in an unreceptive silence; it is like a destructive missile which is hurled into future conversations, creating further havoc wherever it goes.

Finally, Eliashib was not sensitive to the seriousness of sin. Had he lived closer to God, he would never have allowed Tobiah to live within the sacred precincts of the temple. It had been built to honour God, not to promote self. But, by over-familiarity with holy things, the priest became careless about spiritual issues. He knew that *no Ammonite . . . should ever be admitted into the assembly of God* (2) but his mind had become absorbed with other issues. He was no longer the obedient servant of the Word that every priest was expected to be. He did not conform to the priestly ideal, so

---

[8] Rom. 16:17–18; 1 Cor. 5:1–7; 6:1–8; Phil. 1:15–17.

persuasively described by Malachi. His work for God 'called for reverence'. The ideal priest 'stood in awe' of God's name. 'True instruction was in his mouth and nothing false was found on his lips'. He walked with God 'in peace and uprightness, and turned many from sin'. But, as with many of Malachi's priestly contemporaries, Eliashib had 'turned from the way' and, doubtless by his bad example, 'caused many to stumble'.[9] Though Malachi's prophetic ministry is likely to have pre-dated Nehemiah, its moral and spiritual exposure was starkly relevant in this period between the governor's departure after the rebuilding and his return from Persia. It indicates that Eliashib's sin was not a solitary one. During Malachi's time the people had become materialistically minded, their tithes were withheld and the priests had discredited their office. It has much in common with the situation discovered by Nehemiah when he came back to Jerusalem for his return visit.

Nehemiah saw Eliashib's act for what it was – an offence against a holy God, a public denial of the priority of spiritual things, and an act of blatant disobedience to Scripture. Nehemiah could not view Eliashib's action as a friendly gesture to an influential visitor. He called it by its proper name. It was not a kindly thing; it was *an evil thing* (7). Every believer needs a greater sensitivity to sin. All too easily, the ugly thing gradually becomes tolerated, even viewed as the possibly useful thing, then the permissible thing, and finally the attractive thing. It does not happen in a moment. Standards are lowered gradually and imperceptibly. Sin becomes known by another name. We accommodate at one stage of life things which earlier would have been totally unacceptable. That is how great empires have decayed; the disintegration takes place gradually from within. That is how good characters are destroyed. That is how some Christians have been spoilt – by failing to see sin as Nehemiah saw it, the *evil thing* which ruins the choicest things and, by undetected infiltration, corrupts the best of lives.

The identification of the problem demanded drastic, public and immediate action. It was not the time for reflection, delay or compromise. The narrative conveys the prompt action and emotional intensity of the drama: *I learned about the evil thing . . . I was greatly displeased and threw all Tobiah's household goods out of the room. I gave orders to purify the rooms, and then I put back into them the equipment of the house of God, with the grain offerings and the incense* (7–9).

The bad was speedily removed and the good immediately restored. Nehemiah acted exactly as Jesus did five centuries later. Christ also found Jerusalem's holy place cluttered with things which defiled its

[9] Mal. 2:4–9.

glory, contradicted its holiness and marred its witness. On entering the temple courts, the worshipper's mind was immediately diverted from the Lord's praise to the trader's profits. But the place was built to glorify God, not to further commercial enterprise. It was to promote enduring spiritual enrichment, not passing material gain.

Like Nehemiah before him, Jesus tipped over the merchants' stalls and the money-changer's booths. The market-place had supplanted the holy place. Secularism had come to dominate life's priorities. In Jesus' day the sin was all the more serious and offensive. The selling was taking place in the Court of the Gentiles, the area where non-Jews were permitted to listen to God's Word and pray. The traders had supplanted the seekers. That is why Jesus reminded the indignant offenders of Isaiah's memorable words: 'My house will be called a house of prayer for all nations.'[10] Such blatant misuse of the temple could not be tolerated. The temple was for foreigners seeking the Lord, not for those who did not honour him. It was hindering God-fearing Gentiles from hearing unique teaching and sharing in supportive prayer.

Nehemiah's temple narrative, like that which describes the cleansing of Jerusalem's later temple, has important things to say to us about how easily, even imperceptibly, damaging things can displace helpful things in our lives. Paul used temple imagery in his holiness teaching to the Corinthians. Christians in Greek cities were used to seeing impressive temples and wayside shrines to pagan deities. He reminded a Greek audience that 'God . . . does not live in temples built by hands'.[11] During Christ's ministry on earth, his human body became the temple of God, the locus of revelation, sacrifice, forgiveness and intercession.[12] The Lord's present temple is still not to be found in a material building, but in human life. Paul told the Corinthian church that God's Spirit is resident in two places: a human body and a spiritual community.

The apostle says that, now Christ has ascended, the body of the Christian believer is the temple of the Holy Spirit; he indwells our lives. Paul uses the argument to urge the Corinthian believers to ensure that the temple of their human life is kept free from defilement. Their lives belong to God. They 'were bought at a price', therefore, they are to 'honour God' with their bodies.[13] There was a great deal of immorality and uncleanness, damaging and potentially destructive *household goods* in Corinth, just as there was in Jerusalem's temple, both in the time of Nehemiah and of Jesus. The body is meant 'for the Lord', and is not to be polluted as it was by the Eliashib-and-Tobiah partnership. Damaging things can soon corrupt the believer's life, things we possess or ache to possess, see

[10] Is. 56:6–7.   [11] Acts 17:24.   [12] Jn. 2:19–22.   [13] 1 Cor. 6:19–20.

or want to see, hear or have heard, done or desire to do. The temple of Christian personality is a vulnerable dwelling-place and needs to be kept free from defiling influences. The cleansing can be costly. Jesus described it vividly in his teaching. The covetous hand must be severed, the avaricious eye removed. Sacrifice is essential to holiness. Delay is dangerous. Lack of firm resolution can prove morally and spiritually disastrous. As Jesus says, 'It is better for you to lose one part of your body than for your whole body to be thrown into hell'.[14] Christ presses the point home, as does Paul, in the context of sexual temptation. In times like ours, when permissiveness is actively encouraged and sexual offences rampant yet connived at, the warning is specially relevant. For God's glory, at Christ's command and by the Spirit's strength, we need to throw out anything which defiles the temple of our bodies.

In another letter to Corinth, Paul makes a different use of the temple imagery. He tells the believers that their corporate life is also the Lord's temple: 'For we are the temple of the living God. As God has said, "I will live with them and walk among them".'[15] Just as sin can have a devastating effect in the life of an individual, so it can seriously defile a Christian community. Local churches are also vulnerable. They too can become littered with Tobiah's *household goods*, sins which the enemy spawns – unworthy clutter, unspiritual diversions, unhelpful talk, unsanctified ambitions, godless rivalries, selfish preoccupations. Paul had all those problems at Corinth. All such things need to be identified and removed if the local church is to enjoy God's presence, reflect Christ's likeness and convey the Spirit's message effectively to an unbelieving world. There was a surfeit of damaging *household goods* at Corinth, and Paul was courageous enough to expose them though, in the eyes of some people, it cost him his popularity to do so. Some of the believers there had turned a blind eye to 'impurity, sexual sin and debauchery'[16] – all too common in Corinth, but totally impermissible within the temple of their corporate worship, fellowship and witness. Nehemiah was the first courageous hero to cleanse a temple but he was not the last.

2. God's servants neglected (13:10–13)

It is certain that, had they been employed in Jerusalem as they were meant to be, the Levites would have challenged Eliashib's *laissez-faire* policy of encouraging an Ammonite to live within the temple precincts. It was part of their work to teach biblical principles and maintain high spiritual standards. But their ministry soon became marginalized as the prescribed gifts for their support began to

---

[14] Mt. 5:28–30.   [15] 2 Cor. 6:16.   [16] 2 Cor. 12:20–21.

dwindle and eventually dried up altogether. God's plan was that they should be totally maintained by the people's tithes and, for that reason, when the country was divided, they had not been allocated specific tribal territory in Judah. The Lord was to be their inheritance.[17] They were to devote themselves entirely to spiritual work, with their upkeep provided by the people's regular gifts of a tenth of their income. That was the promise made earlier by those who reaffirmed their commitment to the covenant: 'And we will bring a tithe of our crops to the Levites' (10:37). Those who set their seal to the covenant had made their promise, 'We will not neglect the house of our God' (10:39). Yet, within a relatively short time, God's house had been seriously neglected once again, by sins both of commission and of omission – by what was done (providing a home for Tobiah), and not done (presenting the gifts for the support of the Levites).

The allotted gifts for the sacrifices were to be brought to the priest at the storerooms occupied and defiled by Tobiah's person and possessions. The ministry of the temple was no longer effective within the spiritual life of Israel. This fifth-century period when Jerusalem's spiritual life became lax, its priesthood careless and its Levites unsupported, is reflected in the teaching of Malachi. He describes a time when spiritual leaders were content to give him less than the best.[18]

Malachi also denounces those who divorced their Israelite wives in order to marry foreign women,[19] possibly so as to gain financially by a new marriage, thus opening up new trade contacts with neighbouring people. Similar conditions are reflected in the situation Nehemiah discovered on returning to Jerusalem, when 'men of Judah ... married women from Ashdod, Ammon and Moab' (23). The enemy has more than one way of establishing a destructive bridgehead into the life of God's people. An Ammonite man may well be evicted from the temple, but there are plenty of Ammonite women now living at the heart of Israel's spiritual and moral life, the family. They have been excluded from the temple, but they have gained a foothold in the home.

Malachi's central theme is the non-payment of tithes. He pleads that these obligatory offerings for the upkeep of the Levites be brought to the temple.[20] Nehemiah knew how crucial the Levites' work had been in teaching the Word (8:7–9, 11) and, as singers, encouraging the worship (12:47–48). Robbed of necessary support, these men had been compelled to go and work on the land in order to maintain their families. With neglected teaching (Levites) and diminished worship (singers), Jerusalem's spiritual life was markedly impoverished. The people appointed by God to maintain high

[17] Nu. 18:20.   [18] Mal. 1:6–9.   [19] Mal. 2:10–16.   [20] Mal. 3:8–10.

standards were no longer there to do so. It is little wonder that the laws about Sabbath were disregarded and those about marriage ignored.

One sin follows hard on the heels of another. When God's Word is not read, studied or taught, serious defects are bound to follow. Jerusalem's culture was quickly secularized. Materialism became Judah's new god. Studied indifference to God's Word became the order of the day. It mattered no longer what God thought and what the Levites taught. Everybody pleased themselves. It was a recipe for moral, marital and spiritual disaster. People who persistently refuse to listen to the God who loves them cannot hope to live satisfying, resourceful and useful lives.

The payment of tithes for the Levites' support was crucial for the continuance of their work. The priests could exist on the allotted portions of the sacrifices which were brought to the temple, but the Levites had nothing but the tithe money. If that was withheld, God's voice through their ministry was virtually silenced. It is all a tragic reversal of the situation some time earlier when, with hearts full of gratitude and high resolve, the people had put their seals to the covenant and shared with the worshipping crowds who dedicated Jerusalem's walls. At that time the storerooms were packed to capacity with the abundant gifts of God's thankful people (12:44). In those days giving was not an irksome duty. The people were delighted to give for the support of their teachers and spiritual leaders: 'for Judah was pleased with the ministering priests and Levites'. They willingly donated for the ministry of God's Word and work. How easily and quickly things can go into serious decline.

In many parts of the world, excellent work might be done for the Lord if only there were sufficient resources. Imaginative opportunities for service have to be passed by because Christian societies and missionary agencies do not receive enough money to meet present demands, let alone sponsor creative initiatives. Every Christian needs to take this story of Israel's neglect of the Levites as both a warning and encouragement. It warns us against a materialistic outlook which fails to act generously toward others, and it encourages us to think seriously about proportionate, systematic, regular giving. Without making it anything like a legalistic obligation, many Christians throughout the world have made the Israelite tenth a useful minimum guideline when allocating the amount they give to the Lord's work.

Just as Nehemiah had cleared those temple rooms of unworthy things, so now he is determined to fill them with good things. Jesus' parable reminds us that in human life 'empty rooms' are a potential hazard.[21] Nehemiah organizes a team of helpers (see pp. 251–253) to ensure that the *tithes of grain, new wine and oil* (12) which were meant for the Levites (10) are brought to the newly vacated rooms. Now they begin to be used again for their original purpose. Nehemiah knows that it is never enough to concentrate negatively on the exposure of evil; the ideal leader also encourages the promotion of the good.[22] It is possible for church leaders to acquire highly sensitive mechanisms for recognizing what is wrong but to be less imaginative in promoting what is right. Nehemiah did both. Without the expulsion of evil, the good cannot prosper; without the promotion of the good the evil will return.

3. God's day misused (13:15–22)

When God entered a covenant with his people, he gave visible signs to demonstrate his love for them and commitment to them. Supremely, he gave them a book (law), a place (tabernacle, then temple), a ministry (priests and Levites), and a day (Sabbath) at the end of each week which they were to devote exclusively to him. So far in chapter 13 of Nehemiah, we have seen how the first three of these outward signs had become seriously defiled: God's Word had been disobeyed (1–3), his temple desecrated (4–9) and his ministers neglected (10–11). Now we see how his day had been disregarded.

On his return, Nehemiah found that, not only in the 'holy city' but also in Judah's surrounding communities, there was no appreciable attempt to keep the Sabbath special. The seventh day was much like any other day. This weekly outward sign of their commitment to God was no longer evident to an unbelieving neighbour. By their disobedience to God's Word, they had come to worship the unseen idols of contemporary culture. The invisible gods of humanism, secularism, materialism and pluralism had taken the place of the only true God. The occupation of the temple by Tobiah was Israel's sin in microcosm. Just as the Ammonite's possessions had cluttered the temple and kept the Levites' ministry at arm's length, so materialistic interests had marginalized the Sabbath. Gentile visitors to Jerusalem (16) were no longer able to witness, as formerly, the devotion, integrity and loyalty implicit in the weekly act of worship and rest.

Once more, Nehemiah recognized that swift action was urgently necessary. Here again, he is intensely grieved at what he sees, but the earlier displeasure (8) now gives way to righteous anger. He knows that, with this disobedience and preoccupation with materialistic interests, so many other things are at stake. Nehemiah is a man of

[21] Mt. 12:43–45.　[22] Rom. 12:9.

determined action, and something must be done about the nation's sin. Grieving is not enough. William Carey grieved that millions of his late eighteenth-century contemporaries had never heard the gospel. He gave himself to careful geographical research, compiled population-tables and made a globe from the scraps of leather in his shoemaker's shop. He studied the vivid accounts of Captain Cook's travels and gathered persuasive statistics. He wrote his book, *An Enquiry*, to convince fellow-ministers of the world's immense need and the indisputable fact that Christ's commission in Matthew 28:19–20 had never been withdrawn. Something had to be done. It was his determination not merely to study and write but also to act that marked the beginning of the modern missionary movement.

In contemporary society, a wide range of social issues is in urgent need of committed advocates – both men and women of action. It will not do simply to grieve about such issues as abortion, drug abuse, alcoholism, homelessness, poverty, euthanasia. Christian organizations such as CARE compile reliable, up-to-date information to help and persuade parliamentarians about ethical standards, and to encourage church members to pray (a vital dimension) and to act by writing to members of parliament, so involving themselves in contemporary moral issues. To be aware of the need is one thing; to act is another. Inaction is sin, as James points out in his practical and persuasive letter: 'Anyone, then, who knows the good he ought to do and doesn't do it, sins.'[23]

The reason that the Sabbath had been instituted was to recall both Creation and Redemption. God's people were to rest as God had rested, and enjoy doing what God had commanded. In Egypt, the pressurized Hebrew slaves had longed for rest so, in the covenant, all labour was expressly forbidden on this special day: 'you shall not do any work'.[24] Yet, indifferent to God's Word, men and women in Judah's fields were now harvesting (15), doing the very thing the law had expressly forbidden for that day: 'even during the ... harvest you must rest'.[25]

At harvest time, they were not only doing work themselves but also making their servants work, as well as denying their animals essential rest. Their livestock should be enjoying the Sabbath, but Nehemiah noticed that, at harvest time, their donkeys were made to carry heavy loads, a practice directly prohibited by the law.[26] Throughout Judah they were harvesting their grapes, loading their grain, working their donkeys, carrying their produce (*wine, grapes, figs and all other kinds of loads*) and selling their wares, all on the Sabbath, which God had told them to keep as his own special day.

[23] Jas 4:17.   [24] Ex. 20:10; Dt. 5:14.   [25] Ex. 34:21.   [26] Ex. 23:12.

The badge of their promised loyalty[27] was seriously defaced. Instead of putting God first as they had promised (10:28–29), they had put their businesses first. Money and property had become their idol.

This badge of their unique relationship with God was therefore no longer visible to others. Its intention had been not only to honour him and to help them, but also to persuade others; the Sabbath had immense witnessing value. It let other people know how much God mattered to them. In earlier generations, visitors to Israel could hardly have failed to notice how much they honoured God: his will took precedence over their own; his demands overruled their desires. On the seventh day of every week, Gentiles had seen for themselves how much Israelite farmers, tradesmen, merchants, servants, masters, housewives and children loved their God.

Now it was different. Nehemiah saw Phoenicians[28] who had made their homes in Jerusalem treating the Sabbath like any other day: *Men from Tyre who lived in Jerusalem were bringing in fish and all kinds of merchandise and selling them on the Sabbath to the people of Judah* (16). Israelites from the surrounding towns and villages were no longer visiting the 'holy city' to worship on the Sabbath but to attend the city's busy markets, in order to buy and sell their produce up and down its crowded streets. They had abandoned their visible weekly emblem of loyalty and witness. Gentiles were no longer able to discern any distinctive difference between the Israelite believers and people from other countries and cultures.

Nehemiah made a direct approach to Judah's nobles. The leaders of any community have a social and moral responsibility to put things right. Several characteristics of Nehemiah emerge from this narrative about how he responded to Israel's sin.

a. Nehemiah's knowledge of Scripture

Nehemiah's earlier references to harvesting and the loading of donkeys show how well he knew the covenant and the specific Sabbath regulations of the Mosaic Law: 'on the seventh day do not work, so that your ox and your donkey may rest . . . Be careful to do everything I have said to you'.[29] Yet the people had ignored God's Word.

Moreover, Nehemiah twice uses language from the teaching of both Isaiah and Ezekiel when he accuses his contemporaries of

---

[27] Ezk. 20:12, 20.

[28] See D. R. Ap-Thomas, 'The Phoenicians', in D. J. Wiseman (ed.), *Peoples of Old Testament Times* (Oxford: Clarendon, 1973), pp. 259–286, and S. Moscati, *The World of the Phoenicians* (London: Weidenfeld and Nicolson, 1968), pp. 82–87. They were the most accomplished maritime nation in the ancient world (Ezr. 3:7; Is. 23:2–3, 8; Ezk. 27:1–23; Am. 1:9–10) and exported dried, smoked or salted fish, an important part of the permissible Israelite diet (Lv. 11:9; Nu. 11:5).   [29] Dt. 23:12–13.

desecrating the Sabbath (17, 18). Isaiah promised that those who 'keep the Sabbath without desecrating it' will have abiding joy. Ezekiel lamented to Israel's elders the folly of the people's repeated disobedience over the centuries: they 'did not follow my decrees but rejected my laws ... and they utterly desecrated my Sabbaths'.[30] And they were told to keep God's Sabbaths 'holy, that they may be a sign between us' and so that 'they would know that I the LORD made them holy'.[31]

The Sabbath was designed by God not solely as a divinely appointed occasion for physical rest but as a conspicuous symbol that God was the Lord of the Israelites and that they were his people, 'set apart' for his work and witness in an unbelieving world.

b. Nehemiah's use of history

Didn't your forefathers do the same things, so that our God brought all this calamity upon us and upon this city? (18). Once again, Nehemiah draws upon prophetic Scripture, this time citing the instance of brazen Sabbath-breaking in the time of Jeremiah.[32] Back in the sixth century, 150 years before Nehemiah's administration, the people of Jerusalem were doing exactly what Nehemiah found his contemporaries doing when he returned to the city after a period in Persia. The Lord had said to them through Jeremiah, 'Be careful not to carry a load on the Sabbath day', but there they were in the following century at it again, packing their wares on to their donkeys. Jeremiah had said they were not to carry their loads 'through the gates of Jerusalem', but Nehemiah later found them doing exactly that, persistently and unashamedly, *bringing all this into Jerusalem on the Sabbath* (15).

Jeremiah had warned his Sabbath-breaking contemporaries that, if they continued trafficking on God's special day, the Lord would 'kindle an unquenchable fire in the gates of Jerusalem that will consume her fortresses'.[33] Every Israelite knew that Jeremiah's prediction had been devastatingly fulfilled. Those very gates through which her busy traders had passed had been burnt by Nebuchadnezzar's ruthless invaders. New gates had been made and set up by Nehemiah's workers (6:1; 7:1), and now the country's farmers and the city's shopkeepers were in danger of courting a similar disaster in exactly the same way as their disobedient forefathers. People seldom learn from history, but Nehemiah tried to warn the people of the likely consequences of their sin by reminding them of earlier transgression and its evident, frightening consequences.

[30] Is. 56:4–7; Ezk. 20:13, 16, 21, 24.   [31] Ezk. 20:20, 12.   [32] Je. 17:19–27
[33] Je. 17:27.

Jeremiah had contrasted those who travelled from Judah's towns and villages carrying their sacrificial offerings with those avaricious merchants whose hearts were set on what they might grasp for themselves rather than on what they might give to God. The prophet's wistful reference to grain offerings and thankofferings would hardly be lost on people who had withheld their grain from the Levites (15) but were selling that grain for themselves.

c. Nehemiah's resolute action

Nehemiah, however, was not content simply to turn the people's attention to God's Word in Scripture and his work in history. It was a time not simply to hear the warnings of the past but to face the challenge of the present. Nehemiah spoke sternly and acted firmly. He used his gift of direct speech to great effect. He *rebuked the officials* (11) about their failure to support the Levites. He *warned* (15) the traders about selling food on the Sabbath. He *rebuked* Judah's nobles (17) about the breach of the law. He *warned* (21) those inventive merchants who put temptation in the way of the people by erecting stalls outside the gates, luring the weaker Israelite to the other side of the city walls for buying on the Sabbath. He *rebuked* those who had broken their vows of loyalty to God regarding marriage (25). Nehemiah's forthright and uncompromising speech was used to challenge and check weaker people who were living carelessly and behaving improperly.

But God's servant did not only talk; he acted. He confronted the offenders, visited the nobles and challenged the merchants. He took immediate practical steps to rectify a spiritually and morally hazardous situation. He ordered the closing of the city's gates at dusk on the eve of the Sabbath. Only *once or twice* (20) did the artful traders get the chance to erect their Sabbath stalls outside the walls of the city. No wonder *they no longer came on the Sabbath* (21). When Nehemiah spoke and acted, things had to change.

Throughout biblical and Christian history, believers have been grateful for men and women of bold speech and determined action. The heroic example of Daniel and his friends inspired the Israelite people when they were in danger of compromise. As a young man, Daniel acted with trusting resolution, refusing to eat the food provided for him and his compatriots. He insisted on taking a stand for what he knew to be right, and God vindicated him. Later, as a much older man, his determined loyalty was equally unswerving. He refused to change the pattern of his prayer life simply because a pagan king had been manipulated into making an irrelevant edict. Likewise, Daniel's colleagues were determined not to bow down to an idol, however impressive. They believed their God was able to rescue them but told the king that, even if he did not, they would not worship Nebuchadnezzar's image of gold.[34] Over the centuries, the church of Christ throughout the world has been enriched by the inspiring example of men and women who did not only speak fearlessly but lived courageously and did what was right in the sight of God, regardless of the cost. Nehemiah was a man of that calibre, and the life of God's people was better for his devoted work and determined witness.

How significant for us is Nehemiah's Sabbath-restoration campaign? Christians obviously appreciate Sunday as their key opportunity for worship, witness, rest and service, but it is a mistake automatically to transfer the Sabbath teaching of the Old Testament to the Lord's Day of the New. This episode in Nehemiah's ministry is neither to be fervently copied nor summarily dismissed. As we have already seen, these Old Testament situations offer us an illuminating paradigm or model and, whilst this strict Sabbatarianism ought not to be imitated, Nehemiah's story does offer important lessons which can be applied to our use of Sunday and emphasize the need for adequate rest in our lives.

The Israelites' later mistake about Sabbath was in the intense legalism they brought to its sanctions. By the first century, the prohibition about ploughing featured in rabbinic interpretation forbidding the combing of hair. Jesus exposed such rigorous application of the law, teaching his followers that the 'Sabbath was made for man, not man for the Sabbath'.[35] It was intended to benefit them, not irritate them. He deplored the rigid legalism of a synagogue leader, for example, who was angry that a miracle of healing had taken place on the Sabbath.[36] Jesus gave a greater priority to a crippled woman's happiness than to a synagogue ruler's prohibitions. A preoccupation with the legalistic interpretation of the law had obliterated love. The Sabbath was intended for divine glory and human good.

Nehemiah exposed the gross materialism of his contemporaries for whom the acquisition of money had become a greater priority than obedience to God. Their desecration of the Sabbath meant that, as well as denying themselves the opportunity for spiritual worship and physical relaxation, they were also robbing their servants and animals of the right to rest.

Nehemiah was no kill-joy. He knew that the nation could not hope to please God if they wilfully ignored his laws and deprived their workers of essential rest. We ought to avoid rigid regulations and negative prohibitions about Sunday. However well intended, that road may lead all too easily to the very legalism which Jesus

[34] Dn. 1:1–21; 6:1–24; 3:1–30.   [35] Mk. 2:27.   [36] Lk. 13:10–17.

condemned in his religious contemporaries. Nor can we insist that our unbelieving contemporaries automatically endorse our thinking about the best use of Sunday. But we can and should encourage them to believe that the idea of one rest day in each week is God's pattern for humanity, and Sunday is an excellent day for its enjoyment. Jesus said that the Sabbath was 'made for man', not just for the Israelites. One of the saddest things about the increasing pattern of Sunday trading is that it seriously disrupts family life. In contemporary Britain, women make up half the Sunday work-force in shops and supermarkets, which means that innumerable homes are without a mother (or father) on that day when the family might be together and value each other's company. There is evidence that it is already beginning to create serious difficulties for employees who do not wish to work on Sundays, so that some people are fearful that their determination to 'keep Sunday special' may lead to unemployment.

In demanding that his contemporaries set aside that seventh day for the purposes God intended, Nehemiah was emphasizing the centrality of worship, the importance of witness, the necessity of rest and the priority of love. He was saying that loving obedience is better than a full purse.

The prophetic understanding of Sabbath was that it should be an immense 'delight',[37] not an irritating chore. God never demands anything from his people that is not for their good. When Nehemiah's mercenary contemporaries ignored the Sabbath, they were damaging the fabric of their spiritual, physical and social lives. It was too high a price for temporary economic success.

4. God's standards ignored (13:23-28)

Nehemiah exposed those sins of his people which were evident in both temple and market-place; now their transgressions were damaging the nation's home and family life. During his absence, every one of the covenant vows (10:28-39) had been broken, including the people's commitment not to marry partners who did not share their faith. On his return, Nehemiah discovered that *men of Judah . . . had married women from Ashdod, Ammon and Moab. Half of their children spoke the language of Ashdod or the language of one of the other peoples, and did not know how to speak the language of Judah.* Only a few years earlier, as God's people were repairing the walls, the 'Ammonites and the men of Ashdod' had 'plotted together to come and fight against Jerusalem' (4:7-8). Now,

---

[37] Is. 58:13-14.

yesterday's enemies have become today's marriage partners. There is more than one way of destroying a city.

We have already seen (10:30) how crucial it was for Israel's faith that its people did not marry unbelieving partners, yet many in Judah had disregarded this important law. In challenging his contemporaries about their disobedience, Nehemiah uses arguments from experience (23–24) and from Scripture and history (25–26), in the hope that they will realize the enormity of their sin in the sight of God. The offenders had made a series of gross errors and, although we live in a different context and are separated from them by two and a half millenniums, their serious mistake has a relevant message for us: we too can grieve God, ignore the warnings of Scripture and disregard the serious consequences of sin.

First, the offenders had grieved God. Nehemiah identified their sin as *terrible wickedness* in which they had been *unfaithful to our God* (27). Prompted by the materialistic outlook we have already noticed, it is highly likely that these men married foreign wives to promote their commercial interests. During the period of Malachi's ministry, many Judeans appear to have divorced their Israelite wives in order to marry someone from another country and with a different religious allegiance. The prophet exposed the sin of divorce and, though his ministry may not be precisely dated, it certainly belongs to the period that followed the return of the exiles, and may even have been exercised during the lifetime of Nehemiah.

Malachi was distressed that the Judeans had 'broken faith' and 'desecrated the sanctuary the LORD loves, by marrying the daughter of a foreign god'. In doing so, those who had married foreign women had 'broken faith' with their Israelite wives by divorcing them, even though they were bound to them in their 'marriage covenant'. Malachi told them that the Lord hates divorce.[38] For Nehemiah, the most serious aspect of such *terrible wickedness* was that they had not only been unfaithful to the wives of their 'youth' but had also been *unfaithful* to their God *by marrying foreign women.* They had broken their part of the agreement they had made in the covenant promise of exclusive loyalty.

Secondly, the offenders had ignored the plain warnings of Scripture. God had not only given them unequivocal commands about mixed marriages; he had provided stark illustrations in his Word about the dangers inherent in such compromising and forbidden partnerships. Nehemiah hurls a question at the offenders, directing them to a story well known to all their people: *Was it not because of marriages like these that Solomon king of Israel sinned? Among the many nations there was no king like him. He was loved*

---

[38] Mal. 2:10–16.

by his God, and God made him king over all Israel, but even he was led into sin by foreign women (26).

Solomon's offence in this matter had adversely affected their history in the worst possible way. It had led directly to the division of the kingdom. The tragic consequences of one man's sin had written one of the darkest chapters in the nation's history. Scripture made no secret of the disaster: 'King Solomon loved many foreign women besides Pharaoh's daughter ... They were from nations about which the LORD had told the Israelites, "You must not intermarry with them, because they will surely turn your hearts after their gods". Nevertheless, Solomon held fast to them in love.' As Solomon advanced in years, 'his wives turned his heart after other gods, and his heart was not fully devoted to the LORD his God ... He followed ... Molech, the detestable god of the Ammonites. So Solomon did evil in the eyes of the LORD.'[39]

The historian who wrote the books of Kings says that 'on a hill east of Jerusalem', Solomon built altars for 'Chemosh the detestable god of Moab, and for Molech the detestable god of the Ammonites' and that all his foreign wives had their own shrines at which they 'burned incense and offered sacrifices to their gods'.[40]

Nehemiah appeals to the people's understanding of history as well as their knowledge of Scripture, making the important contemporary point that even those who are privileged (or *loved by the LORD*, which is the meaning of Solomon's other name, Jedediah),[41] and who are successful (*no king like him*), can fall into alarming sin. Solomon was treasured by God and applauded by others, and yet he made this awful mistake. It was a stark warning to every Israelite born after him but, even so, many of Nehemiah's contemporaries totally disregarded history's warning about Solomon's disobedience.

The stern terms of Nehemiah's rebuke were shatteringly apposite for those Judean men. Some of them had married women belonging to the precise nations from which Solomon's wives had come from. Women from those same countries were now bringing up their families in Judah – Moabites and Ammonites, the very people who had been excluded from the temple's worship (1–3). An Ammonite had lived for a period at the Jerusalem temple (4–5), but these women had come to stay permanently in many an Israelite home, and, once established there, the potential damage was incalculable. Solomon's sin had been multiplied in their midst.

Thirdly, the offenders were indifferent to the disastrous consequences of their sin. The mother's role in the family is crucial. Normally, she is the one who spends the most time with her children, and naturally they are going to imbibe her principles, copy her

[39] 1 Ki. 11:1–6. [40] 1 Ki. 11:7–8. [41] 2 Sa. 12:24–25; see NIV margin.

lifestyle and, certainly in the case of these fifth-century children, follow her faith. Inevitably, they would speak her language, and so the likelihood of their learning Hebrew was remote. Yet Hebrew was the language in which their Scriptures were written, and when they went to the temple that was the language spoken by priests and Levites. Nehemiah discovered that half of these children in Judah and Jerusalem were fluent in their mother's tongue but had no Hebrew at all. When God's Word was read, they could not understand its message. Moreover, there is little doubt that their mothers, maintaining their allegiance to the gods of Ashdod, Ammon and Moab, encouraged them to pray to such gods and taught them about these native religions.

Concerned about making money, these Israelite fathers had not considered the inevitable effect of their disobedience to God. If more and more Israelites ignored the teaching of God's Word about marriage to an unbelieving partner, then, within a relatively short period of time, Israel's distinctive message would be compromised and weakened to the point of ultimate extinction. The future of Israel's faith demanded their spiritual loyalty and integrity. Whenever we sin, we always involve other people in one way or another. We not only grieve God and damage ourselves; we affect others also.

The incidence of mixed marriage was widespread and not confined to one particular locality or class of people. It had even invaded the life of priestly families where the spiritual responsibilities were normally passed on from father to son. One of the high priest's grandsons had married the daughter of Sanballat (28), another of Israel's bitter opponents. Once again, as with the Eliashib and Tobiah offence, Nehemiah acted swiftly: *I drove him away from me*. It appears that, in some instances at least, the situation was as serious as that which Ezra had discovered in Jerusalem; even priests had entered into forbidden marriage alliances.[42]

Human problems and God's solutions: Nehemiah and ourselves

The sequence of events described in Nehemiah's closing chapter is markedly relevant in a society like our own, adversely affected by secularism, materialism, pluralism and moral relativism.

Secularism has been described as 'an attitude of indifference to religious institutions and practices or even to religious questions as such'.[43] During Nehemiah's absence, a process of increasing indifference led to the gradual erosion of vital spiritual and moral standards in Judah. In this final chapter, it is starkly illustrated by

[42] Ezra 9:1–2.
[43] Larry Skinner, 'The Meaning of Secularization', in Joachim Matthes (ed.), *International Year Book for the Sociology of Religion*, vol. 3 (1967), p. 51.

the damaging conduct of the priesthood. By encouraging an Ammonite to live in the temple courts, Eliashib demonstrated his indifference to God's Word and to his nation's spiritual values; the revealed will of God was no longer a pre-eminent concern. Although the day-to-day functions of the temple were formally maintained during Nehemiah's absence from Jerusalem, the divinely revealed principles for which it stood had been studiously disregarded. Eliashib's permissive behaviour betrayed his heedless attitude both to the teaching of Scripture and to his responsibility as a spiritual role model in the community.

Judah's secularist lifestyle is further illustrated by the nation's studied refusal to provide financial support for their spiritual leaders, the Levites. By withholding their tithe, the Israelite people were declaring their apathy concerning God's Word and the marginalization of their spiritual priorities.

The materialism of God's people was expressed in their total disregard of the provisions of the law concerning the Sabbath rest. In such a culture, pagan traders came to have greater street credibility than Levitical teachers. Money mattered more than God. Contemporary Western society becomes more materialistic with every passing year. The popularity of the National Lottery is evidence of our widespread preoccupation with financial gain. Millions dream of becoming millionaires, yet one winner who has says, 'Life is such a drag now that I can afford anything I want . . . Life has lost its buzz and to be honest it's all a bit boring.'[44] That is one of the sick aspects of materialism; 'the opium of the people', as Herbert Schlossberg describes it. It can never be satisfied.

> All true needs – such as food, drink and companionship – are satiable. Illegitimate wants – pride, envy, greed – are insatiable . . . Enough is never enough . . . That is the horror of the giant in John Bunyan and the wicked witch in C. S. Lewis who give their victims food that causes greater hunger.[45]

Pluralism found a secure foothold in Judean homes when Israelite men ignored the teaching of God's Word and married partners belonging to an alien faith. In our permissive society, the uncompromising convictions and corrective action of Nehemiah would scarcely be regarded as a virtue, but he knew that the preservation of a unique message was at stake. God both inspired and used his steadfast and costly commitment; without such courageous intervention, Israel's distinctive faith could have 'faded away, leaving as little

[44] 'The Daily Telegraph', 28 October 1995, p. 5.
[45] Herbert Schlossberg, *Idols for Destruction: Christian Faith and its Confrontation with American Society* (Nashville: Nelson, 1983), pp. 107–108. I am indebted to D. A. Carson, *The Gagging of God* (Leicester: Apollos, 1996), p. 464, for this reference.

mark on the course of the world's religious history as the Samaritans have done'.[46] Such resolute and informed defenders of the faith are urgently needed in the multi-cultural West. Those who confess Christ need to be able to explain and defend from Scripture their exclusive commitment to him, embody their beliefs in an undeniably consistent lifestyle, and create imaginative opportunities for communicating our incomparable message with both conviction and compassion.

Relativism rejects the Christian conviction that God has provided us with absolute and immutable moral standards, brilliantly summarized in the Ten Commandments. It insists that what is right and wrong is inevitably variable, depending entirely on personal circumstances, local contexts, prevailing customs and the changing patterns of human behaviour. Nehemiah discovered that Judah's people had abandoned their distinctively holy lifestyle and had become accommodated to the religious laxity of their pagan neighbours (1–3). They absorbed the social norms of Phoenician traders (16) and the syncretistic marriage customs of the surrounding nations (23). Nehemiah subjected this deviant conduct to the searchlight of Scripture in law (1–2, 10–11, 15), history (18, 26) and prophecy (17–18). In the context of present-day moral relativism, Christians need to determine their ethical standards by the objective teaching of God's Word,[47] not from vascillating contemporary opinions. They will subject alternative lifestyles to the searching test of Christ's example[48] and his pattern of Spirit-inspired living.[49] In the complexity of modern ethical decision-making, they will value the moral insights of fellow-believers in the wider context of the church,[50] and remember they are not unaided in the quest to shape their moral standards by the message of Scripture, the example of Jesus and the guidance of the Spirit.

In reforming the bleak spiritual and ethical deviancy in Israel, Nehemiah offers us some important insights into God's solution to human problems. The depressing situation confronting God's servant was rectified in five ways.

a. A necessary confession

The book of Nehemiah opens and closes with an acknowledgement of serious human need. Confession of sin, both personal and corporate, forms the introduction to Nehemiah's compelling narrative. Before responding to his people's material deprivation, he

---

[46] H. H. Rowley, 'Sanballat and the Samaritan Temple', in *Men of God* (London: Nelson, 1963), p. 276.   [47] 2 Tim. 3:16–17.
[48] Phil. 2:5–10; 1 Pet. 2:21–23; 1 Jn. 2:6.   [49] Gal. 5:22–26.
[50] Rom. 12:4–8; Heb. 10:24–25.

addresses the greater problem of their spiritual degradation (1:5–7). During the later story, on two public occasions the Israelites confess their sinfulness and rebellion (8:8–11; 13:1–3). They acknowledge that throughout their history they have repeatedly disobeyed God and ordered their lives by selfish standards rather than the message of Scripture (9:5–37). On his return from a stay in Persia, Nehemiah confronted his contemporaries with the sin of worldliness. They had allowed the lifestyles of their pagan neighbours to determine their behaviour. There was no possibility of significant spiritual progress in the life of the community until those gross sins had been exposed, acknowledged and abandoned.

Every major revival in Christian history has seriously addressed the problem of the enormity of sin and its devastating potential for human destruction. The modern church finds it easier to adopt new schemes than forsake old sins. In many situations, the church has marginalized sin and, like Nehemiah's compatriots, allowed a sin-ignoring world to dictate its agenda, altering its message, compromising its standards and changing its values. 'Do not love the world' is a strikingly relevant Johannine exhortation[51] to a generation of Christians in danger of cultural absorption and moral decline. All too often, unconsciously accommodating themselves to contemporary values, churches become preoccupied with marginal things like improved salesmanship ideas, better marketing aids and new leadership patterns. We can find ourselves doing the right thing in the wrong way or for less than worthy reasons. The God-honouring church begins with the reality of sin; it recognizes that, until personal and corporate sin is recognized and confessed, little can be achieved that will last for eternity. Until we acknowledge our failure, we are unlikely to realize our potential.

b. A renewed priority

Sin can never be identified as the malevolent power it is, however, unless it is exposed by the searchlight of God's Word. Central to Nehemiah's message is humanity's urgent need of the biblical message. Long before the palace cupbearer heard about Israel's troubles, he had imbibed the teaching of Scripture. The unique book did not merely preserve stories and sayings from a bygone age; it throbbed with immediacy, vitality and relevance. So, Nehemiah's prayers echo the inspiring language of God's Word; his ambitious ventures are inspired by biblical precedents; his standards shaped by scriptural teaching; and his fortitude undergirded by divine promises. On two great public occasions, the reading of Scripture led directly

[51] 1 Jn. 2:15–17; see also Jas. 4:4.

to a reformation of practice (8:7–12; 13:1–3). It was biblical preaching and teaching which led to a change in human life.

Beguiled by contemporary communicators, the church of our time has marginalized the primacy of expository preaching. Everything must be reduced to manageable 'sound bites'; the media insists that the visual scene and verbal message must have constantly changing variety if we are to capture the attention of reluctant hearers. People will watch their favourite sport or listen to familiar pop music for hours on end, but we are repeatedly told that our contemporaries have a short attention-span and people are incapable of sustained listening. But, when applied to preaching, such reasoning flies in the face of biblical teaching, historical evidence and contemporary evangelical experience. Congregations prepared to allocate prime time to the lively, informed, faithful and relevant exposition of Scripture are communities which meet the deepest needs of the human heart and mind.

c. A decisive affirmation

Nehemiah's message repeatedly confronts us with the greatness and sufficiency of God. It directs the attention away from peripheral issues to the one overwhelming central theme of the book: the incomparable magnitude of God's nature, the utter reliability of his truth, the searching splendour of his holiness, the fathomless depths of his love and the limitless resources of his power. Not everyone would describe Nehemiah as 'one of the most genial personalities portrayed anywhere in the Bible',[52] but all will agree that his substantial accomplishments were inspired and directed by the God who equipped and strengthened him. The dominant note of testimony, sustained throughout the book, deliberately points away from human achievement to divine enabling. Our generation of Christians needs to forsake its triumphalism or abandon its despair and recover its confidence in the superlative magnificence of God. Anything which diverts our attention from our late twentieth-century cultural self-preoccupation and fixes our gaze on the transcendent reality and abundant sufficiency of God will surely be in the tradition of Nehemiah and his associates.

d. A radical commitment

Yet our knowledge of God, however inspiring in its grandeur, can never be left at the level of the merely emotional or largely intel-lectual. If our doctrine of God is thoroughly biblical, it will activate the will. It cannot remain as detached truth, providing little more

[52] North, p. 391.

than an uplifting feeling or an elevated thought. Inevitably and essentially, it will issue in holiness of life. Nehemiah's book is about scriptural holiness as God's prescribed pattern of life for the believer. It is about holiness in the intimacy of daily personal living, reflected in prayer (1:5–11), demonstrated in surrender (2:1–9), expressed in service (2:11–20), tested in conflict (2:10, 19; 4:1–5), manifested in love (5:1–19; 8:10–12) and proved in perseverance (6:1–19; 13:4–31). In the modern world, the holiness of a believer's life continues to be one of the most potent and persuasive evangelistic instruments. Nehemiah's message reminds us that holiness is not a compartmentalized commodity, reserved for churches and Sundays. It was a holiness not narrowly confined to Jerusalem's temple but meant to be evident in Israelite business practice and domestic affairs (13:23). A holy people is the best advertisement for a transforming message.

e. An urgent need

The post-exilic Israelite community was endangered by numerous perils – external opposition, emotional dejection, doctrinal indifference, spiritual lethargy and moral compromise. The times were not unlike our own, and God met his people's need by calling to service a believer alert enough to listen to God's orders. Fifth-century Judah needed a committed servant of God willing to address their situation with realism, urgency and determination, and God found such a man in his servant Nehemiah. The Lord continues to equip leaders, and some of the principles and patterns of biblical leadership can be found in Nehemiah 13:4–31.

Nehemiah 13:4–31
18. Patterns of leadership

Some of the closing paragraphs of Nehemiah 13:4–31 provide a fascinating commentary on the crucial role of the gifted leader. Their portraiture of leadership qualities is all the more compelling because it is presented within a context which demonstrates the bitter consequences of disappointing leadership (4, 29).

The high priest, Eliashib, was directly responsible for the people's spiritual welfare, but he had not supervised with care the life and work of the temple. His namesake (4) had allowed a previously vociferous Ammonite opponent to take up residence in rooms allocated for spiritual purposes and, in doing so, had not only defiled God's house but had also marginalized God's servants, the Levites. The senior Eliashib appears to have ignored the incipient inroads of secularism even when they appeared within the temple's serving personnel. It is possible that, preoccupied with other things, the high priest simply turned a blind eye to his colleague's infidelity. The junior Eliashib's compromising policy imperilled the spiritual life of God's people, marred their witness and discredited his ministry as a priest.

Gross disloyalty in the life of the high priest's grandson (29) had resulted in a similar defamation of God's name. Tobiah had earlier been admitted to the temple and now another enemy, Sanballat, had through marriage become part of the high priest's family. The two men who had most vigorously opposed the rebuilding of the walls had secured influential positions within the life of the people, and they had achieved it simply by manipulating two unspiritual priests.

How could the average person in Israel take Scripture seriously when it had been so blatantly dismissed by the men responsible for its exposition? The priest Eliashib and the high priest of the same name deserved the 'admonition' expressed by Malachi; here were another two of the many priests condemned by the prophet. They had not listened to God, nor had they set their hearts to 'honour' his name. Such priests were meant to turn the people from their sins but, by sinning, they had 'turned from the way' themselves.[1]

The disobedience of these two priests did immense harm to God's people. The story conveys a stark warning to Christians. It is one of those biblical passages with an evident corrective purpose: 'Now these things occurred as examples to keep us from setting our hearts on evil things as they did.'[2] Sin in a leader is extremely destructive. It dishonours God and discredits the offender; it brings the gospel into disrepute and damages the church.

We turn now from these poor leaders to look at three good leadership patterns which are described here.

1. Shared leadership (13:12–13)

When Nehemiah discovered that during his absence the people had broken their promise about tithing their crops for the support of the Levites (10:37), he took immediate steps to rectify the situation. It was vital for the spiritual life of God's people that the teaching and pastoral ministry of these men be speedily restored. Normally the tithes were collected by the Levites themselves, always accompanied by a priest, but Nehemiah realized that at this time new arrangements must be made for paying these dues. After rebuking the nobles for their gross neglect in the matter, he appointed four men to serve as a team responsible for the collection and administration of these gifts, so that people throughout Judah could bring their *tithes of grain, new wine and oil into the storerooms* recently vacated by Tobiah.

The appointment of this small team is an informative cameo of shared leadership with four main concerns.

a. The co-ordination of gifts

The team consisted of four men: a priest, a Levite, a scribe (NEB, 'administrator') and a more menial assistant, Hanan, who may have belonged to an Israelite family of temple singers (12:8). The background, vocation and experience of the four men were different, but Nehemiah deliberately appointed a team with a variety of gifts so that their work might benefit from complementary skills and expertise. If the suggestion about Hanan's family background is correct, Nehemiah had ensured that each of the four main strands of temple service was adequately represented.

A disloyal priest, Eliashib, had misused his office, so it was good that a reliable one, *Shelemiah*, was there to perform duties required

[1] Mal. 2:1–9. [2] 1 Cor. 10:6, 11.

251

by the people's covenant: 'A priest ... is to accompany the Levites when they receive the tithes' (10:38).

Many a Levite had been deprived of support, so it was right that, as their ministry was restored, *Pedaiah* the Levite was there to acknowledge the gifts brought by the people.

A scribe named *Zadok* was necessary for recording the details of the offerings, and all three were helped by a junior assistant, *Hanan*, who could help stack the grain, wine and oil which was brought to the purified storerooms of the temple.

Nehemiah's united team with its diversified gifts is an important model for contemporary Christians. Writing to first-century believers throughout Asia Minor, Peter urges his readers to recognize the complementary nature of gifted ministries. The churches must realize that God's gifts have been individually endowed and generously distributed. They need to be faithfully administered, knowing that servants intent on God's glory always receive necessary strength.[3]

These four men were present at the storerooms to witness (priest), acknowledge (Levite), record (scribe) and handle (assistant) the gifts. Each had a job to do, and they did it as supportive partners.

b. The delegation of responsibility

Nehemiah appointed these four men so that this necessary item of work could be carried out satisfactorily and, given the potential danger of corruption, under the watchful eye of a team rather than an individual. Each member could ensure that the items brought as offerings were allocated solely to the purpose for which they were given. In financial matters especially, it is important for all concerned that such issues are not only done with scrupulous attention to detail but also seen to be done in a thorough and responsible manner. Many a sad story of corruption can be traced to carelessness on the part of senior people who did not consider the temptations associated with the receipt and distribution of large sums of money. Nehemiah believed that there had been enough corruption and mercenary preoccupations in Judah. It was time to begin a new chapter in the ethical and spiritual life of the people. This newly appointed team became exemplars of morally responsible service.

c. The importance of integrity

Nehemiah's primary concern in appointing these particular men was not simply to secure the representation of different members of the temple staff, but because all four *were considered trustworthy* (13).

[3] 1 Pet. 4:11–12.

Nehemiah had been away from Jerusalem for some time so, in selecting the right people, he probably looked to the advice of other people. Yet he made sure that those who formed this important team had, in their different spheres, proved themselves to be honest and reliable servants of God.

The biblical witness frequently insists that character is of greater importance than ability. When Samuel faced Jesse's eldest son, Eliab, he felt sure that a man of fine physique and acknowledged social status was a fitting candidate for kingship, but the prophet had to learn that God is not deceived by merely exterior suitability.[4] He is concerned about 'the heart', those inner qualities that are not always apparent to the onlooker. Nehemiah had confidence in his team because he was persuaded of their moral incorruptibility. Paul maintained that only people of similar calibre should be entrusted with the responsibility of leadership.[5]

d. The primacy of love

Nehemiah had a fine sense of community and believed that, however well his scheme was organized, its purpose would not achieve its potential unless the team believed that givers, administrators and recipients were united in a common bond of love for God and for each other. Those whose ministry would be maintained by these offerings were *their brothers* (13). With the repeated use of this term, the vital theme of mutual love emerges in different contexts throughout the book. Nehemiah regarded all his compatriots not merely as fellow-citizens and fellow-Israelites but as brothers and sisters in the same family (1:2; 4:14, 23; 5:1, 8, 10, 14; 10:29). The *brothers* and their partners must be loved, served, taught, encouraged and protected; in one way or another, all these themes are developed in Nehemiah's memoirs. The 'brotherhood' theme is never far from the New Testament's practical teaching about the church. It reminds us that all who confess their allegiance to Christ belong to each other.[6]

2. Effective leadership (13:30-31a)

In the final brief paragraph of his book, Nehemiah explains that, after the expulsion of the offending grandson of Eliashib, he *purified the priests and the Levites of everything foreign, and assigned them duties, each to his own task.* Nehemiah also *made provision for the*

---

[4] 1 Sa. 16:6-7; 17:28-30.   [5] 1 Tim. 3:1-13; 6:11-12; 2 Tim. 2:22-26; Titus 1:6-9.
[6] Rom. 12:10; 1 Thes. 4:9; Heb. 13:1; 1 Pet. 1:22; 2:17; 1 Jn. 2:9-11; 3:11-17; 4:7-12, 19-21.

contributions of wood at designated times, work which naturally involved women as well as men in every locality throughout Judah. Similarly, the *firstfruits* were to be offered by all the Israelite people.

Once again, we are introduced to another team, though a larger one than the group of four appointed to collect Israel's tithes. Here Nehemiah describes the ongoing work of Israel's priests, Levites and others, and, at the same time, portrays five characteristics of their continuing service. With Nehemiah's encouragement, they faced the future with a desire to work loyally (*purified ... of everything foreign*), responsibly (*assigned them duties*), interdependently (*each to his own task*), persistently (*contributions of wood* brought throughout the entire year) and wholeheartedly, typified in the offering of their *firstfruits*, the very best, for God.

The book's concluding note in these two verses points to the ongoing work and essential partnership of designated leaders and ordinary men and women in Israel. Although brief, its language and ideas deliberately recall the terms of the covenant to which leaders and people had added their seals (10:28–39). The reference to purity, the itemized responsibilities of priests and Levites, the *contributions of wood at designated times* and the offering of *the firstfruits* are an echo of earlier vows made by the Israelites as they promised they would not 'neglect the house of our God' (10:39b).

These two sentences therefore present a miniature of devoted service; they illustrate a cluster of ideals which, here and elsewhere in Scripture, modern believers are encouraged to share.

3. Exemplary leadership (13:14, 22, 29, 31b)

The most outstanding personality in this chapter, however, is Nehemiah himself, the man whose leadership qualities have been evident throughout the story of the physical reconstruction of Jerusalem's walls and the moral and spiritual reformation of the nation. In chapter 13, attention is focused on a group of his short prayers which, at times, read like extracts from a spiritual diary, with occasional passages not originally intended for the public eye. 'The memoirs become a personal outpouring, and we are intruders.'[7] These four prayer-entries reveal four of Nehemiah's basic spiritual attitudes.

a. Nehemiah was earnest in prayer

The four short prayers in this closing chapter can be seriously misunderstood. The introductory plea in three of them, *Remember*

[7] Kidner, p. 130.

me (14, 22, 31), might be thought too self-regarding, but such a judgment overlooks Nehemiah's prayerful approach to the whole of life. Moreover, in the third of the four prayers, *Remember them* (29), he is interceding on behalf of those very priests and Levites who had sinned. Each of the separate encounters described in the chapter concludes with a prayer. Here was a leader who wanted to do everything within the context of daily reliance on God for his guaranteed resources. His memoirs begin (1:4–11) and continue (2:4; 4:4–5, 9; 5:19; 6:14) in impassioned prayer, and his concluding sentences remind us of its sustained priority in the life and work of this reliant servant of God.

b. Nehemiah treasured a deep personal faith

Although necessarily preoccupied with his people's community concerns in their spiritual, moral and social dimensions, this leader acknowledges the importance of a personal experience of God. He treasures the nation's corporate covenant relationship, but when he enters the place of prayer he addresses the Lord not simply as Israel's God but as *my God* (14). That intimate personal kinship has been a vital dimension of authentic believing experience across the centuries. Luther's exposition of Galatians 2:20 ('the Son of God, who loved me and gave himself for me') urges his contemporaries to recognize the crucial importance of those personal pronouns:

> For Christ when he comes is nothing else but joy and sweetness to a trembling and broken heart, as here Paul witnesses ... with this most sweet and comfortable title ... 'Which loved ME, and gave himself for ME' ... Read therefore with great vehemency these words 'ME' and 'FOR ME' and so inwardly practise with yourself that you with a sure faith might conceive and print this 'ME' in your heart ... not doubting but that you are of the number of those to whom this 'ME' belongs'.[8]

Like many hundreds of devoted believers in Old Testament times, Nehemiah enjoyed an intimate personal knowledge of God, a faith which, with the coming of Christ, was to become even more assured, coherent and dynamic for those who believe.

c. Nehemiah was dependent on grace alone

Throughout his life, Nehemiah was a man of vigorous action, but he knew that, although a personal relationship with God needs to be expressed in appropriate works, it can never be achieved by them. He prays that God will show him mercy according to his *great love*

[8] Martin Luther, *Commentary on Saint Paul's Epistle to the Galatians*, ed. P. S. Watson (Edinburgh: James Clarke, 1953), pp. 179–180.

(22). It is the great Hebrew word *ḥesed*, found throughout the Old Testament and variously translated as 'lovingkindness', 'covenant love' and 'mercy'. The term describes the compassionate nature and dependable character of a God who made a firm agreement with his people, and who promises never to forsake those he loves. It denotes 'God's steady and extraordinary persistence in continuing to love wayward Israel in spite of Israel's insistent waywardness',[9] and has already figured earlier in Nehemiah's exposition of the unique love of God (1:5; 9:17, 32). Those who catch a glimpse of the reality, costliness and permanence of that love never imagine for a moment that they can earn God's favour by their works.

d. Nehemiah was conscious of human accountability

The four concluding 'Remember' prayers suggest that Nehemiah treasured an eternal perspective on life. He asks that, in the future, the Lord will forget neither the many 'acts of loyal love' (*ḥesed*) which had characterized his ministry (14) nor the disloyalty of those who had 'defiled' (29) Israel's distinctive witness. His opponents' priorities were determined by social advancement and materialistic gain, but he had worked for God's approval. Blenkinsopp observes that 'to look for assurance that one's life and work are of some worth in the sight of God is hardly an attitude to be despised'.[10] Nehemiah anticipates the day portrayed by Daniel and Malachi when heaven's records of earth's deeds will be publicly revealed.[11]

As Kidner observes, the closing prayer that he might be remembered 'with favour' (29) was abundantly answered for, along with Ezra, he bequeathed to God's people 'a virility and clarity of faith' which has never departed from them.[12] In addition to his administrative skills, enthusiastic reform measures, doctrinal integrity and exemplary lifestyle, Nehemiah has enriched generations of believers by these attractive and perpetually relevant memoirs. Along with every other Old Testament author, he wrote as he was 'carried along' by the Holy Spirit.[13] Through Nehemiah's unforgettable book, that same Spirit who inspired his writings encourages and empowers the believer's obedience to everything that God is still saying to us today.

[9] Norman Snaith, *The Distinctive Ideas of the Old Testament* (London: Epworth, 1944), p. 102; *cf.* Is. 54:8.   [10] Blenkinsopp, p. 357.
[11] Dn. 7:10; Mal. 3:16, *cf.* Acts 10:42; 2 Cor. 5:10; 11:15; Eph. 6:8.
[12] Kidner, p. 133.   [13] 2 Pet. 1:21.